this little Light of mine

Tina Marie Anderson

Lantern
Light
Press

This Little Light of Mine

Copyright © 2025 by Tina Marie Anderson

Published by **Lantern Light Press**

PhilanthropicMischief.com

First edition, 2025

ISBN: 979-8-9986125-0-3

This is a work of nonfiction. Some names and identifying details have been changed to protect the privacy of individuals.

A free digital version of this book is available at PhilanthropicMischief.com.

Printed in the United States of America.

Cover design by Gustavo Caraballo

For all of us,

The ones still sorting, still healing,

still holding the light in the dark.

You are not broken. You are becoming.

Contents

· · ·

Content Note:

This memoir contains references to childhood abuse, sexual trauma, religious control, and psychological harm. While I've done my best to handle each moment with care, some stories may be difficult to read. There is no prize for finishing quickly, so please honor what your heart can hold, and take breaks as needed.

· · ·

Introduction

This memoir is my attempt to make sense of and peace with the unique and frequently tumultuous life I've lived. It's a story of survival, healing, and growth. Of walking through disquieting darkness and discovering the quiet, persistent light within me.

That little light of mine has always been there, steadily guiding me, even in moments when I couldn't see it.

But this story isn't just for me. It's for anyone who has struggled or continues to struggle under similar conditions, or has felt lost in the dark, searching for a way forward.

My hope in sharing my journey honestly and unapologetically is that it might serve as a light for others, too.

This is my story.

This is my light.

And I'm gonna let it shine.

1: The Road

THE UMBRELLA STROLLER WHEELS squeaked against the asphalt of US-19, a busy highway cutting through Port Richey, Florida. The day was overcast, with thick grey clouds stretched across the horizon and no hint of the usual sunshine breaking through. It was unusually brisk for the state, with a high of just 55 degrees—a chill sharp enough to nip at small hands and flush little cheeks. The constant stream of traffic looked somehow subdued under the ashen sky; cars and trucks roared past, their tires hissing against the pavement, a constant reminder of how out of place my three-year-old brother and my fourteen-month-old self were. This was no place for pedestrians, let alone two small children.

My brother Bobby gripped the stroller handles tightly, his small hands steady as he navigated the narrow highway shoulder. "It's okay," I imagine him whispering, his voice small but determined, as if reassuring himself as much as me. Only a toddler, Bobby had already seen enough grown-up routines—perhaps he recalled our mother's fingers fastening the buckles around my waist, or even a cheerful TV parent guiding a toddler into a plastic seat.

Whatever the source, he'd soaked it all in, the way little ones do—quietly, instinctively—and pieced together the steps on his own. And somehow, he managed to load me into that stroller. Even then, he seemed to know my little legs wouldn't carry me far on this journey.

In many ways, that road was the beginning of my story. I have no baby pictures, no original birth certificate, and no keepsakes to prove I existed at all before this moment. All I have is this story, preserved in the records of the Florida court system, documenting the events of December 10, 1981, when two small children were found wandering down a dangerous road with no adult in sight. It was my earliest footprint in the world, made when I was barely old enough to make footprints of my own, and it became the foundation of everything that followed.

We were just two little kids edging our way along a bustling thoroughfare, unguarded and exposed. To any passerby, we must have looked lost, out of place, vulnerable.

I often wonder how many people passed us on that busy road without noticing. How many saw us, observed our noticeably young ages, and decided that there must be a responsible adult nearby, just out of their line of sight? How many couldn't be bothered to care at all?

To us, it was just another day. In my child's mind, there wouldn't have been fear, perhaps only a quiet sense of bewilderment. We were far too young to understand the danger we were in or the reasons why we were on that journey alone.

• • •

As the story goes, our mother needed to go to the store to buy formula for me. In the early 1980s, it wasn't uncommon for parents to rely on formula longer than necessary, whether out of habit or convenience. Frank, the oldest of us three, was just eight years old, far too young for the responsibility of watching his very young siblings. And yet, he was instructed to stay home while she ran her errand.

Frank remembers protesting, worried she might never come back. But with two napping younger siblings in front of him and no real chance of "winning" this argument, he eventually relented. By the time she'd made it halfway down the road, Frank panicked and left the house to follow her.

We'll never know how long we were alone in the house, unaware that we'd been left behind. I wonder what went through three-year-old Bobby's mind when he woke to find himself alone with his baby sister. What drove him to venture out on that journey to find our mother and brother— and, most remarkably, what gave him the intuition to bring me along, taking full responsibility for me as only a selfless child could?

Somewhere along that perilous road, a truck driver spotted us and stopped. The hiss of his brakes and the thud of his boots on the asphalt might have startled Bobby, but he stayed by me, vowing to protect me as best he could.

"Hey there, kiddos," the truck driver might have said, crouching to our level. "Where's your momma?" His voice steady but concerned, his question lingering in the air as Bobby gripped the stroller tighter. I imagine Bobby's wide eyes darting between the man's face and the looming truck, paralyzed, unsure of what to do.

"Let's get you somewhere safe," the driver might have said, his voice friendly, but his motives unreadable. Bobby must have hesitated, weighing something in that small, frantic mind of his. Could we trust this man? He was a stranger, after all...

There must have been something about him, something reassuring in his face or the way that he spoke, that made Bobby comfortable enough to trust him. Maybe it was the simple kindness of showing concern for us when so many cars had passed us by. Maybe it was Bobby's exhaustion. It's even possible that Bobby just thought the big truck was really cool. Whatever it was, he climbed in, and just like that, we were in the hands of a new custodian, a complete stranger, the truck rumbling beneath us as we rolled away towards something unknown.

That day, strangers stepped in to fill roles that never should have been left empty, holding us, asking questions, and making decisions that weren't theirs to make but had to be made. These strangers took us to safety, and social workers would soon step in, their faces likely a mix of concern, a quiet kind of sadness, and that familiar, unspoken recognition that children deserve better than this, and too often don't get it.

The court documents paint a damning picture. Social workers had yet again found us alone and unattended for at least 90 minutes on two separate occasions. Each time, they noted the absence of adults and the sense of abandonment that seemed to follow us like a shadow. Eventually, these episodes built a case that would tear our small family apart, making Bobby and me wards of the state of Florida.

Looking back, I see a childhood teetering on the edge of survival, marked by small moments of grace from strangers who saw us when no one else did. In those early days, we were just children wandering down a road, searching for someone or something—unaware that our path, like our lives, had already veered far off course, shaped by the absence of those who should have been there for us.

• • •

The court documents, neat in ink and legal jargon, told a story of neglect, abandonment, and a family splintered by its own history. They spoke in clinical terms—words like "dependency," "custody," and "neglect"—words cold and foreign to a child. They revealed my mother's desperation, my father's choices, and the reluctant hands of grandparents tasked with gathering the broken pieces of our family. But at the time, these documents and their significance were beyond my comprehension, presented by people whose faces blurred together, whose motivations felt mysterious and unreachable.

While I couldn't yet grasp the details, the road itself was symbolic. It marked the beginning of a journey I'd spend years walking—a journey to uncover who I was, where I came from, and how a fractured family could leave such a lasting mark.

• • •

As I grew older, I often returned to those court documents, replaying them in my mind like a scene from a movie. I imagined Bobby's little hands gripping the stroller tight, the pavement still exhaling its faint Florida warmth despite the unreasonable chill, and the blur of cars speeding past us. The distance we traveled wasn't measured in miles but in the beat-by-beat steps we took to move forward despite our circumstances, learning to be our own safety nets in an insecure world that offered little comfort.

2: The Spark That Started It All

I T ALL BEGAN UNDER the Friday night lights of a high school football game, a small-town ritual where the air buzzes with the roar of the crowd, the hum of teenage energy, and the thrill of believing the world is limitless. That's where my parents, Lori and Marc (short for Marcus), met, caught up in the kind of possibilities you only believe in before life teaches you otherwise.

I know they met that night, but much of what I picture is pieced together from fragments of their story and my imagination. Who they were then—two young people at the edge of something they didn't know would shape the rest of their lives—remains a blend of fact and interpretation. I see my mother with her long brown hair and golden brown eyes bright with the intensity of youth, capturing the gaze of my father with his neatly combed auburn hair and dark eyes. She saw him, too, as he stood lean, serious, watching her in a way that probably made her feel seen like no one else ever had.

Like so many teenage romances, their spark burned bright and fast. Within a year, it became something bigger—a bold, impulsive plan that carried them across state lines. Barely seventeen, my pregnant mother ran off to Alabama with my twenty-year-old father. Because she was underage and without her parents' approval, my father's mother posed as her mother and gave verbal consent over the phone. It was a quick exchange that satisfied the requirement and likely made their defiance feel all the more triumphant.

The legality of their marriage would later come into question. But in that moment, it must have felt like an exhilarating rebellion against expectations, suspicions, and the weight of their pasts. They were two young people carving out a piece of the world they could call their own, defying anyone who said they weren't ready.

Perhaps, in each other, they saw a chance to rewrite their stories. But there are cracks in the fairy tale from the beginning. Their insecurities and silent struggles were already stitched into the seams of their whirlwind romance —unspoken, perhaps even unnoticed, but present all the same. I want to believe they found hope in each other, even if hope alone would never be enough to hold back the shadows.

My mother's family never approved of my father. They saw him as someone who only wanted her for the small sum of money she'd received from a settlement after being hit by a truck shortly before they met—a windfall they considered both a blessing and a curse. According to court records, the accident, along with a childhood bout with spinal meningitis, left her with lasting cognitive effects. Whether whispered in corners or passed through knowing glances, her family harbored their suspicions. And while my father might have feigned indifference, I wonder if he felt the weight of their distrust, especially since, at least in the beginning, some of it was spoken aloud.

• • •

The cracks started small but widened with time. My father later described their life together as strained, weighed down by my mother's mental health struggles and challenges that defied clear explanations or easy solutions. In court records, he claimed she had threatened suicide if he took us away—a moment that revealed just how fragile their life together had become. Whether born of desperation, mental illness, or a genuine fear of loss, her threat became another fracture in the shaky foundation they were trying to hold together.

In court records, my father claimed he left our mother because "she was unclean and unkempt in her housekeeping, did not provide enough hot meals, and was generally incompatible." These surface explanations feel hollow, masking deeper wounds they couldn't—or wouldn't —interrogate. They were too young, too scarred by their pasts, and too damaged by the judgments and expectations of those around them.

• • •

I see my life was shaped as much by what my parents didn't say as by what they did. Their story—part truth, part inherited memory, part fairy tale—became my foundation. I filled the gaps with imagination, crafting a love that held both beauty and cracks. Maybe I've romanticized them, or maybe I've softened their edges to make them easier to carry. Either way, their story lives in me—perhaps not exactly as it was, but in the way I've come to live with it.

In the end, the love that began under those Friday night lights wasn't enough to keep our family together. But it sparked something—a journey that carried me from the edge of a threatening road to a place of understanding and self-love. Their story, flawed and fractured, became mine. And in its cracks, I found my light; stronger and more enduring than I ever imagined. Sometimes, the stories we tell ourselves don't just help us survive; they help us become.

3: A Family Splintered

WHEN BOBBY AND I were placed in foster care, our lives splintered in ways none of us could have expected. Frank, Bobby, and I drifted between places, each with its own kind of unease: our mother's house, where love felt fragile and stretched thin. Our father's sporadic visits, fleeting and unreliable, were like a guest appearance in a life he no longer belonged to. Our grandparents' reluctant support, their home was an obligation rather than a refuge. And the foster homes—temporary, impersonal, never ours to call our own. Each place left its mark, but none fit together. Instead of a whole, our sense of family felt cobbled together, forming a patchwork of mismatched scraps, just as fractured and unstable as the spaces we tried to call home.

Any scenes in my mind of those early days with my mother come not from memory but from the stories I've pieced together, fragments shared by others. The court documents describe my interactions with her during those early days, offering glimpses of a relationship that was already strained.

By the time I was 18 months old, our mother's visits to Bobby and me at the foster home were supervised by a counselor. Reports describe me as happy to see her, but often "puckering up" as if to cry. I resisted being held by my mother or taken from my foster mother, clinging to the only stability I knew. Bobby, still only a toddler, had mixed reactions. At first, he struggled with her leaving, showing what the documents called "emotional trauma" during separations. Over time, though, he adjusted, smiling when she arrived and accepting her departures more easily, "due to his foster parents' patience."

Even though we both appeared to recognize her, the court noted that neither of us could make sense of the situation— how could we? We were too young to understand why we were in this strange place, why our mother came and left, or why she couldn't stay.

Frank remembers our mother doting on me, always wanting a little girl. He described her guttural cries after I was taken, devastated by my absence. "When they returned me temporarily but kept you and Bobby," he said, "she was absolutely crushed. But Bobby and me? She couldn't have cared less about us. She sobbed on the edge of her bed while her boyfriend consoled her, saying over and over, 'We won't let them take the girl.'"

From Frank's stories, life with our mother was a blend of love and chaos. I picture her trying to hold things together in a home that reflected her struggles—messy, fragile, and spilling over at the seams. Dishes piled in the sink, bills and unopened mail stacked on the counter, forgotten leftovers turning sour in the fridge before anyone had a chance to eat them. The floor was scattered with the evidence of half-finished efforts—laundry left in baskets, toys abandoned mid-play, even yesterday's cup of coffee still sitting where she had set it down and never returned. In time, the filth and disrepair grew so severe that the house was condemned— another casualty of everything she was trying, and failing, to hold together.

Did she sing to us softly, her voice a soothing balm, filling gaps with affection to make up for what she felt she couldn't provide? I cling to that image, wondering if, in her own way, she loved us as fiercely as she could. And that was enough, at least, that's what I tell myself.

But our father's presence brought something else entirely. It was structured and orderly—a glimpse of a life with expectations set and met. He didn't visit often, but when he did, there was a rhythm to things. I don't know if any of us felt entirely at ease in that rhythm, but I believe he was trying to offer a version of stability that had always felt out of reach with our mother.

According to court documents, our father had always wanted custody, but his work had taken him to Pennsylvania, where ambition took priority. I don't think it was because he didn't care. It's just that his version of showing up didn't always match what we needed most—love without conditions.

Still, a small part of us looked forward to his visits. If nothing else, for the glimpse into a life that approximated something... normal. It was a life we'd only ever get close to, like standing at the edge of a pool without ever diving in. And even this proximity was consoling in its own right.

• • •

Then there were our mother's parents. After Bobby and I were taken into foster care and the house was condemned, they took our mother and Frank in, not out of love, but because they felt they had no other choice. To them, we were a reminder of their daughter's failures—a burden they neither expected nor sought. Their support came with conditions: they could stay until Frank finished up that school year.

When we spent time with them, we walked on eggshells, desperately trying not to upset the fragile peace they'd constructed around their precious lives. They made no secret of their dissatisfaction, their resentment simmering just beneath the surface. A request by Bobby and my foster mother to visit our mother and Frank on Easter was met with severe resistance from our grandparents. They only agreed after learning the visit would not be overnight and that our foster mother would provide transportation to and from the visit.

And then the months passed by, the school year ended, and so did the terms of their agreement.

With reluctant acceptance that there was no legal placement for their adult daughter, they agreed to let our mother stay, but Frank had to leave. He was placed into foster care immediately, and over the next several months, shuffled between homes.

As a social worker wrote in the court documents, "Mr. and Mrs. Brown have always complained to this agency about its inability to find other living arrangements for both their daughter and their grandson. The Browns have refused to accept any responsibility for their daughter or her current problems. They have difficulty in compromising their plans and lifestyle." Their home was a place of boundaries and rules, a tight-lipped kind of love that felt performative, conditional, and thin.

To them, we were children of chaos, reminders of the very thing they had tried to escape. Their frustrations were palpable, and their disdain for the situation often seeped into the tense air around us, making their home feel more like a caustic holding space than a haven. And yet, they couldn't get rid of us. We were woven into their lives by obligation; family ties that felt more like chains than loving bonds.

• • •

Through all of this, there was Frank, our older brother, the one Bobby and I saw as our protector. To us, he was older and wiser, with an understanding of our fractured world that surpassed anything Bobby or I could grasp. For as long as I can remember, Frank carried himself with a confidence and strength that reassured us. Even in chaos, his presence told us we weren't alone.

When things got tough, Bobby and I instinctively turned to Frank. He was our ringleader—braver and bolder than both of us combined, with a knack for adventure and a resilience far beyond his years. He always seemed to know when to step in, when to pull us close, and when to simply be present as a stabilizing force. More than a sibling, Frank was our guide, our anchor in a stormy world.

But no child should have to be an anchor. Strength like his doesn't come without a steep cost. He bore a heavy weight that should've been carried by the adults around us. That kind of exhausting responsibility doesn't just disappear—it lingers, leaving a lasting mark and reshaping a person.

And yet, somehow, his spirit still found ways to shine. There's one story that stands out when I think about Frank's determination, imagination, and moments of pure heart. I don't remember it firsthand, but I can see it clearly through his retelling.

The Christmas That Almost Wasn't

It was a sunny December day in Port Richey, Florida, and winter break for seven-year-old Frank. Like most boys his age, his days were filled with roaming the neighborhood, building forts, and chasing the kind of harmless mischief that boundless energy invites.

But on this particular day, something unusual caught his attention: trash cans lined the streets, overflowing with crumpled wrapping paper, torn boxes, and festive garlands. He paused, puzzled, trying to make sense of the scene. And then, like a mean jolt of lightning, the realization hit him.

Frank bolted home, breathless and wide-eyed, bursting through the door to share his discovery. "We missed Christmas!" he cried, his urgent voice trembling.

Our mother, seated in her usual spot by the window, exhaled a cloud of cigarette smoke from her worn armchair. Her gaze didn't shift. "Yeah," she replied flatly, her indifference landing in Frank's gut like a brutal punch. Bobby and I rolled around at her feet—too young to respond, and she, too worn out to care. Frank's joy echoed into a room that couldn't hold it.

Frank wasn't deterred. If Christmas had passed us by, then he would bring it back.

With the kind of determination that only a child can summon, he darted back outside. He dug through the neighborhood trash, scavenging whatever remnants of Christmas he could find—garlands, ornaments, scraps of wrapping paper. One by one, he dragged those discarded treasures home and began to build his masterpiece. Piece by piece, he transformed the torn-up scraps into something magical. Soon, a makeshift Christmas tree stood proudly in the middle of the room, adorned with salvaged decorations. He wrapped random objects as gifts —for Bobby, for me, for our mother, and even for our absent father.

When his work was done, Frank stood back, admiring his creation. Then, with a grin that could light up the whole world, he ran to our mother, bursting with pride and excitement. "Merry Christmas!" he exclaimed, beaming as though he'd just conjured joy out of thin air.

But our mother's reaction wasn't what he'd hoped for. When she entered the room and saw what he had done, her face turned hard, disapproving. This should have been her role. Providing Christmas was a mother's job, and Frank's gesture—no matter how well-intentioned—was a reminder that she'd failed. That failure stirred something raw inside of her: an ugly combination of guilt, resentment, and shame. Instead of celebrating Frank's earnest efforts, she lashed out.

"Get all this garbage out of here!" she snapped. "What were you thinking, bringing trash into the house? Get it out!" She turned away, unable to stand the sight of it, as Frank, dejected, glumly did as he was told.

When I think about this story—the missed holiday, the rejection, the way hope and innocence were crushed in an instant—it feels like an unforgettable tragedy.

But when I think of Frank's actions, I see something bigger. I see my big brother building something from nothing in a home where scarcity loomed. Through his actions, Frank taught me that we're never ruined completely. That even the smallest scraps of effort, when done with love, can make all the difference.

• • •

Years later, Frank would reflect on the whole thing with a shrug and smirk, "I wasn't being completely altruistic. I wanted Christmas loot, too. I had it in my head that without a tree, Santa would just assume we were Jews and keep on truckin'."

That's not a tragedy. That's tenacity wrapped in tinsel.

• • •

Even in a story so far defined by fracture, not every splinter cuts the same way.

I have no memories of the foster family who cared for Bobby and me in those early days. I was too young to hold on to their faces or voices, but perhaps I didn't need to. Maybe what they gave me wasn't meant to be remembered in detail but to be felt in my bones—to plant seeds I wouldn't recognize until much later.

I still connect deeply to their kindness when I read the court documents that solidify their presence in my story as clearly as any memory. Warm hands. Soft voices. The quiet and steady patience of strangers who chose to care for two small children when they didn't have to.

At such an early age, I didn't have the language to convey an understanding of kindness or patience, but even without words, I felt the contrast between their care and the chaos I was born into. They showed me a different kind of love—steady and gentle, without strings—that planted the seeds of resilience I needed to grow.

I don't remember their names, their faces, or their voices. But I know that their kindness and compassion showed up in a moment when I needed it most.

• • •

With no support system and no other options, our mother agreed to let our father take custody. The day we left Florida, we took "nothing but the clothes on our backs," as our father would say, retelling the story over the years as if it were a badge of survival. There was no grand farewell—just the dull ache of doors closing and the hum of wheels pulling us away from the only world we had known.

Dad loved to repeat that line, proud of how little we needed, as if traveling light proved we were tough. But in telling our story that way again and again, he flattened what was left behind for us children: our toys, our clothes—yes, but also our home, and *our mother*. He reduced them all to the same inconsequential weight. Things to be left behind and forgotten without a second thought.

Those early days with our mother, however much I imagined them, still linger with me. I can no longer touch that life pieced together from fragments shared by others, but those fragments have shaped my understanding of who I was: a child born from both love and chaos, from a mother who tried in her own way but could not hold on.

We left behind our mother, and now all that remains is Lori. A person, a woman, stripped of her role, reduced to a first name in my story. What she couldn't carry forward, I had to learn to live without. These memories have become a tether to a past I never fully knew, and a compass guiding me toward the resilience I will always need.

These distant, opaque memories, both a lifeline and a wound, have taught me how to manage and carry loss. As very young children, life taught us lessons in survival. That love could be fragile. That family could be both a comfort and a burden. That home might be as unstable as shifting sands. Most of all, like Frank's makeshift Christmas, we learned to endure—and that we could create light out of nothing.

4: A Place to Belong

EVEN THOUGH WE'D LEFT behind our chaotic beginnings in Florida, our new life didn't settle into a period of limbo, a string of temporary stops as Dad tried to build a stable life, juggling a new career in broadcast communications and budding romantic relationships. Our lives became a story of moving, adapting, and searching for a sense of belonging within an ever-changing landscape.

Dad's first new romantic connection started before we left Florida. He connected with a woman named Janet Marbs before he left Lori. She offered him companionship and stability while his relationship with Lori unraveled. But like so much of our early lives, Janet's presence was over in a flash. According to Frank, she kicked us out, forcing Dad to find yet another place for us to stay.

• • •

With nowhere permanent to go, our small family blew through states like tumbleweeds: Florida to Pennsylvania, then Missouri, and finally Illinois—all in less than six months. Each move blurred together, leaving behind the faintest traces of homes that never had the chance to take root. The whirlwind of movement left us unsettled, with instability as our sole constant companion. I have no memory of most of it, no landmarks to anchor those transitions, just a vague sense of motion, change, and the quiet disorientation of everything shifting before I could get my bearings. In those early years, "home" became an increasingly abstract concept.

• • •

Bonnie entered our lives almost by chance. She was a friend of one of Dad's coworkers, but from the moment she walked through the door, she brought a grounding presence that made our fractured family feel a little closer to whole. Unlike so many people who had drifted in and out of our orbit, Bonnie felt permanent. We sensed she wasn't just passing through; she intended to stick around for a while.

Bonnie was a first for us in many ways. She was smart, working as an underwriter for a prominent life insurance firm in Rockford, Illinois. She was responsible, a college graduate, and she owned her own home in Loves Park. And she was stable, with a dependable family network comprised of her mother, father, and sisters, all living nearby.

I don't remember our first encounters with her, but I imagine there was something familiar and comforting in the way she tried to see us—as though she accepted us fully, even though none of us (including her) fully understood what we should be looking at, what we were taking on, or what her presence in our life would mean.

As with Lori, Dad's relationship with Bonnie progressed quickly. I don't know how long they dated, but by June 1983, they were married. For the first time, there was a sense that we could settle, build roots, and create a life not defined by short-term arrangements.

Their wedding photo album depicts a joyful day: Dad, on one knee, playing guitar and singing to her. Surrounding them, we three kids sit nearby, watching with varying degrees of curiosity and awe. The moment radiates warmth, captured in a frame that freezes the melody and emotion in time. Frank reaches out to hold her hand, and Bonnie's red, puffy eyes reflect a powerful emotion—a woman touched to her core. The two of them walk, hand in hand down the aisle, moments after vowing to love one another as long as either of them should live.

• • •

As we began to settle into this new version of "home," my memories coalesced into something I could finally claim as my own. The fragments of my early childhood, once so scattered, started to take shape under the stability of family, complete with loving grandparents, aunts, and uncles—like a gentle light revealing both comfort and complexity in what lay ahead.

Our neighborhood in Loves Park sat perched at an intersection of two worlds. To the west, bustling North Second Street—known locally as N 2nd St—hummed with life. Restaurants, shops, and the small strip mall directly behind our house offered an everyday ease and convenience. But to the east, the landscape shifted, marked by the heavier, grittier hum of industry. Factories and warehouses dotted the street neighboring the junior high and elementary school, a reminder of the working-class heart beating steadily beneath the suburban surface.

As I navigated this new place, both physically and emotionally, a gentle but persistent clarity began to emerge, hinting at the steadiness and the unknowns of what lay ahead. It was here, in Loves Park's blend of suburban calm and industrial reality, that fragments of my childhood memories took shape, finally coalescing into a narrative of my own. It was here, in this shifting landscape, that my own story truly began.

5: The Fragile Peace

I CRIED WHEN DAD and my new mom left for their Hawaiian honeymoon, and I was still crying the day they returned. At just three years old, it must have seemed to them like I'd been crying for the entire eight days they were gone. I didn't know why, but a deep sadness weighed on me, like a shadow I couldn't shake. The babysitter had told my parents that I was sick, but I don't think I was; I was simply sad in a way I could not yet articulate.

When they arrived home, my new mom sat down beside me, gently brushing my hair back, while Dad lingered in the doorway. Her face softened with concern, but his remained stoic and unreadable, as if he were merely an observer in the moment.

"Oh, sweetie!" she said gently. "You're burning up!"

I shook my head. "I'm not sick!" I replied defiantly, unsure of what I was missing but feeling the ache all the same. She stayed beside me as I cried, and for a moment, I felt safe in her presence.

"Oh! Did you miss us? Is that what's going on?" she asked, interpreting my tears as something simple, something familiar.

I nodded, although I knew that wasn't entirely true. I didn't know what I was missing—only that I felt empty in a way her hug couldn't quite fill, even though it felt nice. As she wrapped me in her arms, Dad's expression softened, as if her concern permitted him to care. Together, they hugged me, and it felt wonderful—even if it was not exactly what I needed.

The Shift

That summer, something shifted. I remember my room being warm, bathed in sunlight—a space where I felt safe and happy. I was playing in my room, absorbed in my little world, when Mom entered and suddenly, a chill settled over me. Something was different—there was a tension in the air, stale and suffocating, stealing the warmth from this calm and safe space. She began angrily shuffling things around, muttering under her breath. Her anger wasn't aimed at me, but it blackened the room like a storm cloud, dark and brooding.

I had a sense that I should stay out of her way, but at the same time, I didn't know how. She swiftly grabbed my arm, her grip tight and unrelenting. My feet left the ground as she lifted me with surprising force. In an instant, I was on my back, the breath knocked out of me. For a terrifying and shocking moment, I couldn't get air into my lungs. I looked up, searching her face for sympathy or reassurance—but there was none to be found.

As I gasped for air, I noticed that her face contorted with rage, not concern. She bent down, her nails digging into my sides as she lifted me once more. Before I could brace myself, the floor came up to meet me again, slamming the breath from my body. Each desperate attempt to inhale felt like scaling an insurmountable mountain.

A pitiful squawk escaped me, the only sound I could muster as I writhed on the floor. Her gaze remained fixed on me, still brimming with anger, as though my suffering was an inconvenience. Finally, I managed to gasp out, "I... can't... breathe." I thought, surely, this would change everything— that she'd stop if she only understood how serious it was.

"You can't breathe?" she repeated, her tone mocking the severity of my words. The question offered no comfort, no understanding. I kept gasping, struggling to piece together enough air to survive, wondering if I'd ever breathe normally again.

Her fury didn't relent. She came after me again. This time, I curled into a ball, instinctively trying to shield myself. But her hands found me anyway, lifting me effortlessly. Once more—WHAM!—my back collided with the floor, and the breath I had fought so hard for was gone again.

She doesn't know. She doesn't understand. If I can just catch my breath long enough to say it more clearly, she will hear me and stop!

The commotion must have caught Frank's attention, and he came running to my rescue. He yelled at her, challenging her in a way I couldn't. Their argument erupted into a loud, chaotic barrage. I watched helplessly as she chased him down the hall until out of sight, their footsteps thundering down the stairs. As soon as I could muster the strength, I got up, closed my door, and crawled under my bed. Trembling, my body ached, and my lungs still struggled for air.

Fear and confusion flooded over me; emotions far too immense for a toddler to comprehend. But even then, I knew something had changed—my once-safe world had turned dangerous.

• • •

I don't know if it was something Frank said, or if she simply saw herself through his eyes—saw what she'd done, what she had become in that moment. Maybe my father had words with her when he got home. Or maybe she was afraid of herself. Whatever it was, she never laid a finger on me or my brothers again.

I didn't see that moment as a betrayal, nor did it shatter my faith in her. I believed that she cared for me, and if only she could understand how frightened I was, I thought, surely, she would not have kept hurting me. For a while, I maintained a careful distance—an unspoken, wide berth between my small body and both her unrelenting grip and those long nails—yet a childlike trust remained. I kept telling myself that she just couldn't hear what I was trying to say. Although the feeling of being misunderstood gnawed at me, it wasn't enough to erase the bond I had formed with her. Even then, I clung to the hope that one day she would see and finally understand.

• • •

This memory, raw and unfiltered, remains deeply lodged in the corners of my mind. As I grew older, I learned to compartmentalize, to detach from the violation I incurred. In truth, it never once struck me as "wrong." Even today, thinking of it in first-person terms, I'm not angry or bitter—I feel almost nothing. It is only when I imagine it happening to some other, equally vulnerable child that the full weight of it hits me. That's when I see an injustice.

Maybe it was a survival instinct, or maybe just the way children make sense of things they can't control. I had sensed that her anger wasn't personal—that it was a storm inside her that had nowhere else to go. In that sense, I accepted the pain as normal, telling myself that, combined with my inability to clearly communicate, she simply didn't know any better.

As an adult, I look at photos of my toddler self and am startled at how tiny and vulnerable I was. I can't fathom inflicting that kind of harm on anybody, much less someone so small and vulnerable. Yet when I return to the memory, I feel detached; it's as if I've bypassed any clear "right vs.

wrong." I see the event, but I don't condemn it. I just accept that it was. Only by imagining another child in my place do I feel that rush of outrage on their behalf. And so, I move forward, carrying both a strange peace and a deeper awareness of the harm done—a duality that has become part of who I am.

• • •

The early years with Mom were a strange mix of calm and brewing tension. For a time, she was a source of warmth, a comfort I had not known before. But that warmth was always tempered by something darker, something unpredictable that I learned to navigate.

This was my first real encounter with the storm, the moment safety collapsed into danger, love turned to rage, childhood innocence met an adult's unchecked fury. It was the first time I learned for myself that life could shift in an instant, that the people who cared for you could also bring you pain.

In the years to come, these lessons became part of my survival, part of the way I learned to make sense of a world that rarely made sense. I found ways to adapt, to survive, and even to find strength in the spaces between love and pain. However much effort I put into it by day, my brain kept working it out by night.

Trash Can Vampire

One night, I woke up from a nightmare that left me petrified. In the nightmare, a cartoonish vampire—something resembling a grinning Count Chocula; friendly, familiar, but still a vampire—was chasing me through various rooms in my house. Each time he caught me, he stepped on my foot like a lever, forcing my mouth open as if it were a trash can.

Then, without a hint of hesitation, he would toss trash straight into my open mouth.

The first time it happened, I felt a jarring, almost mechanical sensation, my jaw snapping open against my will, my tongue practically paralyzed. The garbage itself was random and shapeless, and it was foul, like soggy paper mixed with spoiled food and a sour chemical tang. I wanted to choke, cough, or spit it out—anything—but I couldn't manage more than a pitiful gulp for air. The moment I tried to breathe in, I tasted more trash, and panic rushed through me. I felt as if I were drowning in rotten, rancid banana peels.

No matter how desperately I clawed at my mouth or tried to wrench my foot free, the vampire pinned me in place. He'd grin, step down on my foot again, and my mouth would spring open for another round of garbage. Each time, my lungs squeezed tighter, and an icy wave of terror ripped through my body. My heart was pounding so violently that I thought my chest might explode before I ever got a full breath.

This cycle repeated three or four times before I woke up, scared and upset. While the dream's absurd details now seem almost comical, at three years old, it was utterly terrifying. As a result, I couldn't bear to stay alone in my dark bedroom, haunted by those images.

I lay in bed, staring into the darkness, the weight of the night pressing down on me. The silence wasn't comforting; it was vast and lonely, leaving too much space for fear to creep in. I tried to squeeze my eyes shut, willing myself to stay put, to stifle the need for comfort. But the ache in my chest and the images in my mind did not subside.

Slowly, I slipped out from under my Care Bears covers, careful not to make a sound. My breath hitched as I tiptoed toward the door of my parents' bedroom, my heartbeat thudding in my ears. One sound too loud, and I would wake up my father. This was a risk I knew I could not afford to make. Still, I continued. I hesitated at the threshold, my fingers hovering over the doorknob. I knew the door creaked —it always did—but I had no choice. I turned the knob ever so slowly, inching the door open.

Creeeeeeak.

I froze. My entire body went still, listening, waiting, every muscle coiled in quiet desperation and willing my parents to stay asleep. Seconds stretched unbearably.

Nothing.

I exhaled as softly as I could and slipped through the doorway, carefully pressing the door closed behind me. The air in their room was different. Warmer, heavier, filled with the scent of sleep and something that always seemed familiar. My father's presence loomed in the dark, an unspoken threat.

I lowered myself onto the duvet cover lying on the floor at the foot of their bed, curling into its folds.

It wasn't much—just a quiet spot on the floor—but it was enough. I wasn't alone anymore, even if I still had to face my fears on my own. Being near them made all the difference, and eventually, I drifted back to sleep.

When morning came, my parents were surprised to find me there. To my surprise, neither of them was upset—a small but significant relief. My parents' tempers were each unpredictable, and disruptions often carried consequences, but that morning, neither of their tempers flickered to life— and for that, I was thankful.

• • •

I still vividly recall that nightmare, but the deeper terror lay in only now noticing my fear of my parents, even as I needed them. I was just as afraid of them as I was of the cartoon vampire, yet they were my only refuge from the very thing they sometimes embodied.

At just three years old, my dream reflected this tension: a menacing figure, a sense of helplessness, and the paradox of seeking comfort from a source that frightened me. Even in sleep, I was grappling with a reality that felt both dangerous and impossible to escape, my subconscious knitting together symbols it hoped I would one day understand.

6: Moments of Joy, Threads of Expectation

I WAS FOUR YEARS old, and it was my birthday, a day I should remember for its own sake, a special day just for me. It had been a typical late August morning, holding a slight fog and mist that carried a poetic effect and let me feel like the earth was waking up with me as I ate my cereal at the breakfast bar, happily kicking my legs away on my stool and gazing out the small kitchen window overlooking our backyard. By late morning, there wasn't a cloud in the sky, and the sun shone down in the way it does when you know it's going to be a great day.

That morning, Dad took me to Chuck E. Cheese in Rockford, Illinois. "Just for a little while," he said, as if even my four-year-old self could understand that time was precious. We weren't there for long; it was just a stop on his way to something far more significant. My baby brother Markie (short for Marcus) had been born just the day before.

In the foyer of the plaza, the sound of Dad's whistling filled the air, bouncing off the cool orange-brown 6-inch tiles with black grout and floor-to-ceiling windows. He whistled when he was happy—truly happy—and that day, he was practically beaming, as if rising to meet the sun in its declaration of greatness. I twirled around, letting the sound wrap around me, feeling a giddy sense of joy and pride, as if we were sharing that secret.

Dad's speaking voice held a lot of bass. But his whistle had a distinctly lifted tone. It held a gentility, an almost feminine feeling of warmth and certainty. Dad was a talented singer and musician. I could sit back and listen to him play his acoustic guitar and sing, and let the deep copper timbre of his voice and the perfectly aligned vibration of the strings wash over me like I was relaxing in a warm bath.

His whistle had a natural vibrato and a strength that reminded me of a train in the distance. An unmistakable, unshakeable signal. The sound he could make, seemingly like magic, straight out of his face, was extremely controlled —an audible contradiction to his everyday mannerisms. And the authenticity and warmth of that sound was a stark contrast to the artificial air conditioning that blasted us in the foyer that day in late August.

His whistling was more than just a sound. It was proof. Evidence of something I could only feel—a kind of energy that assured me I was safe to simply exist. In a world where small things could disrupt the peace, simply being myself often had the power to disrupt his happiness. His whistle was like a green light or a flag at a car race signaling that I could proceed safely at full blast. It was a permission I didn't need to ask for, and a freedom I didn't have to earn. His happiness was contagious, and it was something I desperately wished I could bottle and carry with me.

Even now, when people ask me what my favorite childhood memory is, I reply, "Anytime my dad was whistling." It was a sound I associated with peace, with love, with everything that felt whole and good and right in the world.

My fourth birthday represented something bigger—a shift that signaled the start of a new chapter in our family with Markie's arrival. Even at my new spritely age of four, I could feel it. In the air, in Dad's joy, in the way his whistling seemed to fill every corner of the day. His happiness was not just about me—it felt like it was about all of us, about the family he was working so hard to build and maintain.

For a little while, standing in that foyer, bathed in the sound of his whistle, I could believe in the possibility of something whole, something safe and secure—a world where I belonged, not just as a daughter, but as myself.

Learning the Rules

A few weeks after my birthday, I felt another shift. It was picture day at Open Bible, the small Pentecostal Academy I attended while my older brothers were at "real school." What I remember most about that place is the cold, hard floor, made up of that old asbestos linoleum stuff. The teachers always seemed stricter than necessary, at least from my little-kid perspective, and the other kids there thought I was a total weirdo for liking peas. To me, peas were a novelty. We never had them at home. While every other kid turned up their noses (which the teachers overcorrected), I enjoyed them very much.

My teacher had told me that day to "sit on my hands" and "keep still" so that the photographer could take a nice group picture. In the moment, the idea struck me as hilarious. Why would anyone sit on their hands? It was so silly! It was the kind of ridiculous instruction only a four-year-old would find funny, and I couldn't help but giggle.

The room's nervous energy made me feel wiggly and alive, like laughter was bubbling up and couldn't be contained. So, when the camera flashed, there I was—grinning from ear to ear, caught in a moment of pure, unfiltered joy. Sitting on my hands.

A few weeks later, when Mom saw the photo, her reaction wasn't what I had expected.

"Tsk." Her tongue clicked in disapproval. "Why didn't you sit nicely and smile like the other children? You ruined the picture."

I didn't know how to tell her that I wasn't trying to be disruptive—that my joy in that moment was real, uncalculated, and mine. Instead, I absorbed her disappointment like an unspoken rule I hadn't known existed.

"I'm sorry," I said, accepting that I had done something wrong, even if I didn't understand what it was.

"If you were sorry, you wouldn't have done it in the first place!" she replied, without looking at me.

Her words planted the seed of a lesson I would carry for years: *Why can't you be like everyone else?*

And the message was clear: Some people's joy existed freely. Mine had to be carefully placed.

• • •

Dad's happiness, his whistle, was already in motion, safe and undisturbed, something I could step into without consequence. But my own expressions of joy had conditions. If they appeared at the wrong time, in the wrong way, they could trigger disapproval. Especially when they were different from everyone else.

It was a dance I would come to know well—balancing what felt natural to me in one hand, and the weight of other people's unspoken expectations in the other. All the while learning when to suppress myself to avoid punishment or rejection.

The cost of stepping outside the lines became very clear early on for me.

Slowly, I began to realize that my natural instincts—my laughter, my curiosity, my energy—weren't always welcome. Over time, I learned to keep those parts of myself hidden, saving my true self for the safe confines of the four walls of my room.

"*Not here*," I'd tell myself, as if the world outside my bedroom walls couldn't handle the pieces of me that didn't fit neatly into its expectations.

I didn't stop being joyful. I didn't stop feeling like myself. I just learned to read subtle hints, body language, expressions of face, and even more obvious expressions like whistling as a sort of temperature check.

When I look at that picture now, I feel a mix of emotions. I don't see a child who failed to conform—I see a child caught in the moment, one of pure joy, being exactly who she was. I see someone who hadn't yet learned the cost of fitting in or the weight of holding herself back. But in the eyes of those around me, it was a lesson that I needed to learn—a skill that would eventually become second nature.

7: Shaping Shadows

I WAS A CAREFUL observer of the world around me. Each day brought lessons—not the kind taught in school, but those learned by watching and listening, absorbing the unspoken rules of family and society. In my earliest memories, I remember feeling energized by other people's company. Whether I was at school, in a room full of relatives, or running errands with my parents, that buzz of conversation and collective energy was exciting. Every new face was a possibility, another set of stories for me to unearth.

But somewhere along the way—after enough scoldings, enough sideways glances through gritted teeth, enough snapped fingers cast my way to just as quickly snap my attention, and enough repetitions of my father's sharp, "Tina, when are you going to learn to keep your mouth *shut*?"—I learned to retreat. The sheer effort of trying to anticipate what I should or should not say, the mental and emotional gymnastics I put myself through so I wouldn't break whatever fragile peace existed, was more exhausting than the joy I got from sharing my curiosity. Over time, spending too much time in the company that once energized me became more draining than it was uplifting.

Quiet became safer than curiosity. I noticed that silence kept peace. Peace was something I learned to cherish more than anything. So, I watched. I listened. And slowly, the outer world—those strained smiles, those unspoken expectations—took root inside me, shaping my shadows and teaching me, wordlessly, that speaking up often came with a cost I wasn't sure I could afford to pay.

The Narrow Way and the Broad Way: A Child's Dilemma

"Which path do we choose, kids?" The teacher's voice rang out with authority, and little arms shot up around me: "The Narrow Way!"

Five-year-old Tina sat still, perplexed.

What? That doesn't make any sense.

The Narrow Way and the Broad Way was a lesson taught in Children's Church, part of the holy-rolling Pentecostal church my family faithfully attended every week, sometimes twice. My family had sampled churches all over town, most of them dancing-down-the-aisle, speaking-in-tongues, laying-hands-on-the-sick, charismatic Pentecostal.

I remember walking through mega-churches that felt like they had been carved from marble and precious stones, where the women's painted faces and hairdos were as lacquered as the pulpits. Their style of dress, along with their family's, seemed to match the architecture: polished, coordinated, intentional.

As I poked at the fraying hem of my own dress and fidgeted with the hole in my tights, it didn't surprise me that we didn't stay long in places like that.

In 1985, the church we were attending was called Family Worship Center. It had a much more relaxed vibe—a lot less cathedral, a bit more bowling alley. The dark faux-wood paneled walls in the foyer, the tired industrial carpet... it wasn't plush like those other places, but it was welcoming enough. It was the kind of place that you'd be interested in sticking around long enough to bowl, but not a minute longer.

And so, it was in the low-lit recreation room of that church that I wrestled with the concept of the Narrow and Broad Way. As I understood it, based on the large picture displayed in front of the rows of child-sized chairs, the Broad Way meant fun and laughter and parties, while the Narrow Way led through dark, scary woods filled with unknowns. My wild imagination did not help. Why would anyone choose the path that looked like the setting of a horror movie?

I studied the faces of the kids jumping up and down all around me, arms still up in the air and shouting, "The Narrow Way!" I was genuinely confused. *What did I miss?*

• • •

I can't help but laugh with my younger self. The kids around me weren't wrestling with theology—they were just giving the "correct" answer. At five, the biggest decisions any of us faced was whether we wanted chicken nuggets or macaroni and cheese for lunch.

But as life moved forward, I came to understand the magnitude of choosing right from wrong. Concepts like the Narrow and Broad Way don't sink in until you've done—or been impacted by—something catastrophically wrong.

• • •

When I was a year or two older, I stole a pack of grape Hubba Bubba bubble gum from the grocery store. I don't recall my exact intent, only that I wanted the gum. I hadn't dared to ask if we could buy it because I already knew that the answer would be no. My decision was deliberate—I took the gum, I hid it, and chewed it with great zeal and pride later at home in my room.

No longer concerned with concealment, the pack and the wrappers from the two or three pieces I had stuffed into my mouth were right there on the floor in front of me when Dad walked in—and there I was, happily and mindlessly chomping away at it.

Dad marched me back to the store with my piggy bank and made me hand over all my life savings to the clerk. Her kind attempt to wave it off, "That's okay, honey," was no match for Dad's resolve. Without a word, and without waiting for my submission, he snatched the piggy bank from my hands, placed it on the counter, and walked me straight back out.

I lost the gum. I lost my life's savings.

I earned a heavy belt whipping when I got home. And I learned a lesson about value that far exceeded those measly coins.

Dad's actions were severe, but they weren't random. They were deliberate, and their meaning only started to come into focus as I got older and I began to wonder:

What did he know that I didn't yet?

The punishment he handed down was hard for both of us. It must have been humiliating, dragging his sticky-fingered daughter into the store, laying bare her failure in front of strangers. But he did it anyway. And he followed it up with pain, maybe because he thought that's what it took. Maybe he didn't trust his words to be enough.

There was something different about Dad's demeanor that day. It was saturated in disappointment for sure. Anger was there. But there was something else threading through it all, too. Something deeper. Was it fear? Was he afraid of who I might grow into if I believed I could take what I wanted and suffer no consequence?

Was he *protecting* me?

• • •

As an adult, I've seen both sides of the Broad Way: the intense thrill of instant gratification and the devastating consequences that often follow. In the biblical lesson, the Broad Way is the easy path, the one most people choose. The Narrow Way, by contrast, is harder. It's often lonely, uncertain, and riddled with doubt. It's rarely fun. It requires honesty, humility, and discipline—the kind of integrity that isn't glamorous and often feels unrewarded.

I think back to that little girl in the children's church, puzzling over why anyone would choose the narrow path. She couldn't yet understand that life's hardest choices often lead to its greatest rewards.

And even then, I was already learning something deeper— not just the courage to take the harder path, but the courage to question *any path* before choosing it. The courage to challenge the blind choice in any one way, even if—or maybe especially when—everyone else is excitedly in agreement, and I didn't fully understand why.

The Book Fair

I had an insatiable love for reading. Teachers rolled out reading programs that felt like gifts from the heavens themselves. Read five books, get a free pizza? Was this some kind of joke? I needed somebody to pinch me so I could believe it. All I had to do was read five books... and you're just gonna give me a free pizza? The only thing greater than my appetite for pizza was my appetite for books!

I remember another kid in class, Kenny, nudging me one day as I was finishing up yet another form. "You know you don't need to actually read any of those books," he said, glancing down at my neatly filled-out list. I was proud that I had genuinely read those books, and I wasn't taking any chances on missing out on free pizza. Besides, once I collected enough pins for myself and my brothers, my parents would take us all out to Pizza Hut to cash them in, earning that little outing for my family felt amazing. "It's not like anybody checks them," Kenny continued, his voice interrupting my imaginary family pizza night, complete with a table overflowing with personal pan pizzas.

I paused to consider his words. I understood them in the order that he spoke them, but I was confused as to why I would need to lie about reading. I loved reading! I concluded that we obviously did not share the same problem, so without acknowledging him further, I gleefully carried my form to the front of the classroom and asked for a fresh one.

For all my love of reading, though, I was limited to whatever my local library had in stock. The school book fair was a highly anticipated event, one that filled me with both excitement and a pang of longing. For most kids, the book fair was a chance to spend their allowance on shiny new treasures, but for me, it was a fantasy—a place where I could flip through pages and inhale that intoxicating "new book" smell, knowing I would never get to take those books home with me.

The school librarian's voice pulled me out of my daydream. "You going to get that book, Hun?" she asked, bringing me back to reality. It was a small question, but it forced me to confront the uncomfortable truth: I didn't have any money to spend.

"Nah," I replied, closing the book with a feigned indifference. "It just doesn't seem all that interesting. I think I'll save my money," I lied. In that moment, I began a dance I would come to know well—the dance between desire and shame, between yearning for something I knew I couldn't have and pretending not to care. I walked away, memorizing the title and cover, hoping it would be enough to fill the empty space where ownership should have been, or until it hit the library shelves, whichever came first.

Years later, when my own child brought home a Book Fair flyer, I could not contain my excitement. "The Book Fair! I can't believe it! They're still doing these?! Oh, sweetie, you're going to *love* it!" A fellow lover of reading and collecting books, his enthusiasm matched mine as he headed off to his kindergarten class the morning of his very own Book Fair. I was surprised, then, when he returned home with stickers instead of books, casually explaining that he'd given his leftover money to a friend whose mom couldn't afford to send her with any.

My mind wrestled with conflicting emotions, pride in his kindness, confusion at his lack of interest in The Most Epic School Activity Ever, and a nagging awareness of my childhood shame. His gesture was pure and free of the overthinking and self-consciousness that had plagued me. To him, it was a simple act of kindness. To me, at that moment, it was a reminder of how we can learn so much when we let go of what we think we know. Even though I'd hoped to relive my own excitement through him, I'm relieved and humbled that he chose his own path, leaving kindness in his wake.

Treasure Hunting in the Alleyway

My brothers and I were not street urchins, but I can see how some of the stories from my childhood might make people wonder. We had a home, a roof over our heads, warm meals, and clothes on our backs—everything we needed. We also knew better than to ask for anything more.

What we lacked in abundance, we made up for by seeking out new opportunities.

Our house was a 1,200-square-foot, two-bedroom, one-bath ranch on an otherwise quiet residential road behind a mini-mall in Loves Park, Illinois. The mini mall's anchor store was called Union Hall, an early discount department store that ended up getting swallowed up by the very industry it helped pioneer. "If it's not at Union Hall, you don't need it!" That was the catchy slogan I recall adults repeating when referring to it. The rest of the indoor mini mall was a variety of around fifteen specialty shops, their tenants changing frequently.

To most people, it was just a strip of stores and a back alley of loading docks and dumpsters. We saw a treasure trove. My older brother Frank had a way of seeing the world differently. Where most people saw dumpsters and semi-trucks, he saw possibility. And through him, so did I.

Frank was the mastermind behind our childhood escapades. The semi-trucks were his first discovery. They came regularly to deliver everything from Pepsi and Frito-Lay products to clothes and toys. Frank discovered that if he asked the drivers, "Do you have any extras?" they sometimes said yes. One day, he came home with snacks and treasure in hand, his face lit with excitement. From then on, we knew there was free stuff to be had in that alleyway—but Frank, ever the resourceful older brother, quickly figured out his success rate improved dramatically if he sent his younger siblings instead.

That's where I came in.

I still remember standing there, looking up at these towering men in their uniforms, nervously stammering out my inquiry about extras. Sometimes they said no, but when they said yes? Jackpot. A can of soda, a bag of chips, sometimes even something truly magical, like a small toy. Those victories felt like winning the lottery.

I was never expecting the coolest new action figure or a Barbie—it could have been a doll missing an arm, a random puzzle piece, or even a baby's rattle, for all we cared. Having a toy we didn't have before made it priceless. Any new treasure opened some new storyline in my imagination: maybe I would stage a "rescue mission" with my brothers while wearing a plastic fireman's helmet, or pretend I was a caretaker feeding my tiny plastic child. It never occurred to me to wish for anything specific, so having even the smallest new plaything felt miraculous—like some cosmic reassurance that, for once, the answer could be yes.

Years later, in conversations with my brothers, they confessed that neither of them had a high success rate. Frank doesn't remember sending us because he got a *"no,"* but he also doesn't remember *not* doing it. Either way, I believed it would work, and somehow, either by luck or willpower, it did.

Sympathy might come more easily to a trucker when faced with begging coming from a little girl rather than a little boy.

And then there were the dumpsters. Where other people saw trash, we saw treasure. There were boxes of food—things we would never have had otherwise, like Kudos bars or Goobers candies. Sure, some of them were past their expiration dates, but they were perfectly fine to us.

The dumpsters also held things far more valuable to us as kids: toys. One day, Frank came home cradling a Teddy Ruxpin in his arms. I couldn't believe it. Teddy Ruxpin was the kind of toy I would have never dreamed of owning—it probably cost a hundred dollars. My heart could have leapt out of my chest, I was so excited as Frank handed him to me. I held him immediately close to my body, hugging him with all of my might. There was no way I was going to let this fantasy escape me!

I sat down and held him in my lap to inspect him further. He had this cute little tuft of hair that I ran my hand over. My fingers traced his khaki-colored overalls where the hook and loop fasteners were sewn in on each side. Instinctively, I lifted one side to the tearing sounds of the hooks separating from the loops, and then the other.

His wide, sparkly brown eyes stared back at me as I turned him over to inspect his back, lifting the fabric to expose the cassette tape player. I couldn't believe this one was *mine*. We tinkered with it before concluding he was broken. But it was no worry because Dad, with his infamous tinkering ability, fixed him. Even if he had remained broken, that bear became my most prized possession. I loved him more than anything else I owned.

And then Chuck E. Cheese came to our town. Fortune smiled upon us and placed it right in that mini-mall in our very backyard.

In those early days, Chuck E. Cheese had a fatal flaw in its system: they didn't mark the redeemed tickets. Once customers turned in their tickets for prizes, the store employees tossed the leftover stubs into giant trash bags and threw them into the dumpster. This was the kid equivalent of striking gold.

At first, we couldn't believe our luck. Frank led the charge, dragging those bags straight out of the dumpster and around to the front of the store. With no shame whatsoever, we'd take the unmarked tickets to the counter, redeeming them for prizes that felt like winning twice. We'd walk out of there with armfuls of cheap toys, grinning ear to ear, feeling like the kings and queen of the mini mall.

But, as with all great cons, it didn't last. The Chuck E. Cheese employees caught on—probably because we were dragging the trash bag full of tickets in the same bag it had been thrown out in. Not exactly the smoothest criminals.

Soon, the discarded tickets started showing up in the dumpster, covered with orange spray paint, making them useless. For a while, we'd still try to salvage what we could—picking through the bag for the clean ones—but the effort outweighed the payout. Eventually, we left the tickets alone, but the thrilling memories of those early victories stayed with us.

It wasn't just the free snacks and toys that made that alleyway special—it was the building materials. The pallets and discarded boxes became the foundation for epic forts, constructed with the kind of creativity only kids can muster. To us, those forts were castles, ships, hideouts, whatever we needed them to be.

The mini mall itself held other treasures, too. My friend Jenny's mom, Sally, opened a drapery shop there. We spent countless days in the shop's basement, surrounded by bolts of fabric and refrigerator-sized boxes. We made dresses for ourselves, outfits for our dolls, whatever our imaginations conjured up, the basement of that drapery shop provided.

Looking back now, it's easy to see how someone might have looked at us and thought: *street urchins*. But that's not what we saw. We saw a treasure trove of possibilities, a world of opportunity hidden in an alleyway.

Though Frank was the one who first taught me about resourcefulness on that Christmas years before, that alleyway is where I first got the chance to practice resourcefulness on my own. That alleyway taught me firsthand that magic doesn't always come in shiny packages. Sometimes it's found in what others overlook or discard. Sometimes it's found in the creativity and determination of a child who dreams beyond their circumstances. Sometimes the excitement and passion of turning trash into treasure goes much deeper than buying ever could.

Where others might see limitation, we saw potential. And that ability to look at the world and see unlimited possibilities within the alleyway, within ourselves, is something I continue to carry with me to this day.

When Moods Shift

One early summer afternoon, we sat around the dining room table. Just like the sticky heat clung to the air, my legs stuck to the camel-colored pleather of my spin-style bucket chair. Dad was at the head of the table, Frank directly across from me, and I watched him with the kind of fascination only a younger sibling can have for their big brother.

Frank was about to eat a tomato. He'd been salting it, savoring the anticipation, completely absorbed in the moment. I watched, curious—was he going to eat this like an apple?—as he took his first big bite exactly like it was an apple—and the tomato juice squirted across the table, landing directly in Dad's face.

It was like watching a slow-motion cartoon that you might find in a flip book: the bite, the splash, the shocked look on Dad's face. To me, it was an accident, nothing more than a funny mishap. But Dad's reaction was swift and intense—his face twisted in anger, and I could feel the mood shift instantly. I wanted to laugh, to share in the humor of the moment. Hard as I tried, I couldn't halt the smirk on my face, but something about Dad's response kept me silent.

That day, I learned another important lesson in moods—the way they could shift in an instant, taking a harmless situation and turning it into something tense, something heavy. I realized that, sometimes, it wasn't the situation that mattered but the temper of the person experiencing it. It was a small, subtle understanding, but it stayed with me, a reminder to always read the room, to tread carefully around emotions that could change in a heartbeat.

Echoes of Judgment

Later that summer, we went out to Pizza Hut as a family—a rare treat, a break from the stifling heat of our small house.

In 1986, Pizza Hut was a special-occasion kind of place. The scent of bubbling cheese and buttery crust hit you the moment you stepped inside, mixing with the faint, slightly burnt aroma of the pizza pans as much as the pizza ovens. The lighting was dim, casting everything in a warm, reddish glow from the iconic stained-glass Tiffany-style lamps hanging over the tables.

We slid into a red pleather booth, the ripped vinyl scraped against my bare legs. The table had that glossy, laminated menu built right in—covered in pictures of oozing deep-dish pizza, golden breadsticks, and frosty pitchers of soda. A jukebox stood against the wall, glowing faintly, waiting for someone to drop in a quarter and bring it to life.

I was sitting across from Mom and Dad when I noticed them glancing across the room, their eyes narrowed, their expressions disapproving.

"That's disgusting," Dad muttered, his voice low. Instantly, my curiosity piqued. "What's disgusting?" I asked, my voice loud—too loud—and eager, hoping for something juicy and scandalous.

"Shhhhhhh," they both whispered, exchanging looks that only deepened my intrigue. Their gaze was focused on a woman sitting nearby, holding her baby, rocking him gently to soothe his fussiness. To me, it was a perfectly ordinary sight, nothing shocking or offensive. But my parents' reactions suggested otherwise.

I asked again, impatient, "What's disgusting? What happened?" But they shushed me once more, unwilling to explain. I had expected to see her changing the kid's diaper right on the table or something equally foul, but as far as I could tell, she was just holding him.

Later, I pieced it together—that the woman had been breastfeeding, and that something as natural as feeding a baby had triggered their disapproval.

Years later, as I held my own fussy babies, I remembered that day at Pizza Hut. Despite everything I'd come to believe, I still felt it—a quiet tug, as if my parents' disapproval had stretched across time, whispering their judgment into my ear.

It was transgenerational judgment, something I knew was irrational but still couldn't fully shake. So, I covered up my body and my baby each time, even in the sweltering summer heat, careful not to expose anything that might invite the scrutiny of onlookers.

I realized that judgment, like so many other learned behaviors, was something passed down through generations, a quiet shame that lingered in the background of my actions. It wasn't my belief, but it was still a feeling I had inherited—a silent lesson tucked away in my memory. And though I knew better, I carried that awareness with me, a reminder of how powerful those early lessons could be.

Fear, Logic, and Spitballs

Dad was angry. Six-year-old Tina's brain got busy trying to figure out why. I see myself now, as if from the outside—this small girl with chestnut brown hair and similarly colored large and innocent eyes, scanning the room. Scanning the face of her father, whom she adored and feared in equal parts. Scanning the faces of her older brothers, who were seated beside her on the couch, meaning no one was going anywhere until a problem had been solved.

Everyone wore a poker face, guarding their real emotions until something more substantial happened and they could reveal their cards. I searched their faces for a hint as to why we were all lined up militaristically on the couch that night. Did they show fear, worry, concern, or some quiet knowing of why we'd been lined up like soldiers?

This wasn't just discipline—it was theater. Dad seemed to relish these moments. Lining us up like soldiers was part of the performance, and his favorite weapon wasn't something he could hit us with—it was messing with our heads.

Dad stood up slowly. He removed his leather belt from his pants loops with a deliberate slowness. He made sure that we caught a full view of the length of the leather and its edges and slowly folded it in half before pulling the ends apart quickly into a sharp CRACK!—a sound that cut through the air like gunfire. I was sufficiently terrified. This went beyond fear. It hollowed me out and filled the space with silence.

If either of my brothers' faces had let a hint slip, I missed it. My fear had a way of holding me hostage inside myself, as if burrowing inward was my only safe place to be from any random storm that was brewing in our family home. I was also very focused on not peeing my pants.

My brothers and I sat, motionless, scanning the room and probably each other for possible answers. Dad's sharp question broke the silence: "Who did it?"

Silence.

This was a familiar order of events. I was never sure how or why my parents thought their style of stern questioning would ever give them the answers that they desired. I knew, logically, that owning up to my mistakes was the "right" thing to do, and I also knew it was almost never the "correct" thing to do, even if it did mean sparking more ire before someone either got caught in their lie through questioning or broken down towards a confession.

What I knew in this moment was that exactly none of us would be leaving that couch until someone did get caught or confessed.

"Who. Did. It," Dad's question lowered to that all too familiar slow growl.

I genuinely had no idea why we were there. I also couldn't find evidence of what someone had done based on anyone's faces or anything in the room. I started to wonder if anyone had done anything, and maybe this was all just a simple misunderstanding.

I said as much, breaking the silence from the couch brigade. "Whaaa-what happened?"

Dad's eyes held strong on me. He sometimes had a demeanor that seemed to defy physics. The energy behind his facial expressions could hold me in a stasis that even today I can't quite describe.

"What happened? Oh, I'll show you *what happened*."

He motioned for us to follow him.

One by one, we each got up from the couch and reluctantly followed him down the hallway to the bathroom, where he stopped.

I've never been able to hide my face. I had no idea what could possibly have happened in the bathroom, and I would bet that my face held all the ideas that were swirling around in my imagination for all to see, still hard at work trying to puzzle its way out of my terribly confusing and snowballing discomfort.

I must have had a quizzical look on my face that matched my state of mind. And I wonder if my brothers' faces held the same look, because Dad very frustratingly pointed into the bathroom and somehow more sharply than before snapped, "Look."

One by one, we poked our heads in. I saw the bathtub with the shower curtain somewhat ajar, the toilet, the sink, and the bathroom rugs. Absolutely nothing seemed out of order. I sense that any look of confusion intensified on my face, my eyebrows probably reaching new ways of contortion to express that I didn't have one single clue what we were supposed to be looking for.

"*The ceiling*," the familiar even-toned low growl returned.

I looked up. There, on the ceiling of the bathroom in our family's small home, were what appeared to be tiny wads of... toilet paper? Tissue, maybe? Something like that.

Well, if I thought I was confused before, this sight only made it worse.

How did those tiny wads of paper translate to the intensity I was gripped by? I could not reconcile the situation, let alone make sense of the alien invaders on our bathroom ceiling.

We were marched back into the living room, back to the couch.

"So, *who did it?*" Dad asked again. Impatience had long settled in, and he was trending towards being broken himself. Because this time the questioning was still firm, but far less "someone will cease to exist any longer because of this!"

Again, silence.

"Well, you all are going to sit there until *somebody* confesses!"

We all understood the rules.

Dinner? Gone.

Dessert? Forget about it.

Going to bed? Not happening.

It didn't matter how long it took. Dad would outlast us. We knew he had much higher stamina.

He left us to discuss among ourselves, like a jury might deliberate innocence or guilt of a defendant in their own midst.

When he was well out of earshot, I expected Frank to speak up. Frank was usually the enforcer when Dad left the room, his impatience sharper than Dad's questions. Bobby's silence was heavier, like he was afraid to even breathe. Me? I was the one lost in the tangle of confusion and fear, wondering how to escape.

But I don't remember either of my brothers speaking up.

So, we just sat in silence.

After a while, Dad came back into the room. "Well? Who did it?"

Silence.

"Look, if you confess now, your punishment will be less severe than if we keep dragging this out," he offered. The soothing tone was somehow worse than the anger. It was eerily calm. It was bait.

Silence.

He left us again. And again, we continued to sit in silence. Being left alone among other people always forced me to address my thoughts. I could say I did it, and we could get this all over with. If I did it and the punishment was lighter, maybe it wouldn't be so bad. And no matter how bad that might be, my punishment is never as bad as what my brothers would get, especially now, and after all of this.

I was tired. I knew the consequences. I didn't know exactly what I was being accused of, but I knew what punishments looked like in our house. I knew that my brothers weren't going to budge. I weighed this against the rising anxiety in my chest, which held me uncertain and powerless. I concluded that eventually I'd be punished anyway—I might as well be in control of *something*.

When he returned to the room, the impatience had returned, "Anybody ready to confess? Who did it?"

That returned impatience in his voice was enough to get me to doubt my plan, but not enough to stop my mouth, "I did. It was me." I said, my eyes lowered to the ground, like a beaten and submissive dog.

"You?" Dad asked, his tone unchanged.

"Yes, it was me."

A few moments passed. "How?" he asked, again in the same tone.

I hadn't thought that far ahead. I didn't anticipate that he would ask for the detailed process of the crime. "How?"

My detective work turned to fiction, crafting a story that fit just enough pieces of the puzzle to end the interrogation. I knew that it looked like paper, and it was a bathroom, so I offered, "Well, I was in the bathroom, and I took pieces of toilet paper, and rolled them up into little balls."

Dad was looking straight at me when his face turned quizzical. Something wasn't adding up...

"How did you get them on the ceiling?"

Oops. I've got to think of that, too? I got back to work, thinking fast. I was all of four feet tall, so there was no way I would've been able to put them on the ceiling standing on the ground. But we did have those bar stools in the kitchen... I reasoned that the height of those chairs plus my own height would place me within reach of the ceiling, and my mouth started moving.

"I went into the kitchen, and dragged one of the bar stools in, and I took those toilet paper balls, and I put them onto the ceiling."

Whew, that was a close one. Good job, brain!

Dad's face changed. It looked like he himself was broken, not me. "*Why would you do that?*" he asked, still firm, but with little tension, like he was relieved and could finally relax now that the case was closed, but now there was a sense of betrayal that I needed to speak to.

I said, "I don't know." It was the answer I gave when I didn't know.

I don't remember details of my punishment besides that I was spanked. I remember details of my brothers' punishments throughout the years; they'd involve creative objects like dowel rods, ping pong paddles, and more. My own corporal punishment from Dad was always either with a belt or his hand, never anything else.

• • •

I never blamed whichever one of my brothers had done it. I never felt a bitterness or resentment toward them, just a curiosity. I've always wondered which one did it, and why neither of them ever confessed, even years later. As I reflect on it now, it strikes me that their silence might have come from something deeper, something heavier than I considered at the time.

This memory is more than a snapshot of absurdity. It's a reflection of how fear twisted logic, how survival meant crafting stories no one questioned, and how discipline often replaced understanding in our home.

Even now, I wonder: Was Dad's belief in my confession a sign of exhaustion, or was he simply unwilling to see the truth? Or did he see right through it and follow through on punishment out of pride? Perhaps he thought it might teach whichever one of my brothers did it a deeper lesson, or that if I was lying, I deserved punishment anyway. Maybe it was some combination of all these reasons—or something else entirely. I'll never know.

In our house, the story didn't have to make sense, it only had to end.

• • •

These fragments of childhood—seemingly disconnected moments of whimsy, discipline, and discovery—painted a picture of a life filled with contradictions. Each memory, whether absurd, profound, or painful, carried its own set of lessons, teaching me to navigate a world that often felt contradictory and unpredictable.

Through these moments, I learned to hold contradictions within myself: that joy and shame could coexist, that creativity could bloom in the face of scarcity, that fear could coexist with love. I saw how the same people who provided stability could also create instability, how the lessons they taught, whether through love or punishment, could leave lasting imprints, both good and bad.

As I grew, these contradictions became a part of me. They taught me to question, to seek, to wonder about the world beyond what was immediately visible. I learned to see possibility in limitation, to find beauty in the overlooked, and to navigate the delicate balance between conformity and authenticity.

Above all, I learned that the most profound lessons often came from the quiet spaces between joy and pain, between what was said and what was left unspoken. They were lessons in resilience, in adaptability, and in the power of finding strength amidst the contradictions of life.

8: Volume Issues

L OOKING BACK, MOST OF my parents' friends were remarkably kind, patient, welcoming, and understanding. My parents had one particular set of friends with whom they'd swap babysitting duty from time to time, a couple with a son who was around Markie's age, then two, and a baby girl.

I think the dad's name was Drew, and maybe the mom's name was Mary. She seemed like a Mary. Drew had this uncanny ability to quote the Bible by scripture effortlessly and without pretense. It was like God's word poured directly out of his heart and into the room.

But more importantly, this family introduced me to Juicy Juice.

Juicy Juice. Real fruit juice. If you were raised like we were— on a steady diet of chemical water (a.k.a.. Kool-Aid)—then you'd understand how life-changing this was. One of my earliest visceral memories is tasting that rainbow of real fruit juice for the first time.

To this day, I have the most wholesome idea of people and families who drink Juicy Juice, and that is thanks to Drew and Mary.

One night, Drew and Mary were babysitting us at our house while my parents were out. I don't remember where they went, but they weren't home, and Drew and Mary were in charge. Like any other night, we Anderson kids were horsing around in the basement family room.

"Horsing around" usually meant wrestling matches or play-fistfights. Sometimes, we'd jump off one of the top bunks onto an unsuspecting sibling below. We had rules, of course. We weren't neanderthals. No hitting in the face or the crotch. Even I, as the only girl, knew that last one, though I didn't entirely understand it.

Of course, horsing around typically ended the same way: someone got hurt. That night, that *someone* was me.

One of my brothers broke the cardinal rule and kicked me right between my legs. I crumpled to the floor, howling like a banshee. Mary came running down the stairs, her face full of concern, to find me rolling on the carpet, clutching myself dramatically.

"What happened, honey?" she asked, crouching down beside me, her voice notably soft and kind.

This was new. Concern? Not mad, not anger—but actual concern for my well-being? I wasn't used to this kind of attention. For a moment, I soaked it in like sunlight. But then I realized I'd have to explain what happened because, despite my best effort, I could not seem to will myself to stop crying.

And that's when the panic set in.

These were my parents' friends from church. Church-going people. Wholesome, Juicy Juice-serving Mary. How was I supposed to explain this to her? What words could I even use? Could I say "crotch?" "Nuts?" Was "dick" off the table? My brothers said that word sometimes to describe the area between their legs, but was that a *bad* word? What did it even mean?

I spiraled. Too much time passed as I debated my options. Mary leaned closer, her eyes full of love and concern. "Sweetie," she said gently, "you have to tell me what happened so I can help you."

I shook my head, doing my best to signal that I didn't know how to explain. Mary misread my hesitation, her face shifting to alarm. "It's okay," she almost purred, soothingly and lovingly. "You can tell me."

Finally, I blurted out the safest, middle-ground explanation I could think of:

"He kicked me in the balls!"

I didn't just say it—I *wailed* it, amplifying my distress and turning my performance up to Oscar-worthy levels.

Mary, to her credit, didn't flinch. She stayed calm, completely undeterred by my dramatic outburst. Then, in the most gentle, serious tone imaginable, she said:

"Sweetie, you don't *have* any balls."

From behind me, my brothers burst into laughter, and I couldn't help but join in. Mary started laughing too, which signaled that I wasn't in trouble for swearing. Soon, the whole room was filled with joyous laughter. Not because it stopped hurting, but because it helped me forget that it did.

The Candy Man's Game

To our close-knit church, he was a man beyond reproach. A beacon of Christian values. A model of warmth, generosity, and kindness. He was The Candy Man—a title spoken with great affection.

Every Sunday, without fail, he'd be there sitting in the church foyer, dressed in his neatly pressed slacks, button-down shirt, and jacket, a beaming smile stretched across his face. He was everyone's friend, shaking hands, slapping backs, handing out peppermints and butter scotches like a currency of goodwill. His pockets were always full of a seemingly endless supply of sweets he offered freely to the children who crowded around him.

"Go on, reach in and grab one," he'd say with a chuckle, giving an encouraging nod. And so, we would.

One by one, little hands would plunge into the depths of his pockets, searching for treasure. He'd grin down at them, his eyes twinkling with something that looked like nothing but pure delight.

"Now, don't tell your parents how much candy I gave you!" he'd joke, wagging a playful finger and a laugh.

And the adults would laugh with him, shake their heads, *Isn't he just the best?*

He loved the children, after all. He let them sit on his lap. He let them tug at his sleeves, at his graying hair. He was harmless. A great guy. A pillar of the church, embodying all that anyone there learned about patience, graciousness, and lovingness.

When The Candy Man called a meeting, people showed up. They showed up because he had concerns. He had something to say. And when a man of such unimpeachable moral character spoke, people listened.

My parents were there, his wife, their Bible study group, the pastor, the Children's Church leaders—all gathered in the fellowship hall. The room had a bank of windows along the back wall with mini blinds in various states of open and closed. It had the same industrial carpet as the rest of the church, as well as the old faux walnut paneling along all of the walls. The two wide doors leading to the fellowship hall— normally held wide open as an invitation to all—were now closed.

I stood in the middle, small, seven years old, in this room where our Children's Church group often played hot potato, feeling the weight of all of those familiar faces staring at me with suddenly unfamiliar eyes.

"Tina has been swearing and using the Lord's name in vain," his wife hissed, her voice dripping with scathing disappointment. Her words hung in the air, sharp and judgmental, while I stood there. Small. Frozen. Trying to comprehend what I'd done wrong.

I knew better than to swear in public, especially in front of church members. I wasn't stupid. I hadn't done what they accused me of—yet here I was, a sinner in their eyes, a "bad girl" in need of redemption. My small mind wrestled with the accusation.

Also: "the Lord *in my veins?*" What does that mean? How could I even stop that?

I ran everything I had learned about religion from that Pentecostal church and others like it that we attended as I grew up.

He is supposed to be in my heart. How did I manage to mess that up? And what does this lady know about that?

I felt the judgment of the group pressing down on me, their disappointment suffocating me. My gaze darted to The Candy Man, the one adult I'd been silently pleading with in my heart to step forward, to make this all go away.

He had always been nice to me, always treated me like I was special, and I clung to the hope that he might defend me, might tell them that I wasn't as sinful as they seemed to believe.

But he never looked at me. Not even once.

Earlier that summer, The Candy Man and his wife were at our house for a good old-fashioned barbeque picnic. We had invited them and a few other people from the church over to go swimming and enjoy a summer day in our above-ground pool in our backyard at our home in Loves Park.

I remember I wore my two-piece bathing suit. Well, it was sort of two-piece. The top and bottom were hot pink in a sort of popcorn shirt material. It had a stretch to it that suggested that I might get to wear it well into adulthood. It also had these black elastic suspenders that were covered in neon colored music notes and connected the top to the bottom.

I remember that bathing suit because The Candy Man helped me take it off in my room, which was in the basement. And I remember it was sort of funny the way he stood in my doorway as I was distractedly playing in my room, but I was supposed to be changing into dry clothes.

And I remember it was funny the way he told me that my parents had sent him in to help me change because I didn't need any help changing my clothes.

And I remember trusting him as he lay me down on my bed to remove my most favorite not two-piece swimsuit to "help me change."

I don't let myself surface memories beyond that. They are there—I can feel it in the way my stomach twists just before the door in my mind slams shut. I remember the detail of a small picture on my wall in its white wooden frame, and yellow gingham mat, of a single white and yellow flower. And I remember carefully listening to him as he left my bedroom, that we would need to keep it between us because "they wouldn't understand."

I remembered that and I remembered my promise. And if I could keep that promise, then I could not possibly be the swearing, lying, sin-filled little girl before them that day.

I was confused as the adults continued, joining hands in a circle around me, their heads bowed, voices rising in prayer over the "sin-filled little girl" they believed I had become.

It felt like I was shrinking, growing smaller and smaller under their scrutiny. I wanted to disappear, to melt into the floor, to be anywhere but in the center of that room that used to be full of laughter and safety but now felt like a condemning hot potato circle from hell.

As I cowered in that circle, surrounded by the adults who claimed to love and protect me, something happened that I haven't been able to fully explain, even now. Their hands rested on my head, my shoulders, my back, as their voices rose in prayer. They spoke of cleansing and redemption, calling out the sin they believed lived in me. But I deflected all of it—the hands, the words, the weight of their judgment. My body, my mind, and my heart pushed it all away.

And then, something else filled the space.

It wasn't a person in that room. It wasn't the touch of their hands or the cadence of their prayers. It wasn't even something I had the capacity to name at the time. But I felt it —I felt held—loved, even. Not by them, certainly, and not yet by myself. It felt as though something far beyond me had stepped in, wrapping me in a sense of purity and clarity that I couldn't possibly have conjured on my own.

I felt absolved—not of all wrongs, because I was a child, and children make mistakes. But I was innocent of the sin they accused me of that day, and I knew it with a confidence so strong it was undeniable, because it was—from this side of my eyes, The Truth. These people were Wrong. Their prayers, their judgments, their collective certainty—they were Wrong. And this knowledge didn't just live in my head; it anchored me in a way I'd never felt before.

It felt bigger than me, bigger than them, bigger than that room. It was outside this world, and yet it was there with me that day, holding me.

That feeling stayed with me, quietly but firmly, long after I left the circle. It didn't stop the pain of what had happened, the betrayal, the isolation. But it reminded me that their words didn't define me. That my truth was mine, and that it mattered.

They prayed over me for what felt like hours. The cadence of their voices was like a chant, repeating words of repentance and cleansing that I didn't understand but felt were meant to purify something in me that didn't belong. My heart was pleading silently, "I was not going to tell *anyone*, ever!"

Looking back now, I realize he'd done this on purpose. But back then, I didn't realize that this was his way of ensuring my silence, of making sure I knew who held the power. By accusing me of sin, he had tainted me in the eyes of the very people who might have protected me. With his wife by his side and the group's collective trust in him as The Candy Man, he had the perfect cover to make sure no one would believe me if I ever dared to speak out, which I never would have. It took me years to realize that what he had done to me in my bedroom was even wrong.

After church, we had to make a stop at the grocery store. I started to get out of the car, but Dad turned around from the driver's seat and said, "Not you. You're staying right here." I caught Mom's eye. In that moment, I felt what she must have been feeling, and I noticed that her face held a pained expression and what felt like shame and embarrassment. I offered as earnestly as I possibly could, "I'm sorry!"

"If you were sorry, you wouldn't have done it in the first place!" she replied, her eyes not leaving mine, and then she and my brothers closed their car doors, leaving me alone with Dad in the car.

He looked out the window, his tone casual, like we were discussing what we'd have for lunch. "Do you want your punishment now, or when we get home?"

"W-what?" My voice shook, startled and confused by the question.

His head turned, his gaze fixing on me, impatient now. "Do you want your punishment now? To get it over with? Or do you want to wait until we get home?"

Hadn't I been cured by whatever happened back there at church?

I didn't know how to answer. Part of me wanted to scream, "I didn't do anything wrong!" I wanted to explain, to beg him to believe me. But I was small, and he was my father, and I could feel the impatience building in him. Any resistance would be viewed as insubordinate and only make things worse.

I weighed my options, reasoning that a spanking in the car would be quick, though embarrassing, with people around.

But if we waited until we got home, maybe he'd forget. Maybe, at the very least, he'd be calmer. "Home," I whispered, keeping my eyes down.

When we got home, he led me into the living room and sat on the edge of the recliner, his expression unreadable. I knew better than to try to run. I knew that any resistance would only make things worse. So, I walked toward him and lay across his lap, awkwardly positioning myself, feeling the humiliation seep into my skin as he pulled my pants down.

In that moment, I went somewhere else. It was a place I'd often go, a place where I could separate my mind from my body, where I could hide from the pain and shame that felt like they were swallowing me whole.

I don't know how many swats I received across my rear end by his bare hand. It wasn't something anybody ever agreed to in advance, or that we had the luxury of preparing ourselves for. Any spanking he doled out that afternoon paled in comparison to the deeper, darker form of punishment assailing my heart and mind.

When it was over, I pulled my pants back up, my face burning with embarrassment and something deeper. I wasn't crying, but the sadness clung to me like a second skin. I was beginning to understand that even here, in this place where I should have felt safe, I was alone.

And at the same time, I understood and even accepted my father's perspective. From everything Dad knew about that day, I had sworn in church, which was a totally punishable offense. Even though I didn't do it, he didn't know that, and I didn't hold my punishment against him.

• • •

The Candy Man's wife made my life miserable after that. Her gaze was sharp, filled with disdain, and every time she saw me, I could feel her judgment. Years later, because of her changed behavior, I wondered if she had had a sense of what had really happened. Did she know? I had become an outcast in my church, marked by the accusation he'd placed on me. His silence, his cruelty disguised as piety, had cast a shadow over me that I instinctively knew I couldn't escape.

This was the moment when I began to realize that "good people" could be anything but. That even the church, with all its teachings on love, kindness, and forgiveness... could be a place of betrayal. And that the people who claimed to protect and love you could be the very ones who turned a blind eye, or worse, who actively joined in casting you out. Even if they didn't know the truth. And especially if they did.

In hindsight, I know now that his accusation was a calculated move—a way to isolate me, to make sure that if I ever spoke up, my voice would be drowned out by the judgment of those around me. He had taken away my power, my trust, my innocence, and left me alone with the knowledge that even the people who should protect me could not always be trusted.

Are You Guys Jehovah's Witnesses?

Some moments stay with you, not because they were monumental, but because they perfectly encapsulate the chaos, humor, and absurdity of growing up with siblings. This is one of those moments.

Frank had a knack for mischief that was subtle enough to fly under our parents' radar but effective enough to leave an impression on us younger kids. Frank's specialty wasn't yelling or roughhousing—it was planting ideas. Intentional or not, they were little seeds of chaos, and he knew exactly which minds would water them.

I must have been around seven or eight when Frank casually dropped one of his most memorable pearls of wisdom into our lives. We were all hanging around, bored, as kids often are, when he casually mentioned, "You can usually spot Jehovah's Witnesses. They're the people who walk around all dressed up, looking nice for no reason."

Now, to be fair, this was delivered with such casual authority that it never occurred to me to question it. I mean, Frank was older. He knew things. And what did I know about social norms or religious practices or even what a Jehovah's Witness was? To me, religion meant Pentecostal fire and brimstone—hours-long sermons, altar calls where people collapsed in emotional outbursts, danced chaotically up and down the aisles, and strict teachings about heaven and hell. It meant knowing exactly who was saved and who wasn't. But Jehovah's Witnesses? That was a new one.

My parents would certainly have known. They would have recognized them as a distinct religious group, separate from our own. And Frank? At fourteen or fifteen, he probably knew this, too. His choice to introduce this particular piece of wisdom to his younger, more gullible siblings now seems far less random than I had assumed at the time. I never thought to question his intent. If Frank said something, then it must be true.

Armed with this newfound "knowledge," I took it to heart and promptly started applying it with curiosity. Anytime I spotted someone who looked a little too polished for the occasion—maybe they were wearing a suit, or a particularly fancy dress—I'd boldly ask, "Are you a Jehovah's Witness?"

I have no idea how many innocent people I tormented with that question. Polite businesspeople who were probably just trying to go about their day suddenly found themselves on the receiving end of my unsolicited interrogation. I couldn't seem to find anyone who would admit to being one, which only deepened my sense of curiosity and commitment to finding one.

The moment it all came to a head was one Sunday afternoon at Sears. Sears was one of those quintessential American destinations, an anchor store in every bustling mall and a household name in department store retail. It was a pre-Amazon one-stop shop, a place where families could spend an entire afternoon picking out new clothes, comparing home appliances, and maybe even indulging in a soft pretzel or bag of popcorn along the way.

The store itself was cavernous, with displays for absolutely everything from Kenmore washing machines to rows of glittering jewelry counters, and the hum of shoppers was near constant. It was the kind of place where kids could wander, spouses might separate to tackle their errands, and every department offered its own small world of possibility.

Into this everyday suburban scene stepped my family and me, our weekend ritual more or less set: start in the clothing section, meander through the shoes, and wind up testing lawn mowers or vacuum cleaners for no particular reason. It was a routine we never thought twice about until that Sunday, when Sears became the stage for the drama about to unfold as I spotted them, a couple across the bustling showroom. They looked *perfect*. They were dressed to the nines, standing out like they'd just stepped out of a fashion magazine. My little brain fired on all cylinders. This was it. This was them. This was my moment.

Without hesitation, and with all the enthusiasm my small lungs could muster, I shouted across the store:

"HEY! Are you guys JEHOVAH'S WITNESSES?"

The chaos that followed is seared into my memory. Heads turned. Conversations stopped. Somewhere across the aisles, a display of vacuum cleaners stood witness to the aftermath of my outburst.

Our parents? *Super* not amused.

Dad gave me the kind of glare that could turn water into steam. Mom's face cycled through embarrassment, disbelief, and frustration in rapid succession. I braced myself for the scolding I was utterly confused about but knew was coming, but not before catching a glance at Frank.

There he was.

Frank, with the biggest shit-eating grin plastered across his face. He looked like a kid who had just won the lottery. Vastly different from my parents, he wasn't mad. He wasn't embarrassed or mortified. He was *delighted*. I could see it in his eyes. He'd been biding his time, waiting for the perfect moment when one of his younger siblings would put his plan into action in a way that he could witness firsthand.

It was his masterpiece, and I had delivered it right to him.

Later, after the storm of parental fury had passed, I started to piece together that maybe Frank's advice hadn't been entirely sincere. He had set me up, knowing full well what might happen, and he had gotten exactly what he wanted: chaos and entertainment at my expense.

• • •

I cannot think about that moment without laughing now. Frank's grin, the stunned silence of the Sears showroom, the way our parents practically evaporated from embarrassment—however many strangers on the random end of my interrogation—it's all so vivid as it replays in my mind.

While I'm sure Frank wasn't thinking about "teaching lessons" that day, I can't help but reflect on how much he shaped my childhood. For better or worse, he taught me how to find humor in the absurdity of life—and how to laugh at myself when I inevitably stepped in it.

So, Frank, if you're reading this: Well played.

9: Learning the Rules

I LOVED THE HOLLYWOOD DINER, a place filled with cozy warmth, the smell of burgers, and endless plates of golden-brown fries. It was a treat for us, a family outing that felt luxurious in its own modest way. As a family of six, trips to a buffet-style restaurant like this one offered a rare chance to indulge. For me, it meant piling my plate high with goldfish crackers and chocolate pudding, and for a few minutes after we ate, it meant exploring the arcade corner where my brothers and I could press buttons and pretend we were playing unless we encountered one of those rare opportunities where someone left a stray quarter nearby and one of us actually got to play.

One winter evening, as we prepared to leave the diner, I spotted something on our table: a crumpled dollar bill.

I kept a close eye on it. I knew better than to make a scene. Dad or Mom would probably spot the forgotten dollar before we wandered too far away. I lingered at the table. I lingered a bit longer. And then I realized that no one else had noticed the dollar on the table. *Activate!*

"DAAAAAAD! You left a DOLLAR on the table!" I yelled, dollar waving in the air like a flag, chasing him through the bustling diner.

By the time I reached him at the counter, his face had hardened, and I immediately knew I had done something wrong. He gritted his teeth and growled through a forced smile, "*Put it back.*"

Confusion overwhelmed me. Why was he upset? I was just trying to help. Money wasn't something we had an abundance of, and I knew saving every bit was important. Leaving a dollar behind seemed like a mistake.

"But Dad, you left this dollar on the table," I persisted, not quietly, staring down at it, hoping he'd see the sincerity in what felt like my heroic act.

His expression darkened. *"When are you going to learn to keep your mouth shut?"* he hissed. That phrase was the full stop, the one that meant I'd crossed an invisible line.

He handed me a few more dollars, his jaw clenched, and ordered me to "go put this on the table. Now." My cheeks burned as I walked back, feeling the weight of other diners' eyes on me, more confused than when I started.

• • •

I figured it out years later when someone explained the concept of tipping to me. Putting two and two together, I realized that it wasn't that I had done something wrong; it was that Dad was embarrassed. My loud, well-intentioned announcement had revealed his reluctance to part with more than a dollar for service at an all-you-can-eat dinner for a family of six.

That night, I learned that sometimes, despite all of the evidence you may have to the contrary, silence is expected. I began to understand that my father's anger was often not about me, but about something else entirely—the invisible burdens I couldn't yet grasp. As uncomfortable as uncertainty is, I didn't want to hold space for both, but I had to, because I had no other choice.

The Neat Freak

Our home was always meticulously clean—or at least, that's how it appeared to anyone looking in from the outside. But even as a young child, I understood that this appearance of perfection wasn't about comfort or organization; it was about control. Mom had a rigid idea of what "clean" should look like, and anything less than her uncommunicated and ever-changing vision triggered a wrath that turned our house into a warzone.

One summer day, I heard it—the unmistakable call that signaled she was on a rampage. "TINA!" Her voice sliced through the stillness of the house like a warning siren. I froze. This was the beginning of a dreaded ritual I had come to know too well.

I could hear her rummaging through my things before I saw her, each movement heavy with purpose. Then came the loud shuffle of clothes, toys, and anything she deemed "out of place." By the time I reached my room, it was a disaster zone. The neat piles I'd carefully made, my little stashes of treasures—all were strewn across the floor as if a tornado had blown through.

I stood in the doorway, unsure of what to do. If I tried to help, I would be "doing it wrong." If I stayed still, I would be accused of "making her do all the work." So, I chose the middle ground, feigning busyness by moving things from one side of the room to the other, hoping she wouldn't notice.

Then she yanked open my closet doors and gasped. "SHOES PILED HIGH!" she yelled, her voice sharp with disgust. She started flinging shoes over her shoulder without even looking. One of them—a white patent pleather church shoe with a hard heel—sailed through the air and struck me squarely in the forehead. The pain was sharp and immediate, like a hot knife slicing through my skin, but I stayed silent. Crying, I had learned, only made things worse.

My hand shot up to my forehead, and I felt the warmth of blood seeping between my fingers. The sight of red made my heart race, but I didn't dare make a sound. "I'll give you something to cry about" was a phrase I feared more than the pain itself.

I glanced in the mirror and removed my hand to see if it looked as bad as it felt. Blood spurted out like a small, frightening fountain, splattering across the mirror above my dresser. My voice trembled as I spoke, trying to sound calm despite my panic. "Uh... my head is bleeding."

At first, she didn't even turn around, too busy tearing through my closet. "GOOD!" she spat, her words dripping with venom. It wasn't until I repeated, "Uh... it's bleeding really bad," that she spun around. Her face shifted instantly from fury to something resembling concern. She grabbed a t-shirt from the mess on the floor and pressed it against my forehead, and we went upstairs to the bathroom to assess the damage.

The storm had passed.

It left behind the briefest flicker of motherly care that almost made me forget the miserable scene that preceded it.

On the way to the emergency room, she seemed concerned, though I was not sure about what: my well-being, or how Dad would react when he learned about what had happened. Mostly, I was relieved that the yelling had stopped.

• • •

I still catch myself stuffing things into closets and hidden corners, hiding clutter as if it might protect me from something unseen but ever-brewing. To me, "clean" has never been about tidiness—it was about control, about avoiding the storms I couldn't predict or stop. That lesson, like the scar that remains on my forehead, stayed with me far longer than any mess I ever made.

And even now, long after the yelling has stopped, I sometimes feel that old instinct rise—the urge to disappear the mess, to prevent a storm that isn't even coming.

Tina Cries a Lot

When I was in the fourth grade, I was placed in a special class to address "self-esteem issues."

My teacher had recommended it out of concern for certain behaviors I had displayed in the classroom. In the mid-1980s, my parents likely had no idea how to handle me. Just as rigid about following bizarre rules as they were in creating them, they probably felt they had no choice but to support the teacher, possibly in spite of, or perhaps even reinforced by, my crying and pleading.

The teacher's recommendation, my parents' passivity, and my resistance all carried some weight. Starting from Kindergarten, my report cards often stated, "Tina cries a lot," a detail that likely swayed my teacher's concern and ultimately my parents' reluctant agreement. At the time, my parents were navigating their own challenges, shaped by societal norms that discouraged questioning authority and their own limited experiences with how to handle an emotionally expressive child.

"I'll give you something to cry about!" tended to have an opposite effect than what they intended. (I think.)

These factors likely left them feeling ill-equipped and uncertain about how to "fix" me. At the time, I was living through a childhood marked by trauma, and as a poor family, our expectations for what I could achieve were modest at best. So that I needed or would benefit from some help was not off base; it was just ill-timed.

The worst part of this so-called "self-esteem" class was that it was scheduled at the same time as my Reading class, a subject I adored and excelled at. As a fourth grader, I was advanced to take lessons with the fifth graders. Missing that opportunity felt like a cruel punishment.

As if that were not bad enough, the special class was held in the "LD" (Learning Disability) hallway, a place I feared would draw unwanted attention and ridicule from my peers. Back in those days, the "LD" hallway carried a heavy stigma —not because there was anything shameful about the students who learned there, but because our culture hadn't yet figured out how to talk about learning differences without judgment. Just walking into it felt like I was confirming something shameful about myself, and that weight didn't come from the kids—it came from the way society saw them.

All of this amplified my resistance to the class and deepened my doubt in the authority figures or adults entrusted with my "care": the teacher, my parents, the self-esteem teacher, and anyone else who seemed to value compliance or otherwise incorrect sweeping assumptions over listening or understanding.

Besides being "overly emotional," I also had a habit of frequently opening my mouth to challenge my teachers when they were wrong.

My rationale, if anyone had bothered to just ask? I would want to know if I was wrong about something. It's like having a booger on your face. You'd want to know if you had a booger on your face, right?

The teacher being wrong about one thing and leaving the error unchallenged made it really difficult to focus on anything else they said, because I did not (and still do not) know everything, and I would have no idea if anything else they were saying was also wrong.

For me, mistakes might as well have been a metaphor for a fatal flaw in the space-time continuum, requiring repair before life could continue, and I could listen to literally anything else that followed.

Also, I understood that her awareness of her error would make her a better teacher. This belief, that acknowledging mistakes leads to growth, is central to my core. It shaped my approach to authority, making me critical of those who refused to admit fault, and reinforced my commitment to transparency and accountability in my own actions.

And maybe just as important? I personally absolutely loathe having to redo something that I've already done. Doing it the right way helps you avoid having to do it again.

Cue memory of Dad's voice in my ears scolding, "Tina! *When are you going to learn to keep your mouth shut?*" His frustration often echoed the sentiments of those report cards that noted, "Tina cries a lot," followed closely by his familiar refrain, "I'll give you something to cry about." To him, my emotions and outspoken nature seemed inseparable, creating a child he likely felt unprepared to handle. This perception shaped our relationship in ways I'm still unpacking.

I often felt as though my father viewed me as a problem to be solved rather than a person to be understood, which left me questioning whether my natural tendencies were, in fact, flaws to be fixed. Over time, this belief about myself and our dynamic became a driving force in my journey toward self-awareness and authenticity.

I zipped through those workbooks, puzzles, and little game-things as fast as I possibly could so I could get back to the 5th-grade reading class.

I answered every question the teacher was asking perfectly according to what I thought she wanted to hear.

And as far as my teachers and my parents were concerned, the behavior modification class "worked."

In other words, they were satisfied that I could fall in line and conform.

I learned to keep my mouth shut and that Authority, with very few exceptions, was not to be challenged, even When It Was Wrong. This lesson, however, created an ongoing conflict with my natural tendencies to question and to speak up. While it served me in navigating systems that valued conformity, it also left me grappling with the tension between compliance and my deep-seated belief in honesty and justice. Reconciling these opposing forces is ongoing work.

It also taught me that to get what I want (in this case, back to the 5th-grade reading class), I would have to behave the way someone else wanted me to, just because they wanted me to. Even if it wasn't important to me, or something that I wanted.

The behavior modification class taught me how to thrive in a world that I frequently felt I wasn't meant for.

While I did "learn" to keep my mouth shut and feign ambivalence the same as my peers, I have never learned to hide my face. And it typically holds the precise words and thoughts that I have not stopped thinking.

It is both my greatest liability and my greatest strength—this face that refuses to be silenced, even when the rest of me has been trained to.

A Sticky Thanksgiving

Thanksgiving, 1988. Mom convinced our entire family to upend tradition and abandon turkey.

Instead of that golden, familiar bird, she proudly announced that we'd be dining on exotic meats and dipping various ingredients of questionable appeal to a child into expensive and hard-to-pronounce melted cheeses. Fondue, she called it, and she said it with an air of sophistication that made it clear she was proud of this culinary innovation.

To say we were disappointed would be an understatement. Turkey was tradition. Turkey was what all the kids at school would be talking about. Turkey *was* Thanksgiving! And while the adults also grumbled about the deviation from the norm, we voiced our objections loudly and without restraint. Whether out of annoyance or practicality, they eventually gave in. Sparing us the fondue effort, we were served cold-cut sandwiches instead.

The holiday took place at my grandmother's house on Mom's side. Grandma's house was a haven. Everything about it felt cozy, safe, and unchanging. The scent of Caress soap lingered in the air, a smell I can still conjure today as easily as stepping through her front door. It was where I recovered from chickenpox, where I drank Coke straight from the glass bottle, and where I was allowed—encouraged, even—to shove my hand into the cereal box to fish out the toy, with Grandma always standing by in full support, physically, mentally, and emotionally.

But holidays at Grandma's house carried an extra energy, something layered beneath the surface of the warm holiday cheer. There was joy, but it always seemed slightly tinged with something performative, as though the happiness came with an unspoken pressure to deliver it perfectly. It was like the feeling of eating an orange after brushing your teeth: sweet and good on one level, but with a faintly sour undertone that never fully left your mouth.

The adults sat in Grandma's formal dining room at the "grown-up table", while we kids—me, my three brothers, and our cousin, Jeff—were relegated to the smaller kitchen table. This was no problem for us. The adults' world of fondue and small talk wasn't ours anyway. We had cold cuts, cheese slices, bottled Coke, and free reign to goof off and tell fart jokes without the drag of serious adult intervention.

I don't know whose idea it was, but at some point, someone threw a slice of cold cut at the wall. The real surprise wasn't that someone threw it—it was that it stuck to Grandma's wallpaper.

The particular *slapping* sound was delightful, and the fact that it defied gravity by staying there was absolutely mesmerizing. We stared at it, wide-eyed, and then erupted in maniacal laughter. What else could stick to the wall?

Cheese? Yes, it sticks!

The game was on. A slice of ham here, a piece of cheese there, and soon enough, the wall looked like a makeshift deli mural. Our laughter grew louder with each successful stick and failed bounce, and we were completely lost in the rush of our little experiment.

Sweet gherkins don't stick. We knew that, and they went flinging anyway. Because really, they only belong in one place, and that is the trash.

We should've known it wouldn't last.

At some point, an adult—whose face I can't remember but whose stern tone I'll never forget—burst the fun bubble. We froze, our giddy giggles still echoing in the air, and braced ourselves for what was coming. We got the scolding we undoubtedly deserved, a firm talking-to about respect and decorum, though in hindsight I can't imagine anyone actually thought that fondue was the foolproof recipe for elegance, even if it was served on Grandma's formal china and silverware.

As soon as the adult left, we sat in silence for about ten seconds before the giggles started up again, stifled as best as we could manage so as not to attract the attention of any other adults who would ruin our fun.

It wasn't long before the ham and cheese had been cleaned off the walls, and the kitchen was returned to its normal state. But the memory of that Thanksgiving has stuck with me far longer than the deli meat stuck to Grandma's walls.

10: Finding Myself in the Absurdities

APRIL 13, 1989. IT was Bobby's 10th birthday. The house buzzed with energy—a little different from the usual birthday buzz, though. Bobby was going to have a real birthday party at the house, with kids from school, and I knew that he was getting a new bike. That was the big secret, and one I think I had actually managed to keep. I attributed the unusual energy in the house to my relief at finally getting to unload that secret.

Having people over meant Mom was busy cleaning the house, presenting it in a way that was clear in her mind but a total mystery to the rest of us. I did my best to feign alignment with her intensity and, as usual, stay the heck out of her way.

The details of the day are fuzzy. I don't remember what was served, what games were played, or who came to the party. What I do remember—apart from the bike reveal—was the shift that happened when the day started to wind down.

"Ha, ha! Your birthday isn't until the 30th!" Frank exclaimed, snapping the day's carefree energy back into tension.

The commotion that followed was intense. My parents' body language screamed *this is not a laughing matter*, but Frank's face held a glee that would have rivaled a kid let loose in a candy store.

I tried to connect to Bobby in that moment, to imagine what it would feel like if we had just celebrated my birthday on the wrong day. And in that moment, a memory came rushing back—my own birthday, the year prior.

• • •

It was the first day of school, and the teacher had asked the kids when their birthdays were to put them on the classroom calendar for everyone to see. Each kid responded as though they just *knew*. Like knowing your birthday was the most obvious day in the world. When it was my turn, I guessed a random day in June.

I've never been able to hide my face; my teacher must have seen right through it. She headed over to her desk, flipped through the spiral-bound book that all teachers had, which contained the class roster, and she put one hand on her hip, "Hmm."

She headed back over to me, crouching down to my level, her face full of concern.

"Today is your birthday. *You didn't know that?*"

Her worried face didn't match what I knew I was supposed to feel about birthdays. Birthdays were supposed to be fun and exciting. People were supposed to be *happy* when they talked about them. And I certainly was, especially finding out that it was my birthday. But her expression held something different. I didn't know what to do with this contradiction.

So, I shrugged, tried to change the subject, so it would go away. But it was too late, the kids around us had already heard what she said, and suddenly they were all staring at me like I had twelve heads. It was all too clear to me that I should have known when my birthday was and certainly that it was that day... but I hadn't.

• • •

Those feelings flooded back as I watched Bobby's face. I could see him searching for the quickest route to normal— trying to sweep it under the rug, to make it stop, to will everyone to please stop *talking* about it, already!

Between Frank's laughter and our parents' frantic urging for him to chill out, they explained what had happened. Bobby's original birth certificate had the date handwritten in cursive —*April Thirtieth*—but it had been misread as *April Thirteenth*. It wasn't until someone looked at the typed version, showing 4/30, that the mistake became obvious.

Our parents had known about the mix-up for years but hadn't had the heart to tell him. After all, Bobby had always thought his birthday was April 13.

• • •

None of us has forgotten. Markie probably doesn't remember that day exactly, he was too young. But even he knows the story well, as it has been retold by his older siblings countless times over the years. For years, we gave Bobby a hard time about it every April 13th. And Bobby, true to form, always gave a sort of half-hearted, "Ha, ha, very funny," followed by an unspoken plea for us to stop bringing it up already. I wonder now if his annual half-laughs weren't just good sport, but self-protection. The kind that keeps you from reopening a door that never fully closes.

I'm struck by how much of our shared history feels like this: stories that unite us but don't always carry the same weight for everyone. I feel a tug at my nervous system calling me to consider that maybe this isn't simply a funny anecdote, but a reminder of how easily someone's feelings can go unnoticed, and how quickly a person's reality can be rewritten by others without anyone ever meaning harm.

These are the thoughts that echo most for me now. That even the stories we laugh about, the ones we think are harmless, can hold a complexity we don't bother to unpack until years later. It's a humble reminder to look closer, to listen more carefully, to *lean in*, and to honor the parts of someone's story that may hit differently than they hit for you.

A Child's Drawings

I was nine. I know this because the girl Mom babysat for a short time, Stephanie, was seven, and I am almost exactly two years older than her. At nine years old, I had it in my mind to play an art game. I was going to teach Stephanie how to draw something, but I wouldn't tell her what it was until we were finished.

We sat cross-legged on the floor of my bedroom while I walked her through each step as though I were coaching her through a drawing of other mundane things, like a kitten or a rainbow.

I remember specific details of my teaching, and in hindsight, I'm surprised by how detailed both our drawings were. I was proud of myself. And I was proud of her, too. By the end of our drawing session, two little girls had two erect penises on colored construction paper, on full display there on my bedroom floor.

After our arts and crafts session, we played with dolls. Or played house, or went outside to play in the yard. Just like any normal kid, on any normal day.

That evening, everything seemed perfectly normal. Stephanie went home, we ate dinner, and I fell asleep without a care in the world.

Until Dad woke me up.

He yanked me out of a deep sleep. It was dark, late. Dad was *pissed*. He demanded I get out of bed and meet him in the living room upstairs. "*Now*," he growled.

I had no idea what was going on. I had no idea what I'd done.

Upstairs, Mom and Dad sat in the living room. I stood in the doorway, not wanting to come nearer, and knowing that lingering would only make things worse.

I shuffled towards them, each step heavy, resisting with the least effort possible. I did not want whatever was coming to me and could not participate in my own destruction, but I willed myself to, anyway.

Dad's face was one of bewildered disbelief, while Mom sat stone-faced, her hands clenched tightly on her lap. The silence stretched unbearably, thick with unspoken judgment.

"We just got off the phone with Stephanie's parents," one of them said flatly.

This is one of those moments where adults say things and you know they expect an answer, but you don't have the foggiest clue what they're talking about. And then you're thinking too much about how you should respond, and by the time you figure that out, you've completely lost track of the actual question. So, you just stand there, trying to look like you're paying attention while having absolutely no idea what's going on.

I still don't think I have this look nailed down.

I stood there, dumbfounded as to what to say or how to respond to this news.

"They said you led Stephanie through a little... *drawing exercise* today?"

Uh oh, I thought to myself, trying to will the redness from flushing to my face, my body betraying me, signaling a dead giveaway of guilt before I even understood what to feel.

"Oh... yeah!" I managed to stammer. "Yeah, that was fun!"

"Do you... have those drawings, down in your room?"

"Oh, yep! I sure do!" I offered quickly, hoping that honesty would be the best way out of my predicament.

"Why don't you go get them," Dad said, not asking. "We'd like to take a look at them."

My heart sank to my stomach. I thought they'd leave it at that. In the moments before turning towards my room, I really had no idea that I'd done anything *wrong*. But the way they looked and the way they were framing the conversation suggested that I had, in fact, done something wrong. And so, it would be imperative at this moment not to admit to anything.

Downstairs, back in my room, I looked desperately to find two drawings that might pass for something that two different people drew that weren't *that*.

No such luck. It's like I didn't plan for this crime at all.

Reluctantly, I picked up the two drawings, and was left with only gravity this time to propel me back up those stairs to the living room, where my parents were waiting for me. The shame and embarrassment I felt in that moment eclipsed any will I had to stay out of trouble. I was caught red-handed.

I held them in my hands, with the guilty evidence facing me. "Here they are," I said, as if bringing them to the room might still have been sufficient. It was worth a shot.

Dad reached out his hand. "Let me see them."

I handed over the drawings, hoping they might somehow magically transform into something different, like kittens or rainbows, the moment they touched Dad's hands.

I couldn't make eye contact with him. Or her. I was deeply crimson red in embarrassment and shame.

I don't know how much time had passed before one of them spoke up.

"What was going through your head?"

The tonality of exasperation was all too familiar to me. It meant I had really screwed up. It meant I had disappointed them. And it meant I was going to be in for a long night.

Dad had put them side by side in front of him. They seemed to stare back at me as I sat across from him.

As it often does, my imagination went to work. Upside down, the drawings kind of reminded me of corn husks. The hair could pass as the corn hair thingies. It could pass as the WEBLOS Boy Scout symbol I'd seen embroidered into badges that my brothers had. Maybe? I don't know, I guess to 9-year-old-Tina, it was worth a shot:

"Well, we started out drawing corn husks, but that wasn't working out..."

The details of my full imagination as explained by 9-year-old-me escape me, but the way the looks on my parents' faces dissolved from disappointment to relief was immediately noticeable. So I just kept talking until they got bored of hearing me talk about my totally innocent art project.

It must have worked because they sent me off to bed. They wanted to keep the drawings, but said goodnight, and I headed back downstairs towards my bedroom.

"Whew!" I thought to myself as I descended the stairs to the stillness and quiet of the basement. Even if I still didn't know exactly why I was in trouble, I knew that I had probably just avoided a legendary ass-beating.

• • •

Thinking back to my nine-year-old self, in my mind, I was innocent. I didn't feel like I was doing something wrong until I felt like I was in trouble. That's why I scrambled to cover up my "crime." It was a pivotal moment for me—a place where innocence and guilt blurred, and somehow, I had to keep holding space for both.

Even as a child, I felt their silence more than their words. And as I grew, that silence stayed with me.

How could they have missed it? *How could they not see?* And how did no one question why a nine-year-old girl knows how to draw an anatomically correct erect penis?

I imagine 7-year-old Stephanie at her own parents' dinner table that night answering the age old question, "What did you do today?" with, "Tina taught me how to draw a penis!" because I had *explicitly* told that's what we'd drawn.

Was I that compelling a storyteller? Or was it just easier for everyone to believe it was a coincidence?

Fine! Really, I'm Fine!

I was around 9 years old. Frank had recently acquired a 10-speed bike, and it felt like a treasure I wasn't supposed to touch.

But I couldn't resist.

My bike was a standard single-speed with the kind of brakes you pedal backwards to engage. The 10-speed was sleek and intimidating, but exciting with its brakes on the handlebars. I had no idea what I was doing, but I wasn't going to let that stop me.

I propped the bicycle against the bench that ran along the driveway in front of our garage, steadying it with my left hand. I go-go-gadgeted my arm out while walking behind the back wheel and stretch Armstrong'd my right foot up onto the bench, stepping up just high enough to swing my left leg over the seat. I was instantly grateful for my foresight to leverage the bench because I realized very quickly my legs were way too short, and my feet were nowhere near the ground.

I took a deep breath, and I shoved off from the bench, wobbling my way down our driveway. So far, so good!

The plan was simple, and I rehashed it in my mind while I pedaled: I'd take the 10-speed to the end of the road, turn around, and see how fast I could get that puppy going. There was only one intersection to cross on the way back. *Easy enough*, I told myself. I'd just watch for cars, and if I saw one, I'd hit the brakes. No big deal.

I reached the end of the road, turned the bike around, and lined myself up for the return. I could feel the weight of the moment, like fire burning down the back of my neck. I took a deep breath, exhaled, and I was off.

The wind whipped against my face as I pedaled faster and faster. The world blurred. I felt invincible—until I saw the car in my peripheral vision to my right. My brain, prepared for this moment, screamed: *Brake!*

My little feet spun the pedals backward as fast as they could, pumping them with all my strength, but nothing happened. I didn't even have time to wonder why those weren't the brakes.

The car hit me square on my right side. I went airborne.

What happened next is hard to explain. Instead of pain or panic, I felt... held. It was as though something had caught me, gently cradling me from a distance, like I was no heavier than a feather. Even as my body made contact with the pavement, skidding to a halt, it felt soft. Controlled. Like someone or something was protecting me and gently returning my body to the ground. I can still feel that sensation—light, calm, safe.

I opened my eyes. A woman was running toward me, panic in her eyes. "Are you okay? Sweetheart, are you okay?"

I sat up and looked around. My first thought wasn't about me or my body—it was about the bike. My brother's bike. It was nowhere to be seen. I felt a jolt of panic. "Where's the bike?" I managed to croak out.

A passerby pointed toward a tree. There it was, crumpled against the trunk, the front wheel still spinning like a dying top. My stomach sank. *Shit.*

Voices buzzed around me. One of the adults said they needed to call the police. Was that expensive? Another mentioned an ambulance. That definitely sounded expensive.

"No," I blurted out. "Please don't call anyone—I'm fine!" I was anything but fine, but the fear of Dad's reaction outweighed the pain of what had happened. "I'll walk down the street to my house and tell my mom what happened. I'll bring her back here. Please, don't call anyone. Please?"

Somehow, they agreed.

Back at the house, Mom gave me a look I couldn't quite read —half disbelief, half suspicion. It wasn't worry or fear. It was puzzled, like she was trying to piece together a puzzle with missing pieces. Like there was more to the story than what I was presenting.

"No, really," I told her, "There's a lady down there, and some other people, and they're threatening to call the police unless you come down there and tell them I'm okay."

She didn't look convinced.

Reluctantly, she walked back down the street with me to where the car, the woman, and a small gathering of concerned adults were waiting. The puzzled look on Mom's face must have been contagious because now all their faces were wearing it.

"Why do you think she didn't want us to call the police?" "Why do you think she didn't want us to call her dad?" "Where *is* her dad?"

The questions hung in the air, floating around me like fireflies I couldn't swat away. I was feeling dizzy, whether from the impact or the anxiety. My mind was racing, trying to figure out whether I was winning or losing the war on *please, please, please don't tell my dad.*

This was the eighties, long before cell phones, and I had no understanding of what happens when your kid gets hit by a car. Apparently, none of the adults did either. But the next thing I remember, we were back at the house, and I was trying to explain what happened to Dad, who had, against my urging, been called before Mom headed up the street, and had to leave work early.

To this day, I'm not sure if one of those strangers guilt-tripped my parents into taking me to the ER, or if it was something they decided to do on their own. All I knew was that I was fine—*very convincingly, very fine!* I was walking, talking, smiling—fine!

Our family had planned to go to the Hollywood Diner that night, our favorite spot with the kids-eat-free special. I did not want to ruin that—there was no place in the world my siblings and I loved more. I was fine. *FINE.* Saying it aloud might have gotten me accused of talking back, so I kept it to myself, silently willing the evening to go as planned.

Dad looked at me. "Okay," he said. "We can go to dinner first, or I can take you to the ER first. Your choice."

"After," I said. Of course, I said, "after."

Dinner went off without a hitch, like I hadn't just been airborne earlier that day, like I hadn't been struck by a car and crunched my brother's prized 10-speed. Internal injuries be damned—its kids eat free night!

• • •

I can sense that *something* happens whenever something major happens. It's not a feeling I can name, but it is something, because it's definitely not nothing. When something happens, the air feels almost stale. It's a mixture of fear, of uncertainty, and although it is something that I cannot name, it is something that you cannot trust.

We went to Hollywood Diner that night, but that something came with us. It buckled itself into the car with us, wedged itself between us kids in the back seat. It wrapped its arm around Dad as he awkwardly and seemingly unable to stop himself from chattering away.

It's similar to the feeling on a big day like Christmas or your birthday. Where almost nothing can go wrong. There's a runway for miles and miles to make mistakes, but that something hangs delicately in the air, and you can't name it, and you can't see it, but you know it is there. And you can't enjoy it because even if it feels good for a little while, you know it won't last.

We ate, we laughed, we enjoyed the diner's fluorescent glow and sticky vinyl seats, and then Dad and I went to the ER.

No scrapes, no bruises, no broken bones.

The doctors confirmed what I already knew: I was fine.

And just like that, it was gone. That Something. As if nothing had happened at all.

A Christmas Miracle

It was Christmas morning, 1989, the year *The Little Mermaid* was released. I was nine years old, and my entire world revolved around that movie. To say I adored it feels inadequate. I practically *worshipped* it. Ariel, Flounder, Sebastian, I loved them all so fiercely it bordered on obsession. Every song, every frame, every moment of the movie held me in a sort of spell.

I bounded out of bed with the unbridled enthusiasm of a child who still (mostly) believed in the magic of Santa Claus. On Christmas morning our small house was transformed. The living room glowed with the twinkling lights of the tree, and the air felt charged with possibility. My brothers and I dove into our stockings and ripped into packages, our laughter and excitement filling the room.

And then it happened.

Frank and Bobby held up their gifts from their stockings: plush *Little Mermaid* ornaments from McDonald's. One was Sebastian, another was Flounder, and the sight of them made my heart skip. But as I sifted through my own pile of gifts once, twice, and a third time just to be sure, I realized something terrible.

There wasn't one for me.

I froze. I couldn't understand how Santa—magical, omniscient Santa—could have made such a grave mistake. Didn't I love *The Little Mermaid* more than anyone else in this family and possibly the world? Hadn't I been good this year? The injustice of it was too much to bear.

At nine years old, I was in the strange middle ground of believing and not believing in Santa Claus. I had my suspicions, of course. While our fireplace was electric, I climbed up the flue one day to see if I could get outside, onto the roof—but found that it stopped at the ceiling. But I wasn't ready to let go of the idea of Santa. I still needed him to be real.

I decided, out loud and with conviction, to write a letter to Santa. My parents, I reasoned, might overhear my plan and act as Santa's intermediaries if needed—just in case my worst fears about his existence were true.

"I'll just let Santa know about the mistake," I announced. "My ornament probably got left in his sack or fell out of the sleigh. Or maybe it's still at the North Pole! I can understand how busy Christmas must be. I will just leave him a note to remind him, and I'm sure it'll be here tomorrow."

I wrote my letter carefully, explaining the situation with all the maturity and diplomacy I could muster. I made it clear that I wasn't angry, just disappointed—and that I trusted Santa, of all people, the father of Christmas, to be fully able to correct the error. I left the note prominently displayed by the tree, where Santa (or whoever might be filling in for him) couldn't possibly miss it.

The next morning, I woke up with the same nervous anticipation I'd felt the day before. I rushed to the living room and stopped in my tracks. There, sitting on top of my letter, was a *Little Mermaid* ornament.

I stood frozen for a beat, overwhelmed. And then my heart soared. The Christmas Miracle I needed had arrived.

· · ·

As I've grown older, I've come to realize that the magic of Christmas isn't about Santa or presents or ornaments. It's about love. It's about the people in our lives who hear us, even when we don't realize we're being heard, and who go out of their way to bring us joy. It's about believing in something bigger than ourselves, even when the evidence suggests we shouldn't.

That ornament—whether it came from Santa or a tired, overworked parent—did more than make me happy that morning. It kept my belief alive. Not just in Christmas or Santa, but in magic, in wonder, and the idea that sometimes, when we need it most, the universe (or someone who loves us) will conspire to make sure we feel seen.

Toast

One morning, when I was about 9 years old, I woke up with a fierce hankering for some buttered toast. Now, I don't know why on that particular morning I had such a vicious desire for melty butter on toasted bread, but I did, and so I set out to the kitchen to satisfy my craving.

As I lowered the slices of knockoff Wonder white bread down into the toaster, I could practically taste the lightly browned warm deliciousness melting in my mouth. I opened the harvest gold colored fridge by the faux wooden handle and grabbed the Country Crock, set it on the counter and peeled back the lid.

Country Crock is always spreadable, even right out of the fridge, because it is a manufactured butter-like substance, not real butter. But I grew up knowing no different, and I remember feeling especially irritated whenever other people insisted on setting out "real butter" because it inevitably destroyed whatever you were trying to spread the rock-hard, impossible-to-spread substance on. Even now, I insist that it tastes the same!

But I digress.

By now in our story, my bread has toasted to a perfect golden brown, and our old toaster notifies me of its finished work by springing my fresh toast up with that magical "toast is done" sound. I carefully, yet quickly, remove the toast from the toaster to retain heat and maximum toastability, and lay it out onto my napkin, which is waiting on the counter next to the tub of Country Crock. I scrape up a nice layer of butter and lay it on thick, smoothing it out from crust to crust. I grab the other slice and duplicate my efforts to cover my toast perfectly and evenly in golden buttery glory.

I had worked pretty quickly, and at this point, I was rather impressed with my work, and due to my focused, speedy efforts, the butter hadn't even started melting yet.

I pause for only a few seconds to let the butter melt, but quickly lose patience as the nagging drive to enjoy warm, fresh, buttered toast reminds me why I stand here today. I carefully pick up the napkin which now holds my delicious, buttered toast and my mouth begins to water as I feel the warmth of my finished project from under the napkin.

I lay my small breakfast down on the breakfast bar and climb up onto the closest stool. I take a deep breath, giddy with anticipation. I pick up one slice, bring it to my mouth, and take a big bite...

What... (chew, chew) the... (chew, chew)... oh, *yuck!*

FROSTING.

Not golden, delicious, melty butter—frosting! Despite being a Tupperware lady, Mom reused Country Crock containers like nobody's business, and I, at the tender young age of nine, had fallen victim to her extreme thriftiness. Her homemade vanilla frosting, while delicious, was entirely unexpected!

• • •

There weren't a lot of things I could control at that time in my life, but breakfast? That felt like one of them. I was nine, growing more independent, and making my own toast was one small way of asserting that independence. I had my process down—perfect golden-brown toast, just the right amount of butter, the satisfaction of doing something for myself.

And then, just like so many other moments in my childhood, reality came along and said: *Nope.*

A mix-up, a misunderstanding, and suddenly, instead of warm, melty butter, my toast was slathered in leftover frosting, a cruel joke played not by a sibling, but by sheer absurdity itself. It was a minor moment, a small betrayal—

but in a world where bigger betrayals loomed, it felt like a perfect metaphor. Like the fates were conspiring against me.

Looking back, I laugh. Because what else can you do? Maybe that's why I gravitate towards absurdist humor—when you grow up in a world where control is fleeting, you either get crushed by the dysfunction or learn to shake your head, take another bite, and roll with it. Because now that you know it's frosting, you can notice that it actually tastes pretty good!

And you can always be grateful it wasn't bacon grease.

11: Crossroads and Chaos

SOMETIME BETWEEN 1989 AND 1990, Dad got a new job that meant moving to a new state: Ohio. While he started work at the TV station in Canton—his first time serving as Chief Broadcast Engineer—the rest of us stayed behind in Loves Park, waiting for our house to sell and for the school year to end. For a while, it felt like we lived with one foot in each world.

Once school let out, Mom, Frank, Bobby, Markie, and I joined Dad in Canton for what felt like an extended vacation. Arriving in the city for the first time validated my imagination: it was an entirely different world. Eager to learn about our soon-to-be home, I had written to the Chamber of Commerce, and they sent glossy magazines and brochures celebrating local highlights: the Pro Football Hall of Fame, Timken manufacturing, the McKinley monument, sprawling parks, and bustling shopping districts. From what I'd read, Canton, in addition to Ohio, "had it all!" My eyes drank in every detail they could.

As we exited the freeway in our Buick Century, the sun was setting over the busy shopping area called Belden Village. We rolled the windows down, letting the fresh June air wash over us, as if it might help us feel closer to our new home. The evening light cast a golden glow on everything: the car hoods, shop windows, and street surfaces. In that moment, I felt a distinct shift inside me—maybe it was hope? I wanted to believe that this place would be something new, Something different. And exactly what we all needed.

Dad was staying in a furnished apartment while we searched for our next house. To my nine-year-old self, it wasn't just an apartment, it was a dream. Like a hotel, but better. It had everything: couches, beds, dishes, and towels. Why didn't everyone live in a furnished apartment? I decided then and there that when I was an adult, I would. In my mind, apartment life meant freedom. Glamour. Adventure.

One afternoon, while Dad was at work, Bobby, then eleven, announced he'd be making lunch for everyone. Inspired by some cooking show he'd watched on PBS, he dove into the kitchen like a professional chef, completely in his own world. Bobby was making tuna fish sandwiches. A basic recipe, sure, but he approached it like he was crafting a masterpiece. Bowls clanged, drawers opened, and Bobby moved with pride on his face and mastery of his station. Watching him move with confidence and joy, I couldn't help but smile. There's something intoxicating about seeing someone in their element, like watching the stars align, and everything just clicks.

The room buzzed with quiet contentment, Bobby's pride radiating like sunlight as we all gathered and sat down at the table. And then, just as quickly as it came, the light was snuffed out.

Lost in the delight of my own sandwich, I hadn't even noticed Mom taking a bite. So, when her voice slashed through my preoccupation, it felt like a slap across the room:

"Don't you know how to make tuna fish sandwiches?"

Her mouth was still half-full, her body tense. Bobby froze.

My 10-year-old brain got busy trying to figure out how our gratitude could have so suddenly warped into rage. My thought process was interrupted.

"DON'T YOU KNOW HOW TO MAKE TUNA FISH SANDWICHES?" she repeated, her voice rising to an uncontrolled boil.

We all sat stunned, looking at our sandwiches, quizzically. And then each other.

"I'LL FUCK YOUR ASS!" The volume of her voice was so loud it seemed to shake her entire body, the table, and the whole room.

The air left the room, taking Bobby's joy with it.

Frank, then around seventeen years old, laughed. It was funny, after all. *What an absurd thing to say.* But Frank always laughed when tension bubbled over, like a pressure valve releasing. One laugh led to another, and soon the room was in total disarray. Mom's anger spiraled, and Bobby's pride crumbled like broken pieces at his feet.

I don't remember the details of what happened next, and have a hard time looking back and seeing anything besides the absurdity of the scene. According to Mom, Bobby had used too much mayonnaise, and this culinary crime is what had earned her fury.

I remember feeling confused about why it was such a terrible thing. And I remember feeling scared. Through my adult eyes, I can plainly see that it was ridiculous then, and it's ridiculous now.

• • •

For years, when I retold this story, I focused on the surface humor of it.

But writing this out and reflecting on it has brought a deeper layer into focus. Why did she say that? What would prompt a forty-two-year-old, self-proclaimed "good Christian woman" to hurl such vile words at an eleven-year-old boy over something as trivial as too much mayonnaise?

She didn't say it to be funny, and I don't think she said it just to be cruel. There was intent in her outburst. It was meant to wound, like a frustrated toddler who doesn't know his words yet, with a tantrum. To put Bobby in his place, to crush the joy he'd found in the simple act of making sandwiches.

Her words weren't really about the sandwiches or the mayonnaise or even Bobby. They were an outcry of her own pain, stress, and unresolved issues that boiled over in moments like this. It's hard to pinpoint a single cause, but being 474 miles away from her entire family and the only place she'd ever known as home, cooped up in a one-bedroom apartment with four kids ranging in age from six to seventeen, likely contributed to her mounting frustration. In that moment, Bobby was simply the nearest target, someone she could vent her pent-up emotions on with little to no consequence.

And what about the rest of us? Markie, only six, likely didn't understand what was happening but absorbed the tension all the same. I was confused but scared, trying to navigate the storm while staying out of its path. Frank, at seventeen, laughed—probably because he thought it was funny, but probably because it was the only way he knew how to defuse the situation.

As I write this now, I'm struck by the weight of what we witnessed that day, what we lived with every day. Her anger wasn't just loud, it was volatile, unpredictable, and deeply unsettling. And yet, because we could do nothing else, we normalized it. We had no other option.

This story is one of the infamous ones we retell whenever we get together, each of us filling in the gaps in the others' memories. We laugh now, because what else is there to do? But beneath the laughter lies a quieter truth: how quickly joy could be extinguished in our home, and how we learned to find humor in the havoc just to survive.

And yet, even now, trying to make sense of it feels like chasing smoke. Frank and I have revisited this moment more times than I can count, like the Zapruder tape, we turn it over, test different angles, search for a logic that never appears. Even her sisters could not explain her behavior. The best we've come up with is that she felt powerless, and these moments of unpredictable, crushing rage were how she clawed back control. But knowing that doesn't make it make sense. It never did. And maybe it never will.

The Jeans Realization

I was sitting in my seventh-grade math class, mindlessly fidgeting with my pencil as the teacher's voice droned on in the background. Math lectures had a way of turning into white noise, letting my mind wander far from numbers and equations.

History and science, when taught by teachers who prioritized learning over memorization, could capture my interest. I loved social studies, the way it connected dots between people, places, and events. And I excelled at English, no matter the teacher. I sometimes wonder if I had ever had an awful English teacher, whether I would have even noticed.

But math might as well have been a foreign language. I looked around the classroom, at the rows of desks filled with my classmates—kids I'd been around for years but didn't feel particularly close to. They all seemed to exist on a wavelength that I was tuned out of, a frequency where they just "got" things I didn't. Then one day, something odd caught my eye.

It was just one kid I noticed at first. And then another. And then another. Before I knew it, I was practically spinning around in my chair, noticing and re-noticing the same evidence over and over again.

The pants. Everyone was wearing jeans.

It might seem like a small thing, a detail that should have gone unnoticed, but it was as if someone had flipped a switch in my brain. Jeans. Denim. Everywhere. Row after row, seat after seat, each kid was clad in denim—except me.

My mind went back to my parents' words, the warnings about jeans. "Poor people wear jeans," they had said, as if it were an indisputable fact. It was a story they had crafted for me, a story meant to separate us from others, to show the world that we were different—better, even. But in that moment, I realized it wasn't a story anyone else was adhering to. Here in this classroom, jeans weren't a sign of poverty. They were just...normal. The standard.

I can never hide my face, and it must have been saying something loudly enough for my friend Trice to notice. "What is it?" she whispered.

Wide-eyed, I turned to Trice, whispering urgently, *"Everyone is wearing jeans!"* as if I'd stumbled upon some great revelation.

She laughed, giving me a strange look. "You're so weird!" she said, rolling her eyes. But I could see her amusement.

She laughed.

So I laughed. We both laughed. Her laughter was carefree, mine tinged with embarrassment. I'd been sheltered in ways I hadn't even known to notice until that very moment.

That day marked a shift. Jeans weren't just jeans anymore. They were a tiny rebellion waiting to happen, a silent promise I made to myself that one day, I'd wear what I wanted, not what I was told to wear.

Dreams and Dismissals

I was in sixth or seventh grade, sitting at the kitchen table one evening, absolutely electrified by the day's science class. We'd learned about gamma rays, and at that moment, I was *sure* I'd stumbled onto something revolutionary. The idea burst out of me the instant Dad walked through the door after getting home from work.

"Dad! I figured it out! We can use gamma rays to get rid of cancer!"

I didn't know much about cancer then—just that it was a terrible thing a lot of people wanted to cure. My Aunt Penny had died of it, and my big takeaway from that experience was that it kept coming back, claiming more of her body each time until it ultimately killed her.

Gamma rays, I reasoned, would need to be narrowed in on cancer cells somehow so they didn't destroy the healthy ones. What I had learned about gamma rays was that they killed all cells. And once cells were dead, they didn't come back.

And so there it was, my offering of the solution on a silver platter, straight from the mind of a middle schooler.

He looked down at my papers and books and folders splayed out across the kitchen table. It felt like my own laboratory, holding all the worldly evidence I had at my disposal in the mid-nineties. He placed a hand on the page that held my hypothesis and read it for a few moments.

"That'll never work," he said. Not unkindly, but with a resigned fatalism that only adults seem to master. Then he continued on his ritualistic path toward his bedroom to decompress after a long day.

I felt deflated. My excitement evaporated as quickly as it had come. If my dad, the smartest person I knew, didn't believe in my idea, why should I? Gamma rays, curing cancer—it was just a silly notion. I shelved it in the mental junk drawer where I kept other "childish" ideas. The ones the grown-ups told me weren't worth pursuing, like being an artist. Or a singer.

I wonder if his own parents had responded to him in this way. He had been a lifelong tinkerer, nicknamed 'Giz'—short for 'gizmo'—since childhood. It was a nickname that could have been given either with admiration or exasperation, or perhaps a bit of both. His father died when he was fifteen, so I don't know how much encouragement or discouragement he had growing up. But I do know that by the time I came along, he had already decided which ideas were worth entertaining and which weren't. And mine, at least in that moment, didn't make the cut.

• • •

It wasn't just my gamma ray idea. Looking back, there were a lot of things about me that didn't fit neatly into my parents' worldview. Take math, for instance. To this day, I don't "know" my multiplication tables in the way most people do. I can calculate answers and even have strong competence in mathematics, but I never memorized those basic tables that children are supposed to learn in grade school, no matter how hard I tried. I struggled later, too, when math involved memorizing formulas instead of understanding them.

My parents told me it was because I was lazy. And having no other logical explanation, I believed them. I was lazy. There was no other reason that I couldn't seem to memorize what every other kid my age could. I could plainly see that this came easily to other people and so I must not be trying hard enough. I must be lazy.

Even as I believed I was lazy, I worked around it. I found ways to interact with math that worked for me. I found out that I didn't need to memorize those tables because I could always figure out solutions. But I carried that "lazy" label with me for years, well into adulthood. It became a part of my self-image, even as evidence of the contrary kept piling up.

As I got older, I realized: I'm actually pretty good at math. Once I stopped trying to force my brain to memorize things it didn't want to memorize, and leaned into understanding instead, it all started to click. In college, I even tutored other students. Turns out I wasn't lazy—I just needed to solve the problems in a way that made sense to me.

My brain simply processes information differently than they expected. What my parents and teachers saw as laziness or a failure to conform was really just a mismatch between how my brain worked and how they thought it should.

We like to think that parents, teachers, and authority figures have our best interests at heart. And most of the time, they do. But what I've come to understand is how frequently their advice, critiques, and dismissals come from their own often narrow worldviews.

We all do it. We project our values, fears, and biased experiences onto others without even realizing it. We decide, consciously or not, what's "right" or "possible" based on the stories we've internalized about the world.

But when we impose those worldviews on kids, we risk shutting down their creativity and individuality. We risk silencing their unique ways of seeing the world—the very perspectives that could lead to innovation, progress, or simply a richer understanding of what it means to be human.

• • •

For a long time, I believed the stories other people told me about myself. I was lazy. I was naïve. I didn't think things through. And maybe those things were true in some moments. But they weren't all-encompassing definitions of *me*.

I don't know if there was a single turning point when I began to reject those narratives. It was more of a slow awakening, a series of moments where I realized: *Maybe they were wrong about me.*

Maybe I wasn't lazy; maybe I just learned differently.

Maybe I wasn't naïve; maybe I was optimistic.

Maybe my "silly" ideas weren't silly at all.

With effort over time, I reclaimed my voice. I started to trust my instincts and lean into my natural curiosity. And I made a conscious decision to approach others, especially kids, with a mindset of encouragement instead of dismissal.

• • •

When I think back to Dad dismissing my gamma ray idea, I wonder what might have been different if he'd said, "That's interesting—tell me more." What if he'd leaned into my curiosity instead of brushing it off?

What might I have discovered about myself, about science, about the power of exploration?

Years later, I was stunned to learn in some stray news article that gamma rays are used in cancer treatment. I chuckled at the words staring back at me in black and white print. The very thing I'd blurted out at the kitchen table as a kid wasn't only plausible—it was real. And while it's tempting to enjoy the irony, I mostly just marvel at what might have happened if Dad had taken that spark seriously.

We'll never know, of course. But what I do know is this:

Every time we dismiss someone's idea—especially a child's— we close the door on possibility. And every time we encourage their curiosity, we crack that door open a little wider.

The Weight of a Pencil

"Man, you don't wanna give me your pencil because you're racist," declared Mia Thompson.

My heart sank. The middle school art room, usually a blend of open, buzzy creative energy and the faint smell of acrylic paints and pencil shavings, suddenly felt claustrophobic. The hum of chatter and the scrape of chairs faded into the background as Mia's accusation rang in my ears.

Mia was about my height, just under five feet, but she outweighed me by at least twice my own weight. She walked around with her hands balled up tightly into fists, matching the defiant expression that seemed glued to her shiny, deep-brown face. She typically wore an oversized plaid flannel shirt jacket and baggy jeans, which only partially concealed her distinctly feminine, hourglass figure.

For the early nineties, she was wearing what most kids were wearing, including me. Though I was about as femininely shaped as a two-by-four, and I doubt my own baggy flannel hid that fact for me, either.

Mia seemed completely unconcerned about combing her hair. It always appeared to have a mind of its own, sticking up stubbornly in every direction. She carried herself with a stance that clearly read, "Don't mess with me." At eighty-five pounds soaking wet, I was acutely aware that she could have easily flattened me if she wanted to. Not that she ever had. Still, I made a point to stay out of her way, and I noticed that most other kids did the same.

I froze, no words coming to my defense. Fear and confusion gripped me—fear of what others might think, confusion over whether Mia's words held any truth, and a deep shock at being called something so unimaginable to my younger self.

I am not racist!

My best friend is Black!

I only have one pencil on me!

These thoughts raced through my mind as I tried to make sense of the moment, but none of them made it to my mouth. It doesn't make me racist to resist giving up my only pencil. She should've brought her own supplies!

Despite my inner protests, I watched as my hand moved almost involuntarily, handing over the pencil. She snatched it with disdain, scoffing, "Racist." Her voice carried a sharpness that sliced through me, leaving me stunned and ashamed.

A wave of amplified discomfort hit me. I wanted her to stop calling me a racist. I wanted to stop feeling like a racist. And yet, the moment I gave her my pencil, I felt as though I'd betrayed myself. If I truly wasn't racist, why did her words bother me so deeply? Why had I caved under the weight of them?

If I'd been accused of lying, cheating, or stealing, I would have stood up to her with conviction, confident in my truth. But here? In this moment? I wasn't sure I even felt qualified to determine whether I was racist or not. That uncertainty stuck with me long after the pencil was gone.

• • •

There's another element to my reaction, and it's where my own reckoning began: What if it hadn't been Mia Thompson? What if it had been one of the popular kids asking for my pencil?

If Anna Hartwell, one of the long-blonde-haired, perfectly dressed girls who held social power like currency had asked me for my pencil? Would I have hesitated?

Probably not.

Not because Anna deserved the pencil more than Mia, but because the urge to fit in, to please the right people, would have overridden any sense of fairness or principle I thought I had.

And that was unsettling.

Because it meant that my decision wasn't just about race, it was about popularity. Unfortunately, when I dig deeper, I know it wasn't *not* about race, either. It was about race and power and class, the unconscious calculations my brain had already learned to make by the age of twelve.

• • •

White people who don't believe they are racist loathe being called racist. It feels like an attack on character, a fundamental misjudgment of who they are, rather than a challenge to reflect. I know because I felt it.

Looking back, I don't think Mia was trying to have a conversation about race. I think she was annoyed. Maybe she just wanted a pencil and called it like she saw it, reacting to her own unconscious biases. Maybe she knew that calling a white girl racist would make said white girl uncomfortable, and maybe she found that funny. Maybe she wasn't wrong.

What I know now is that racism isn't just about malice. It's also about the small, instinctive hesitations, the unspoken hierarchies that shape how we move through the world.

Mia saw something at that moment that I wasn't ready to see.

• • •

I can't wrap this memory in a neat bow. It wasn't a revelation, just a crack in the surface—one of many I've felt throughout my life.

On reflection, I can't know Mia's heart or motives, but I know my own. And I know that I am still a work in progress. If the same situation unfolded today, I'm sure I would handle it differently. I might say, "You may be right, but I'm not going to give you my pencil because I only have one. I can help you ask around to see if anyone else brought more than one that you can borrow."

Not because I owe Mia anything, but because I believe in meeting people where they are. Because I don't want to let my own defensiveness keep me from doing what I know is right. Because I know that it's not avoiding the discomfort, but addressing it, where the real work begins. It's not about self-flagellation or guilt; it's about growth, about learning to see the world—and ourselves—more clearly.

The Great Pop Heist

It didn't take much to spark an adventure between Bobby and me. Just sixteen months apart, we were practically joined at the hip. Dad even referred to us as "Bert and Ernie." We shared an unspoken understanding—a silent agreement to chase what we wanted, without much forethought about rules or consequences.

One summer night, Bobby and I hatched what we thought was the most brilliant plan of our young lives. The Kmart down the road kept cases of pop outside, and we noticed that they were unattended after hours—the tempting, elusive stacks of sugary, fizzy goodness just waiting out in the open. The plan was simple: in the middle of the night, we'd sneak out, ride our bikes over, and liberate a couple of cases. It was the ultimate heist.

The night arrived, and we initiated the execution of our plan with the precision of seasoned spies. We snuck our bikes out through the back door of the garage, careful not to trigger the electric garage door that would alert our parents. We solidified our grand plans at the end of the driveway, adrenaline spiking as we prepared to pedal into the summer night.

Bobby led the way, his bike slicing through the warm summer night as we coasted down the road. I followed close behind, keeping a lookout for any headlights that might force us to duck into a ditch. We'd discussed and agreed in advance: if we saw any cars, we'd hide. If the Kmart parking lot lights were too bright, we'd retreat. Simple rules, easy enough to follow.

About halfway there, I detected headlights coming up from the road behind us. I veered off the road, plunging into the ditch, and held my breath, just like we'd planned, hoping the car would pass by without incident. The white light of the headlights intensified, and suddenly, red and blue lights tore through the night.

I froze, heart pounding, carefully lifting my head just enough to watch in horror as Bobby kept pedaling, seemingly oblivious to the police car right behind him. "Shit!" I whispered, watching him disappear down the road. As soon as the coast was clear, I shot out of the ditch, pedaling as fast as I could to get back home, panic fueling every push of the pedals.

I put my bike back in its exact spot, slipped inside, and dove into bed, pulling the covers up over my head. My heart thudded in my chest as I lay there, wide-eyed, wondering what was happening to Bobby. Did they catch him? Had they taken him to jail? Would they let him off with a warning? My mind raced through a thousand scenarios, each more dramatic than the last.

After what felt like hours, a car pulled into the driveway, its headlights slicing through the blinds of my bedroom window. My stomach dropped as I heard a knock at the front door.

Shit.

Messing up my hair and rubbing my eyes, I shuffled to the front door, doing my best to look like I'd been asleep the whole time. "W-what's going on?" I asked, feigning confusion.

The officer, unimpressed, asked me to get one of my parents. I hesitated, knowing this was only going to get worse. "They're sleeping. They're gonna be really mad if I wake them up," I said, as quietly as I possibly could. The officer repeated himself, more sternly this time: "Please go get one of your parents."

Whatever punishment followed must have been severe, judging by the way my entire body still tenses at the thought. But the details are gone. And that in and of itself says more than memory ever could. I'd been punished before. I'd be punished again. By this time in my life, it was routine. Expected. Not worth committing to memory. There was nothing remarkable to keep. All I know for sure is this:

Bobby, my closest conspirator, had ratted me out.

That night, something more lasting was etched into me: a fracture in the trust I'd placed in Bobby. In my eyes, we had a pact, an unspoken bond that had held us together through so much. That bond now felt fragile, if not broken entirely. I didn't walk away from that night angry—the consequences of my actions were my own. I walked away having learned that even the closest partnerships could falter when fear and survival came into play.

"Aren't you even going to apologize?" Mom demanded.

"You always say, if I was sorry, I wouldn't have done it in the first place," I replied, doggedly, with the tiny sliver of energy I had left. I noticed a shift in her expression, but I didn't have the emotional bandwidth to sort it out. So I turned around, walked quietly to my room, closed the door behind me, and tried to get some sleep before I had to start getting ready for school.

12: Shadows of Sunday

I T WAS A SINGLE photograph, black and white, with his name beneath it: Ricky Lawrence, age nine. The boy stared back at me like a ghost from the past, a stranger who had shaped my life in ways I still struggle to comprehend. I stumbled across the photograph while digging through online archives.

The newspaper described how, at just nine years old, Ricky had run away from home, declaring he was going "to live with the bums" in Chicago. This foolish quest was charged with a desperation that spoke volumes about his life, a childhood steeped in abandonment. His mother had left him. His father was absent. He was the oldest of several siblings, all of whom were placed in foster homes. His great-grandmother had taken him in but eventually found his behavior too difficult to manage, leading to his placement in a boys' home. Ricky's reality was one of rejection, isolation, and displacement—a storm of neglect no child should ever have to endure.

Eerily and heart-wrenchingly relatable.

At eighteen, his struggles only deepened. While incarcerated, Ricky and a cellmate set fire to their mattresses in a desperate attempt to escape. The image of those two young men, confined and hopeless, resorting to such reckless measures, is haunting. Their attempt failed, and they were returned to jail under harsher punishments, a stark reminder of a system that punishes but rarely rehabilitates.

Around the same time, he became entangled in a court case that hinted at an even deeper wound. He accused a man named Edwin Lavern Stahl of contributing to his sexual delinquency. The details were laid out in a brief newspaper article, with language as vague as it was telling.

Ricky testified that Stahl had taken him to a motel when Ricky was seventeen, but the defense focused on discrediting him. His record of detention at the Durand Farm School and the Illinois State School for Boys was introduced as evidence against his credibility. The jury deliberated for just over an hour before finding Stahl innocent.

Reading this decades later, I couldn't help but notice what wasn't said. The charge of "contributing to the sexual delinquency of a minor" was a legal catch-all at the time, often used to address situations society didn't have the words—or the courage—to confront. In 1969, cases involving same-gender attraction were rarely named outright, and the language surrounding them often obfuscated the truth. Was Ricky the victim here? The phrasing and details suggest he might have been, but the courtroom wasn't a place where boys like Ricky found justice. Instead, his detention record and his admission of frequenting a tavern underage were used to paint him as delinquent, as if his credibility as a person could be erased by his circumstances.

The article offers no insight into how Ricky felt about the verdict, but I can only imagine it deepened his sense of vulnerability and invisibility. To stand in a courtroom filled with people—each performing their roles with practiced decorum—a judge, lawyers, and jurors, to tell your story and be met with disbelief—what does that do to a person? How does it shape the way they see themselves, or the world around them?

This glimpse into Ricky's life is a painful reminder of how broken the systems are that we assume are meant to protect us. Ricky was just a boy navigating a world that had already discarded him, his voice drowned out by prejudice and the weight of his past. The system didn't see him as a person at all; it saw him as another problem to be managed, another piece of evidence to sweep under the rug.

When I found this article, I felt a surge of anger, not just at Stahl, but at the defense, the jury, the judge, the world that allowed someone like Ricky to fall through the cracks. What could his life have been if someone, anyone, had listened and believed him?

The trail of newspaper clippings ends there. What happened to Ricky between those moments of desperation and his entrance into my life is a void once again left only to my imagination.

• • •

When I met Ricky, "Rick," as I knew him, he was no longer a boy in black and white. He was a grown man, the adult son of Jackie, a good friend of my parents. Jackie lived alone on the outskirts of Rockford, Illinois, in the country. She was like a second grandmother to me, her home a place of warmth and indulgence where I could escape the tensions of home. Sundays were spent running wild on her property, the freedom intoxicating and comforting all at once.

Jackie was a survivor of her own horrors. She spoke openly about the abuse she endured during her marriage, often in graphic detail that far exceeded my maturity and understanding as a child. Her television still bore the bullet holes from the night her ex-husband shot at her across their living room.

"That was the night I kicked him out," she'd say, her voice tinged with defiance.

When Jackie moved to Ohio shortly after we did, it felt like a piece of home had followed us. Sundays would become a ritual again. Not long after, Rick moved in with her. I was told that he was a year or two older than Dad, with a mysterious past that no one fully explained, including why he was living with his mother. Jackie's reluctance to discuss him, paired with the way she watched me when he was around, made me feel uneasy. At the time, I couldn't specify why.

• • •

That summer I turned eleven, I got to spend the weekend at Jackie's and was helping her unpack boxes in her new home. That first night, the living room was sparse, with little more than a television and a pile of blankets where I planned to sleep. Though he had his own bedroom, Rick announced that he'd sleep in the living room too, "to keep me company."

Jackie hesitated in the hallway but ultimately left us alone, wishing us goodnight as she walked down the hallway to her bedroom and closed the door. Her unease lingered in the air like a warning I didn't understand.

As the television flickered with *Ren and Stimpy,* Rick began talking. I was annoyed by his intrusion at first. We didn't have cable television at home, so this was my rare opportunity to watch Nickelodeon. He started sharing stories of his time in prison, the art he'd created, and the poetry he wrote, and this piqued my interest. I'd never met anyone who spent time in prison before. And I loved art and poetry.

He asked if I'd like to read some of his poetry and grabbed a notebook off the shelf. It had an almost childlike cover with puffy, textured *Precious Moments* figures on it.

His words were dark but oddly fascinating. I enjoyed art and poetry myself, so I stayed engaged, asking him questions about several aspects of his writing. I was a precocious eleven-year-old girl, or so I had often been told. I imagine my engagement with his poetry made him feel seen in a way he'd never been before.

"Can I brush your hair?" he asked, seemingly out of nowhere.

The request didn't seem strange to me. I had brushed Dad's hair on the floor of our living room at home probably a thousand times. Even though no one ever offered to brush mine, I didn't think twice. In the bathroom where my brush was, I quickly ran through it to smooth it out—my hair has always been unwieldy.

Back in the living room, I handed him the brush and sat down in front of him, letting him fumble awkwardly with it. As he tugged at my scalp with an unfamiliar clumsiness, unease crept in. I didn't say anything. I was still young enough to believe adults always knew best—that they always had good intentions.

When I told him I was tired, I took my brush back to the bathroom, brushed my teeth, and returned to my blankets, but something was different. He had moved his bedding closer to mine. Too close. But I didn't want to make a big deal out of it. I lay down, pulling the blanket to my chin, trying to ignore the growing discomfort. Moments later, I felt his hand on mine.

My body stiffened at the crossroads of knowing right and wrong. This felt wrong. But was it?

Was there harm in his touching my hand? I took it through my mental model of seeing plenty of people holding hands and decided that there wasn't anything wrong with it.

I relaxed a little. The room was dark and quiet. I lay there awkwardly and willing myself to feel less awkward when I was interrupted. "Do you think you'd be my girlfriend when you're a little older?"

I thought about his poetry. I thought about Dad, who would be very disapproving of our age difference, but then I thought about the future and wondered if, when I am older, the age difference will make a difference anymore?

"Sure," I shrugged, finding no reason *not* to be his girlfriend when I got older.

"When you're older, we can do things like *this*."

• • •

Rick's presence turned Jackie's home into a place I dreaded. Over nearly four years, Sundays, once a sanctuary, became suffocating. I tried to avoid going altogether, producing any excuse to stay home or finding ways to keep busy when I couldn't. But my parents, self-absorbed in flea markets and various crafting projects under some illusion they'd get rich off of any of it, left me at Jackie's alone with Rick more often than not.

On my fifteenth birthday, it all came to an end.

Jackie and Rick came to our house to celebrate, a break from the usual routine of going to their place. I was outside, setting up the backyard for my friends, when Rick snuck up behind me, making strange noises that grated on my nerves like nails on a chalkboard and reaching out with his hands in a pinching motion towards my breasts. He lunged toward me, his intentions clear.

But this time, something in me snapped. Enough.

I dodged his hands, spinning away from him with a speed I didn't know I was capable of. With the fierce determination that only fear and anger could inspire, I turned to face him, with a fire behind my eyes I'd never felt before.

"If you *ever* fucking come near me again, *I will end you*," I growled, my voice low and steady, the words laced with not a threat but a truth that represented absolutely every fiber of my being.

For the first time, he backed off.

I watched him retreat, and a wave of relief washed over me. In that moment, I found a piece of myself I didn't know I had —a strength forged in defiance, a courage born out of survival.

Four years. Two hundred and eight Sundays. That's how many opportunities he had to invade the fragile spaces I tried and failed to keep safe. I managed to escape a few of them, but not enough.

There was nothing I could do to stop it, so I did what I had learned to do best—I adapted. I accepted the parts I couldn't change and focused on what I could.

My saving grace was a Super Nintendo.

My parents, citing "anything not of God is of the devil," wouldn't allow one in our home, but Rick had one. And if I had to be in that trailer with him, at least there was something that I could look forward to. I clung to those pixels like a lifeline, treating them like an end goal, a checkpoint in a game I never wanted to play.

I studied patterns. I got creative in ways to evade or at least delay the inevitable, sometimes managing to escape entirely if my parents and Jackie came back earlier than expected.

It took me years to come to terms with my behavior in survival mode. Over those four years, I went from being a little girl to an adolescent. I crossed natural lines of human growth and development while blurring them at the same time. I never stopped resisting going over there. I assume my parents chalked up my resistance to some kind of teenage angst.

At first, I only had the quiet tug at my instinct that something was wrong. At my young age, my trust in adults was higher than my sense of right or wrong. But eventually, I knew. I crossed that line of understanding, of recognizing what was happening was wrong. And then came the unbearable weight of knowing, while still being trapped in it, and having no way to make it stop. The colossal mind fuck of those four years and decades that followed still prods at me. My adult brain, now allegedly "all knowing" of right and wrong, wrestles with the innocence of my eleven-year-old self, the one who had no way out.

It took something from me that I will never get back.

And I have had to learn how to live with that.

• • •

Looking through those newspaper clippings decades later, learning more about Rick's story, I am struck by the layers of brokenness that led to his actions. His childhood, his incarceration, his rejection by the world—it doesn't excuse what he did, but it forces me to confront a question that gnaws at me: Do people become monsters because they are treated like monsters?

Is it a natural human response, when your back is against the wall, to lash out at whatever or whomever is in your path, even if it's just an eleven-, twelve-, thirteen-, or fourteen-year-old girl? Do people become so consumed by their own pain, their own sense of entitlement, that they believe the world somehow *owes them* something for what was taken— that they forget what it felt like to lose *their own innocence*? If they can't have it, does that mean *no one can*?

And where does my anger belong? At Rick, for what he did? At his mother, Jackie? She had been strict, firm, but loving towards me, yet she had abandoned him, her own son. At the system that failed him so profoundly that he became my tormentor? At my parents, who left me alone with a known ex-convict, Sunday after Sunday?

What he did will never be okay. But his actions do not define me. I am more than the Sundays he robbed me of, more than the moments he tried to reduce me to something small and silent. I stand here now, holding onto the power he could never take, telling my story—for the little girl who fought to survive and the woman who refused to let his shadows define her.

I refuse to let the silence he imposed be the final word. His actions left cracks in my path, but they did not decide where I would walk.

I used to think that I was alone. I thought I was the only one. But I know that I am not.

I tell this story for every little girl who ever whispered a defiant "FUCK YOU" into the darkness, their voices shaking but still their own. For the eleven-year-old me who deserved safety and love. For the adults who carry the weight of stolen Sundays of their own, unsure if they'll ever feel whole again.

To anyone who still stands in the shadows of what was taken, your light is still yours. It is waiting for you, fierce and unbreakable. And when you're ready, when you take even the smallest step toward reclaiming it, you will see: they never had the power they wanted you to believe they did.

That power belongs to you.

13: Cracks Beneath the Surface

EVEN AT ELEVEN, I was a shrimpy kid, and too small to ride the Zipper alone. That much was clear. The ride operator barely glanced at me before jabbing a finger at the height requirement sign. I turned to Mom, my only shot at getting on the ride.

She hesitated. I could see it in the way she shifted her weight, in the way her lips pressed into a thin line. She wasn't a ride person. I don't recall ever having seen her on a ride. So, I was surprised that even though it was a reluctant agreement, she had agreed to ride with me.

The moment we climbed in, I could tell something was wrong. The ride operator slammed the lap bar down, and it snapped loudly into place. A sharp sound escaped her—a noise I'd never heard her make before. I turned and looked at her, but she was preoccupied with trying to adjust herself, struggling to shift the metal bar that had wedged deep into her stomach. There was no give.

The Zipper started up, and for the first few rotations, she was quiet. Uncomfortable, shifting, but quiet. And then the cages started to spin.

"Stop the ride," she gasped.

I glanced at her, startled. She was gripping the bar, her fingers clawing at it, as if she could pry it away from her body by sheer force.

"STOP THE RIDE!" Her voice was louder now, edged with raw panic.

Then the cage flipped, and her breath hitched in a way that terrified me.

"I CAN'T BREATHE!"

I had never heard her say those words before, not even in anger.

That's when I started yelling, too. "HEY! STOP! SHE'S HURT!"

The ride operator didn't move. Didn't react. Just stood there, watching, laughing.

I didn't know if he thought we were playing, if he had trained himself to tune out the screams of kids on this ride, or if he simply didn't care.

And then, just as suddenly as it started, the ride slowed. I don't know if it was our turn to stop or if, by some miracle, he finally heard us.

When the cage unlocked, Mom practically stumbled out, gasping for air. She wasn't just in pain. She was humiliated. I could feel it radiating off of her.

We left the carnival without a word and never talked about it again.

At the time, I only understood a fraction of what had happened: she had done this for me. She hadn't wanted to, but she did it anyway. And I had never wanted her to get hurt.

It would take years before I fully grasped the other layers— how our bodies, even our suffering, could be treated as spectacle. How cruelty could be so casual. How humiliation, once endured, rarely finds its way back up to the surface to be processed aloud.

That day, I learned how easy it is for someone's pain to be ignored when people think it's all just part of the show.

Fitting the Frame

It was picture day in middle school. The photographer fussed over me. "These outfits just aren't meant for girls with... your kind of body!" She adjusted the straps and tugged at the fabric, trying to make me fit into something I apparently wasn't designed to wear.

Comments about my body seemed to be everywhere, as though my size was some sort of community project everyone felt entitled to weigh in on.

"Does she eat enough?" a lady at church asked, poking at my arm.

"She must eat like a bird!" one of my parents' friends joked, her laughter trailing behind like a knife cutting through the air.

"You're too skinny to be a cheerleader!" Mom told me when I mentioned trying out for the squad.

"You'd look better with a little more meat on your bones," Dad commented when I asked how I looked in my dress moments before heading out the door for a school dance.

These weren't cruel people. They believed their words were gentle, maybe even concerned. But concern isn't a shield from harm. Their (probably) well-meaning comments landed like thudding weights, pressing down on me, reinforcing a sense that something about me was fundamentally wrong.

Though no one explicitly told me to shrink myself, each suggestion that I "fill out" or "fit in" communicated something else entirely. I internalized their words, translating them into a quiet narrative: *Yes, I am small. So, I will just be small.*

• • •

By my teenage years, I had perfected the art of smallness. I didn't rock the boat. I spoke softly. I avoided eye contact. I had learned that being small wasn't just about my body, it was about my thoughts, my voice, my presence. I folded and molded myself into whatever shape I thought was required of me, working tirelessly to fit into a frame I didn't create, but somehow felt obligated to fill.

I look into the big brown eyes of my younger self in the portrait that was taken on that picture day, and I see someone trying desperately to disappear. She didn't realize that in contorting herself to meet others' expectations, she was minimizing pieces of herself—pieces she'd spend decades fighting to reclaim.

They were right about one thing: I was a skinny kid. You only needed eyes to see that. But my size wasn't the real problem. The issue was how easily my body became an invitation for others to define the space that I was allowed to occupy. It was never really about the clothes. It was about how others expected me to fit.

Over time, I began to reject the whispers urging me to shrink. I started seeing my size, my thoughts, and my voice not as things to fix or minimize, but as fundamental parts of who I am.

Now, when I think about that girl on picture day, I want to tell her this: *You were always enough. You never had to fit —you get to define what fits you.*

Stories We Read, Stories We Tell, Stories We Ignore

By the time I reached middle school, thriller fiction had become my genre of choice, and R.L. Stine was unquestionably my favorite author. I couldn't read his books fast enough, often devouring them under the light of the small lamp in my room, long after bedtime. The protagonists in his stories constantly faced perilous, impossible choices, navigating danger and deception with cleverness and courage.

I didn't just read them for entertainment; I read them to learn.

Those characters showed me how to survive under pressure, taught me the value of critical thinking, and demonstrated how to face my fears head-on. What I didn't realize then was how much those lessons would help me navigate the complexities of my own turbulent life.

But not all stories were neatly contained between book covers. Some spilled out into the real world, messy and unresolved, demanding answers I didn't have in the days long before the World Wide Web put everything at our fingertips.

Aside from our township library (which I regularly begged my parents to take me to visit), the Pfeiffer Middle School library was my go-to source for exploration and discovery. Built in 1975, it was one of the newest schools in the Perry Local Public School District, and by the early 90s, it still felt impressively modern. The air inside carried a distinct freshness, retaining its "new library smell", mingled with the subtle scent of aging pages and polished wood.

One afternoon, as I browsed the sections beneath the larger-than-life dramatic painting depicting the infamous duel between Aaron Burr and Alexander Hamilton, curiosity compelled me to approach the librarian. Feeling both nervous and determined, I asked a question I believed to be straightforward: "Do we have any books about Amy Fisher?"

Her face twisted in a way that told me I had just stepped into forbidden territory. "Why on earth would you want to read a book about that little *tramp*?" she snapped, her tone sharp and dismissive.

I didn't know how to respond. The words stung, not because I agreed with them but because they revealed and aligned so much about how Amy Fisher's story was being received. The headlines had painted her as the "Long Island Lolita," a teenage girl accused of shooting a woman in the face. But that wasn't the story I saw. To me, Amy Fisher wasn't a villain—she was a sixteen-year-old girl manipulated by an adult, Joey Buttafuoco, whose role in the tragedy was downplayed, even excused, by a society eager to place all the blame on a girl.

At twelve, I didn't have the words to explain why her story resonated so deeply with me. But I knew there was more. I needed to know what Joey had said to her and what promises he had made. I needed to know that I was not alone. But the headlines offered no answers. Only judgment.

I was already carrying my own silent story by then. Two grown men had crossed boundaries they never should have, and while no one called me a "tramp," I felt the weight of societal blame in other unspoken ways. I knew what it was like to carry shame that wasn't mine, and to be judged for the actions of adults who should have known better.

Amy's story wasn't just sensational. It was familiar.

The media had turned her into a caricature—a cautionary tale about teenage rebellion—but I saw the layers that they ignored. She was just a girl manipulated by a man with power. And the world around her had failed to protect her.

Reading R.L. Stine had taught me to look for the "why" in every story, to understand the motivations and circumstances driving people's actions. But in Amy's case, the "why" was deliberately obscured. Society didn't want to ask why a sixteen-year-old girl had been in that position. They didn't want to confront the power dynamics, the manipulation, or the systemic failures. They wanted a villain, and Amy was an easy target.

It wasn't until years later that I finally got to read Amy's account in her own words. Everything I had suspected was true: her story was far more complicated than the headlines suggested. She had been lied to, manipulated, and discarded. The librarian and the media who called her a "tramp" had missed the point entirely.

Amy Fisher's story helped me realize how often we ignore the complexities of people's lives, how quick we are to judge without understanding. It showed me how the narratives we accept, and the ones we reject, shape not only how we see others, but even how we come to see ourselves.

In Amy, I saw myself. I saw the weight of shame and the desperation to be understood. And I saw the importance of asking the hard questions, even when the answers aren't easy.

I devoured stories to learn how to survive. But the stories that society doesn't want to tell or even acknowledge are often the ones that teach us the most.

Amy Fisher's was one of them.

The Pool

My parents were always bouncing between fitness kicks, a trend that felt ubiquitous in the nineties. Sometimes it meant home workout tapes, sometimes it meant dragging us to a fitness center, where they'd send us off to the kid-friendly areas while they halfheartedly committed to their latest health phase. I didn't care either way, gym visits always meant one thing to me: swimming.

I loved the pool. The moment we stepped into the locker room, I could already hear the echo of splashing water and smell the sharp tang of chlorine. I changed quickly, eager to dive in, but as Mom and I were heading out, a pair of teenage girls behind us started giggling.

Not just laughing—giggling. The kind that carries an edge with it.

I snapped my head around, scanning their faces, trying to piece together the joke. What was funny? Who was funny?

Mom didn't turn. She just muttered, "Ignore them." Then I noticed: they were targeting her.

Out in the pool, I forgot about them. For a while, anyway. The water was its own world, separate from everything else. But then the lifeguards blew their whistles—five-minute safety check, everyone out. I climbed onto a lounge chair next to Mom, wrapping my towel around my body.

The girls were still there. Their group had grown now, and a couple of teenage boys had joined in. I watched them, wary, not liking the way they seemed to be building up to something.

I watched as two of the boys got up. I tried to keep them in my peripheral vision as they walked past us, so that it wasn't obvious that I was watching them. One of them turned his head, barely even slowing down as he tossed the words over his shoulder:

"You really need to shave—gross."

Mom stiffened. She didn't look at them. Didn't look at me. Just stayed frozen, staring straight ahead.

I blinked. Confused. My brain raced to decode it. Shave what? What was gross?

I thought about what I looked like. I looked at Mom.

Nothing out of the ordinary. Nothing to see here!

It wasn't until we were packing up to leave that I started to put it together. She stood up, gathering our things, and in that instant, I saw what they had seen—what they had been whispering and laughing about since the locker room.

Thick, dark hair. Peeking out from beneath her swimsuit.

I pointed. "Is that what those kids were talking about?"

I wasn't asking to be mean. I wasn't asking her to embarrass her.

I was still trying to put the puzzle pieces together, still trying to understand what had just happened.

Her face flushed; her movements rushed. "Oh, I don't know," she said dismissively, shoving things into her bag. "Who knows?"

And that was that. We left. We never talked about it again.

At the time, I didn't understand what it meant to feel shame over your body in this way. I didn't fully understand how it felt to become the joke. But I did understand what it meant to pretend something wasn't happening. To tamp it down, to act like it didn't matter, to hope that if you ignored it long enough, it would just go away.

And that's what stuck with me the most.

Not the insult, not the laughter, not the hair.

The silence.

The Cost of Speaking Up

Bobby had been held back a year, and we were both in seventh grade. I would have been twelve, so he would have been thirteen. The day went on like any other until I was called to the principal's office late in the afternoon. That sudden announcement sent a familiar jolt of panic through me.

What had I done? What was about to happen?

As I walked down the hall, my mind scrambled, frantically replaying my recent actions, but nothing came to mind. When I reached the office, I saw Bobby sitting outside the nurse's room, his face beet red and streaked with tears. He didn't look at me, and I felt my stomach drop. Something was seriously wrong.

Inside the principal's office, the news hit me like a freight train: Bobby had reported Dad for abuse. The principal wanted to know what I had to say about it. My brain buzzed with panic.

Reported Dad? What was Bobby thinking?

My thoughts raced as I imagined the consequences. What if they believed him? Would we be taken away? Would we end up in foster care again?

Frank's horror stories about foster care replayed in my mind —the kind of harm that left visible bruises and deeper wounds you couldn't see. Things so dark that Frank, who never seemed afraid of anything, carried his awful experiences like a weight he couldn't put down.

Whatever was happening at home, we could handle it as a family, I reasoned. But foster care? That was worse than anything.

The night before, Bobby had gotten into trouble—something trivial that I can't even recall now, but it had been enough to spark Dad's attention. The argument that followed escalated quickly. I sat frozen in my room as Dad's voice thundered through the house, hurling the same slur at Bobby over and over: "faggot."

It was a word I didn't fully understand, but I could feel its venom, its intent to wound. Bobby yelled back, which only made Dad angrier. The confrontation ended with Dad smacking Bobby around and, in the chaos, ripping out the earring I had helped Bobby pierce just a few weeks earlier, with nothing more than an ice cube and a sewing needle.

To this day, I don't know if Dad ripped it out intentionally or if it was an accident. But Bobby's ear had bled, and his face was swollen with fresh hurt, both physical and emotional. That moment had clearly been another breaking point for Bobby, and as I pieced it together, it must have been the moment he decided to report Dad.

Now, sitting in the principal's office, I felt the weight of it all crashing down on me. When the principal pressed me for details, I froze. My mind told me there was only one option: Don't get hauled away to foster care.

"He's lying," I blurted out, my voice trembling. "He does this sometimes—makes things up for attention." The words tumbled out, a reflex born of fear and survival. I painted Bobby as a troublemaker, someone who exaggerated or fabricated stories to get his way. Bobby did get into trouble, but it wasn't the whole truth, and deep down, I knew it. But it was the only way to keep us safe.

The principal leaned in, his expression softening, as if he didn't entirely believe me. That made me double down. "Our parents aren't abusive," I insisted. "Bobby's just mad because he got into trouble last night," I explained as though it would erase everything he had said. As though it would make the entire situation disappear.

Then, the police arrived.

My heart pounded as they entered the room, their presence transforming an already terrifying situation into something far worse. I repeated my story to them, desperate to sound convincing, to protect us from the unknown consequences of Bobby's actions. The fear of being taken away, of losing what little stability we had, and the unknown knowns of foster care were too overwhelming.

When Dad showed up at the school, his face was a mix of disappointment and concern. That concern confused me. For a fleeting moment, I thought maybe this wouldn't be so bad. Maybe everything would be okay. Dad even had his arm around Bobby, hugging him as we walked out to the car—a rare gesture that gave me hope. But as we climbed into the car, an eerie silence settled over us. It wasn't the kind of silence that came from relief; it was the kind that signaled that a storm was brewing.

When we got home, Mom was in the kitchen, boiling spaghetti, and the smell of it filled the house. For a moment, everything felt normal. Sensing the call of dinner, Bobby appeared, having climbed the basement stairs that opened beside the kitchen. He paused on the top step, just shy of entering the room. "What are you doing here?" Dad asked flatly, his voice devoid of emotion.

"I—I thought I heard dinner was almost ready," Bobby stammered, his confusion evident. He looked at the table, already being set, confirming that he'd interpreted things correctly.

"This is a family dinner," Dad said, in that same chillingly flat tone. "You're no longer a part of this family."

Bobby froze, his face a mixture of disbelief and heartbreak. He stood there for what felt like an eternity, waiting for someone to tell him it was a joke or a misunderstanding. But no one did. Mom walked past him without a word, carrying a pot to the table. Markie and I exchanged helpless glances but said nothing. Speaking up would only make things worse.

Eventually, Bobby turned and went back downstairs. I stared at my plate, no longer hungry. After dinner, Dad disappeared, and then we heard it:

The sounds of Bobby being beaten.

Each blow echoed through the house, a visceral reminder of what happened when someone stepped out of line.

I didn't see Bobby again that night. I knew he didn't deserve to be beaten like that—nobody ever did—but I was angry at him for turning Dad in and risking all of us being sent off to foster homes (Frank was an adult by then).

In my mind, he was gambling with all of our lives, not just his.

• • •

Years later, I'd reflect on that day and the impossible choices we both made. Bobby had the courage to speak up, to tell the truth, knowing full well the risks. I, on the other hand, let fear guide me. I thought I was protecting all of us, but in reality, I was only protecting myself and the fragile semblance of normalcy I was desperate to preserve. As the only daughter, I still didn't have it "easy," but I did have it a whole lot easier than my two older brothers.

For Bobby, that day must have been devastating. It meant he wasn't safe at home, at school, or even with the authorities. Where does a child go when every avenue of protection is closed off? Even I wasn't safe, because calling him a liar and failing to speak up on at least his behalf amounted to a betrayal.

I'll never know the full impact of my betrayal on him, but I carry it with me now—a reminder of the cost of silence and the ways fear can strip us of our humanity.

Would life have been better if we'd been taken away? I'll never know. It might have granted us better childhoods, or maybe it would have led us down even darker paths. What I do know is that the life we continued to live after that day was unbearably hard. Especially for Bobby. And for all the strength he showed in that moment, it feels like the world— and I—let him down in ways that still haunt me.

• • •

For so long, I've been frustrated by the world's inability or unwillingness to try and understand someone else's perspective before casting judgment. It's a trait I've seen in leaders, in family members, even in strangers, and it has always felt like a personal affront to my sense of fairness. But as I sit with these memories of Bobby, as I peel back the layers of my own judgments against him, I realize I am not innocent of this, either.

How easy it was to label him as the troublemaker, the idiot brother, the one who couldn't get it together. How quick I was to dismiss his struggles without asking myself what it must have been like to walk in his shoes. I was so caught up in my own survival, so focused on protecting myself, that I didn't have the capacity—or maybe the courage—to truly see him. To understand what it must have felt like to solely endure most of our parents' rage after Frank left. To know that no matter how hard he tried, he would never feel like "enough" in their eyes.

This isn't an easy thing to admit. It's far more comfortable to sit in my frustration with the world than to hold a mirror up to myself. But the truth is, I judged Bobby long before I ever tried to understand him. And I can't help but wonder:

How many times have I done this to others?

How many times have I failed to extend the very compassion I demand from the world?

Emotions: Unlocked

I was sprawled out on my bedroom floor, listening to Rock 106.9 WRQK on my purple boombox. I had my window open, letting the breeze come in, and I could hear the blinds tapping against the sill every time the wind picked up.

I was in that teenage, restless space of not knowing what to do with myself when a song started playing that I'd never heard before: *What's Up?* by 4 Non Blondes. Something about it made me sit up and turn up the volume.

"And so, I cry sometimes when I'm lying in bed, just to get it all out, what's in my head..."

The words felt like they were opening a door. Before I even knew what was happening, I started crying—really crying. I hadn't cried like that before, not for no reason, not just because of a song. But the song kept going, and I just let it happen. I leaned into it, feeling every word echo something inside me that felt like permission—permission to notice something. To feel.

For a few minutes, I connected to myself in a way I hadn't ever been before. It was like all the layers I'd built around myself were peeling back, and for once, I didn't have to pretend to be small or quiet or hidden. I could just be.

When the song ended, I turned my radio off and sat there in the silence, letting it sink in. And before I knew it, I heard myself whisper,

"I want my Mommy."

It was weird, hearing that come out of my own mouth. I didn't even know what "Mommy" meant. But in that moment, I let myself need it.

And it felt so, so, right.

That was the first time I felt myself take up all the space I needed.

The Butter Knife Conundrum

It was one of those days, walking home from the bus stop, when I could just feel that something was going to go terribly wrong. Maybe things had been going too well for too long. Maybe I developed a sense for it.

I remember taking my time on that walk down our road that day. A sharp sting in the air signaled summer's end, though the colorful sweater and teal leggings I wore suggested it wasn't quite winter yet. I was in between extremes. I looked up at a cloud-dotted sky and breathed in the fresh air.

When I got home, I was relieved to find that my room was just as I left it. It wasn't uncommon for my "Spidey senses" to mean that I'd come home to find all of my stuff piled on my bed which meant I wouldn't be eating dinner, or going to bed, until everything had been put away. And the "right" way. Which I never felt sure of, as it seemed to be a sort of moving target.

As I walked in, everything seemed pretty normal. Ominously so.

Outside the safety of my bedroom, Mom sat on the couch, our shih tzu, Princess, nuzzled close to her. I don't remember exactly what she was doing. Watching TV, probably. Maybe reading her Bible.

I just remember the quiet.

It felt suffocating, especially in contrast to the fresh air outside.

Why was it so quiet?

Those were the days when Frank and his wife, Carly, lived in the basement. I wasn't sure if they were even home, it was so quiet.

I lingered in the hallway there between my bedroom and the living room, gauging the safety of the stillness in the air. It seemed suspicious, but there was no physical evidence of anything telling me otherwise.

I took another good look at Mom as I walked towards the living room. Reading her body language. Reading her face. Reading the room.

Again, I had no logical explanation for whatever I felt. There was no supporting evidence of anything amiss. So, I sat down on the couch next to Princess, scratching her head.

Princess was always next to Mom on the couch. That day, she was mashed so tight against her, I wondered if Mom had sat down on her that way. Princess didn't seem to mind. She seemed to enjoy me scratching her head, lifting her head so that I would scratch her chin.

"Everything... okay?" I asked, absentmindedly, my attention still on the dog.

She didn't lay into it right away. It sort of ramped up. I don't recall the details of the ramp-up, just the punchline:

"Frank is a son-of-a-bitch!"

And—I can't explain what happened to me in that moment. I knew full well that keeping my mouth shut when things ramped up like that was the best option. For all of us. Especially me.

I knew that, and the image of Dad gritting his teeth, growl-warning me, "Tina, when are you going to keep your mouth shut?" is one that is forever etched in my mind before I say anything.

But something in me on this day switched, like permission. Like an injustice. Like SAY THE THING. Like holding on to a hot coal and you must unload it before it burns you.

Fire!

"How would you like it if I called *your* mother a bitch?" I asked.

No attitude, no tone. Just flat. The words had formed into a question that way in my head, leaving my lips without incubation of thought.

In my 13-year-old mind, I heard my brother being called a bad name. And I was taught not to call people bad names.

And not only that—if she was calling him a son-of-a-bitch, that meant she was also insulting my biological mother. In one breath, she had hurled insults at two people: my brother and the mother I still romanticized. Back then, I imagined her as the perfect mother, her longing for me just as much as I longed for her, and at any given moment, she would appear back in our lives to whisk me away, and we'd live happily ever after. Hearing her name twisted into an insult felt like a direct attack on that fragile dream.

So I asked again, genuinely:

"How would you like it if I called *your* mother a bitch?" I wanted to *know*.

I had felt the tension from down the road, so it didn't technically go from zero to a hundred in a fraction of a second. But that is what it felt like I was observing in what happened next:

"How *dare* you call my mother a bitch! She has been nothing short of a saint to you kids!" Mom bellowed out.

I felt the heat rise in my face, not because I thought she was wrong, but because I knew I'd hit a nerve I didn't fully understand.

Her mother was not a bitch. I loved my grandma, her mother. She really was a saint towards me and my brothers.

My mind was hard at work trying to figure out how to separate the thing that I said from the thing that I meant and the thing that was heard when Mom interrupted it:

"Who taught you to swear like that?"

I blinked. I didn't feel defensive or combative. This question genuinely perplexed me. All I had done was repeat the thing that she had just said.

This felt like a trap. I had backed away from her on the couch. Princess had jumped down.

I decided to keep my mouth shut. Whatever happened next, I was not going to win.

"Who taught you to swear like that?" she persisted.

I didn't know what to say. I knew what she was asking, but I knew it was a setup. By then, Frank had either heard the commotion or just happened to be coming upstairs to grab a snack.

Hearing that Frank was in the house felt like relief and also like reinforcement. Like a witness. Like whatever happened next, it was going to be navigable because someone else would have been there to talk about it.

Her frustration rippled through the room. Her hands clenched tightly into fists. "WHO TAUGHT YOU TO SWEAR LIKE THAT!" she yelled now, shaking the couch as she swung her arms up and drove them down into the couch, demanding an answer.

"You did!" I quipped. I definitely quipped. There was a tonality. An attitude. And it was like *I've just had enough* in word form. Because it was true! *She* taught me how to swear.

I sat there, helpless, watching as Mom, calm just moments before, erupted before me like an emotional volcano. Her fury ignited in an instant, launching into the same well-worn rant I'd heard so many times before, one I could almost recite by heart:

"I guess I'm just the worst person ever. I used to be a good person! I USED TO BE A GOOD PERSON! After all the things I've done for you? You ungrateful little bitch!"

She started praying passive aggressively vigorously aloud for herself and the child demon before her that was triggering her. "Lord, give me strength!"

This was a common occurrence; I was used to this.

Her fervent prayers were eclipsed by what happened next:

"I'm going to kill myself!" she exclaimed.

"I'M GOING TO KILL MYSELF!" she yelled again, getting up from the couch and stomping towards the kitchen. Her footsteps thudded across the floor, each step vibrating in my chest like a drumbeat. Next, I heard the sound of the silverware drawer flinging open madly. The clatter of metal against metal rang out, sharp and jarring, as if the drawer were echoing her mood.

I stayed back in the living room, unsure of what to do and trying to understand how this had escalated so quickly.

I could hear Frank in the kitchen with her, the wall between the living room and kitchen separating us. I let my imagination fill in the blanks about what was happening in that room.

"You aren't going to kill yourself, Bonnie." He said in his classic Frank tone. It was matter of fact. And probably sounded condescending to her, then around forty-five years old, coming from Frank, then around twenty.

Even as I stood frozen in the living room, I was grateful for Frank's presence. He always had a way of defusing things, even if Mom's reactions to his tone sometimes felt like pouring gasoline on a fire.

I heard a twist in his voice. Was that a laugh? A chuckle?

"You aren't going to kill yourself with a *butter knife!*"

I peeked around the wall into the kitchen.

There she was, standing next to the open silverware drawer, butter knife pointed right at her chest, like she'd plunge that extremely blunt utensil into her sternum any time soon.

I also let out a chuckle. I couldn't help being overwhelmed by the absurdity of the scene. It was probably an uncomfortable laugh, or maybe I did it in solidarity with Frank. We were an ultra-religious family. Suicide was a big ole no-no that would send you automatically to hell. The Do Not Pass Go, Do Not Collect $200 kind of hell.

So, I had an understanding that her threats were surface-level. At 13, I was certainly not equipped to understand the magnitude of whatever emotion was on full display for me, but the threat of unaliving herself plus my imagination had her standing in the kitchen holding something much more menacing than a butter knife.

I don't recall how that big event officially wrapped up. I know it concluded with an outburst of violent crying and a lot of "Just wait until your father gets home!"

But there it was, another in-between moment. And there I was, suspended between absurdity and chaos, unsure of where any of it would land, yet knowing somehow it always would.

I wasn't sure if I'd get in trouble, but I knew one thing: I wasn't the one out of control here. Dad would see that.

"Yes," I remember thinking to myself. "Just wait until he gets home."

14: Lies, Lessons, and High Notes

I WAS A CHOIR kid with a pretty decent voice. I frequently tried out for solos and landed them, more often than not. So, when Mr. Kendrick, my eighth-grade choir director, approached me after class one day, it shouldn't have been a surprise. But it still caught me off guard.

Mr. Kendrick was maybe an inch or two taller than me; he was probably about 5'3" or 5'4". He had startling sky-blue eyes and short silvery hair neatly brushed to the side. His skin tone had a greyish and almost transparent hue, and I'd guess he was probably in his late fifties. He always looked sharp, dressed neatly in a button-down shirt and slacks, and his shoes had a consistent shine as though they were freshly polished.

Based on his meticulously pressed appearance and impeccably shined shoes, I'd guess he was what Dad would call a "military man." Yet, his demeanor defied the stereotype of any military man I'd ever encountered. He spoke gently, carried immense patience, and radiated enthusiasm for the choir. It was clear he genuinely loved his work.

"I noticed you haven't returned the form for solo and ensemble yet. Here is a piece I think you should consider doing," he said with all the cheerfulness that junior high choir directors around the globe exhibit.

"Oh, right!" I replied reluctantly. "I almost forgot about that! Yeah, that, uh, sounds... great!" I half lied.

I was very much interested in participating in the solo and ensemble, yet I was very much not interested in returning the form. It required a thirty-dollar entry fee I was convinced our family did not have to spare.

I half-heartedly thanked him for the reminder on my way out of class that day and, upon exiting the classroom, promptly compartmentalized the topic so that I would not have to think about going or not going.

The next day, he caught me off guard again. "Did you bring the form for solo and ensemble back? It's due by the end of the week!" He looked at me directly with those bright-blue eyes, smiling warmly with his whole face. While noticing his genuine encouragement, I simultaneously appreciated and wanted to avoid it.

"Yeah, I talked to my parents about it last night. They don't think I'm good enough." I blurted out, without considering anything other than avoiding admitting that we couldn't afford it.

Why? Why did I say that? It absolutely was not true.

His face contorted before I even finished my lie.

"What?" he asked. Not firmly or meanly, but gently, as though he truly hadn't understood.

"Yeah, they just didn't think I'm good enough," I repeated, eyes dropping to the ground as I noticed his confused expression.

"Um. Well, uh. I'm sorry to hear that," he said, attempting to compose himself. "We'll miss you there!" he added, in an effort to remain supportive and encouraging.

My stomach twisted. I felt so terrible walking away from class that day. I felt like my legs were trapped in thick steel boots due to my whopper of a lie. But as the bell rang signaling the end of class, I compartmentalized it again, hoping not to think about disappointing him.

I was surprised when I walked in the door after school that day and Mom immediately interrupted whatever thought train I was on, "Got a call from Mr. Kendrick today."

What? Why? *Why couldn't he just leave this alone?*

"He said there's this solo and ensemble thing, and he really wants you to go. He even offered to pay. But do you? Do you want to go?" she asked, not looking up from whatever she was reading when I walked in.

"Yes, I would love to go!" I blurted out, again without thinking.

"I'd have to drive you there, and it's over an hour away. Are you sure that you want to go, though? I'm not going to drive you halfway across the state for you to half-ass it!" she said, now staring me down, as if she were peering into my soul for evidence of truth or untruth.

I had lied enough, and even though I could feel the line of questioning was meant to steer me in the other direction, I opted not to lie again, "Yes! I would love to go. I think I would do well, and he thinks so, too!"

• • •

I went to the competition. I scored the highest marks for my solo and both ensembles that Mr. Kendrick suggested at the last minute. If he was going to be paying for it, the least I could do was show up for him.

Some guilt has remained with me all these years about having lied to Mr. Kendrick. At the same time, I'm grateful that he persisted and pushed past my lie. He didn't have to do that, but he cared enough to follow up, to try to make a difference in my life.

I find evidence woven throughout my life of this type of behavior: kind, outstretched hands of almost perfect strangers. Adults who took the time to look after me. People who, for some reason, spotted some potential in me and shone a light on it before I ever knew that 'potential' was a thing that I could possess. And I am forever grateful to Mr. Kendrick for having the sense, and no doubt courage, to push past what he thought he knew, and to proceed with curiosity.

I would have loved to have been a fly on the wall that day to know what all was said. I can assume that he hadn't told Mom that I said my parents told me I wasn't good enough. I would have been instantly in trouble for lying and not allowed to go based on that alone.

What had he told her? What had she told him?

I'll never know. I am left with gratitude, though, and I cherish this small act from an almost perfect stranger. He touched my life and gave it a nudge in a direction that it wouldn't have without it.

Babysitting and Boundaries Broken

I was fourteen, and it was supposed to be the summer of freedom. I'd be staying with Carly, Frank's now ex-wife, babysitting my nephew Nathan for twenty bucks a week and an endless supply of Basic cigarettes. Carly had a night job, which meant I had the run of her place, a stuffy townhouse in the projects in Canton, Ohio.

Babysitting my nephew felt like a huge responsibility, and the townhouse, barely cooled by the window units upstairs, felt more like a cage than a space of independence. I was in this weird in-between developmentally as well: old enough to be trusted with a toddler but still just a kid myself, trying to figure out where I fit in.

One sticky summer night, while I was watching *Casper* on TV, Carly's "boyfriend," Jim, knocked on the door. Jim was a regular fixture in Carly's life—a married man who'd often show up with beer and pizza. He was twenty-six and talked about leaving his "crazy" wife, like he was just biding his time until he could be with Carly.

I told him to come in, barely looking up from the TV. He handed me a deep-dish pizza, the kind with caramelized cheese on the crust and crispy pepperoni—the good stuff. I thanked him. Nathan was already asleep in bed, so I figured he'd just drop it off and leave, but he settled in on the couch.

"You might get scared here all by yourself at night," he said, almost like a promise. "I'll just stay until Carly gets home."

I didn't think much of it. Jim had always been around, never threatening, always just there. He liked good music, he liked to hang out, play cards, and have fun, and he was friends with Carly, so he was harmless... right? I also wanted to make a point to be nice to him. He'd told me that he had a recording studio in his apartment and that he thought I had a great voice, and he'd love to record me sometime. He could be my big break.

My eyes moved to a paper bag that he held in his hand, which held the shape of a bottle. "Do you mind if I have a beer while I'm here?" he asked. I remember thinking it was a weird question.

Historically, he and Carly would throw back beers without asking me for permission. They would also let me have a bottle or two. I don't remember if I answered. He pulled the 40 oz bottle out of the bag, opened it, took a big swig, and sat down a lot closer than I liked, next to me on the couch.

"You wanna swig?" he held the bottle out to me.

"Sure." I took a swig.

The movie Casper is a roller coaster of emotions. Never one to mind the ride, I was no doubt teary-eyed and hugging myself on my side of the couch and my own little world inside my head when I sensed him looking over at me.

"Oh, hey!" he said softly, edging closer, covering me with his body and his arms.

They felt heavy.

They felt good.

I openly started crying.

"Hey. What's going on?" he said gently. So gently. He put his hand under my chin and lifted my head so that my face was square with his.

I did not know why I was so emotional. I had no words to explain what had overcome me.

Sure, the movie had triggered emotion, but not in the proportion to which it was exiting from my body. "I... I've just never been hugged like that before." I managed to say, huge tears squeezing out of my eyes as I stared into his.

That was true.

But the words I'd formed to explain didn't click the way a genuine root cause does for me when I am exploring them. Especially regarding a big emotion emanating from me like that.

It wasn't the hug.

He pulled me into his lap, like a baby, his arms wrapped tightly but gently around me, cradling me. His heavy arms held me awkwardly for I don't know how long.

I felt too big to be held that way.

And at the same time, I loved the way that it made me feel.

I felt safe.

I felt cared for.

I felt his hand start to go up the back of my shirt.

I froze.

I wanted to believe it was all in my head, that he was just being nice. He kept pushing, and I kept freezing.

I had already submitted to being held like a baby, even though it felt awkward, it also felt really nice, familiar. I let him do that. But when he started kissing me, it stopped feeling nice. He told me not to be a baby about it.

So, I wasn't. But I was only fourteen. And as I felt the weight of his twenty-six-year-old body suffocate me, I let it blot out any remaining semblance of infancy that might have dared to remain.

"I don't like this," I managed to say, loud enough to be heard but not in a cry like a baby.

"You did this to me," he replied with a smirk that made my stomach twist, pressing the weight of his body against me, hard.

"You can't leave me hanging."

• • •

That night, something in me broke. I didn't know what it was like to feel safe, but I knew what it felt like to have the illusion of safety ripped away. Amidst this conflict that I was desperately trying to process in real-time, I wanted to believe that he was my friend. I wanted to believe that deep down, he cared about me.

Now, as an adult, I can plainly see what he was doing, the way he was blurring lines that should never have been crossed. He took advantage of my innocence, wrapped his intentions in kindness, and made me feel like I had no choice but to submit and be grateful.

I was fourteen.

I did want to be held.

To be comforted.

To feel like I mattered.

But not like that.

Church Pew Psychology

Our family attended Harvest Christian Center, a small, non-denominational evangelical church in North Canton, Ohio. It was notably led by a woman pastor, Sharon Edwards, something that felt both exciting and groundbreaking to me as a teenager. Separate from some of the bizarre culture in the church, I genuinely enjoyed her messages and found myself leaning in, captivated by her sermons. However, the adults around me offered a complicated contrast: during the services, they nodded in agreement, raised their hands in praise, and spoke passionately in tongues, but behind Pastor Sharon's back, they whispered doubts about whether a woman should preach and debated the biblical validity of her position.

The church building felt as though it had seen better days. It struck me as run-down, almost forgotten in time, like it hadn't been maintained since it was built. Windowsills had pieces dangling precariously, patches of carpet were noticeably missing or damaged, and doors stubbornly refused to close properly, often getting stuck halfway between open and shut.

One of the girls at church, who was my age and whose family served as missionaries, once shared stories from their travels abroad. She told us about places far worse off than our humble, dilapidated sanctuary, emphasizing the struggles she'd witnessed. Her stories both intrigued and horrified me, especially when she recounted an incident from her time in Bolivia, where men had repeatedly tried to purchase her. The idea left me deeply disturbed, a stark and jarring contrast to anything I'd ever personally experienced.

It was against this backdrop, in a setting both physically worn and spiritually vibrant yet contentious, that we found ourselves attending a special evening church service. I had convinced a few friends of mine to join me, not necessarily because I thought they would find it all that enticing, but because my attendance meant that we could all hang out afterward, and whatever mischief we had planned for that evening outweighed our collective avoidance of church boredom.

My parents, perhaps equally eager to distance themselves from four restless teenagers, sat several pews ahead of us with Markie (who would have been ten at the time).

That evening, amid the usual rhythm of church—singing, sitting, standing, praying, sitting, listening—I experienced an unexpected moment of clarity. As Pastor Sharon preached at the pulpit and my friends whispered and giggled beside me, something urged me to pay attention. The kind of urging that feels like someone grabs your face, with both hands, and says, "Notice This."

In my direct line of sight were Mom, Markie, and Dad. In that order, ahead of me. Dad's protective arm around Markie. All three sitting close. Not in a weird way or anything. Just in a distinctly loving way. Yet, as I observed them, a wave of bittersweet appreciation washed over me.

How lucky Markie was to be enveloped in such clear and undeniable love from both of his parents. I was happy for him.

Throughout the years, it was not that I didn't notice the special treatment he enjoyed. As the family's baby and the blood-born offspring of both his mom and our dad, it just made sense. I noticed it because I exploited it often! That kid could get away with murder, and I knew it! I'd set him up to tape record audio of him swearing on cassette tape so I could use it as leverage to get something I wanted from him later. Which was usually an oath to silence about something I did that would have no doubt resulted in getting my ass handed to me.

He got more Christmas presents than the rest of us. I know this for sure because one year, my parents put all the wrapped Christmas presents under the tree several days in advance. Unable to resist the temptation, I carefully unwrapped each gift any chance I was left in the house by myself, meticulously memorizing the original folds and tape placement so I could wrap them back up exactly as they had been—careful not even to lift the print off the paper with the tape. I'm embarrassed to admit, I did this more than once. Ultimately, knowing what everybody got for Christmas, not just me, ended up spoiling my own Christmas.

These childhood antics highlighted a truth I always noticed. But that evening in church, I started to notice it in a new and different way.

I felt grateful that Markie got to feel the love of his mom and dad. That he had both of his parents in his life, and that he got to sit between their warmth that day. As far as I knew, he never did shitty things like try to blackmail anybody or open everybody's Christmas presents. He deserved it.

• • •

As I sit with this memory now, I'm struck by the sense of genuine gratitude I felt for Markie that day. Not just then, but even now, as I reflect on it decades later, the sole prevailing feeling is as vivid and real as it was in that church pew.

I don't recall ever sitting between them like that. Not once. It just wasn't something that happened for me. I simply accepted it as the way things were, like gravity or the color of the sky. I don't remember wishing for it or even imagining it as a possibility. It wasn't my place. It wasn't my role. It wasn't for me.

It is only now, and looking back on it, that it strikes me as unusual. Somewhere along the way, I had internalized the idea that my role was different, that the closeness and warmth Markie received just wasn't meant for me. Or maybe I believed something about myself—some flaw, some failure—had disqualified me from it. It's nothing I ever thought about with intention, and so I also didn't question it. I didn't fight for more. I simply... accepted.

It's strange to me now, reflecting on it as an adult, because that kind of acceptance feels almost alien. Shouldn't I have been angry? Shouldn't I have longed for the same embrace, the same closeness, the same warmth? But there was no bitterness, no questioning. Just gratitude.

And yet, as I sit with it now, there's a part of me that wants to reach back to that girl in the pew and say, "It wasn't okay, Tina. It wasn't okay for you to be passed over." Because it wasn't fair. And it wasn't a reflection of my worth or my value, even though I quietly accepted it as though it was.

This moment, like so many others, shaped me. It taught me to observe others receiving the love I craved without feeling resentment. It taught me to settle for less, to expect less, even as I witnessed the proof that more was possible. And perhaps that's why it took me so long to believe I deserved more—to believe I could ask for what I deserved.

I've spent years trying to understand how I could feel so much gratitude for Markie without even a whisper of anger for myself. And I think the answer lies in what I came to believe about love: that it was finite and there was not enough for everyone. I convinced myself that the warmth my parents gave to Markie was warmth they couldn't also spare for me. And I accepted that as truth: if there's not enough to go around, then at least he's getting it.

It's only now, with the benefit of hindsight, that I see how that quiet acceptance planted seeds of both resilience and resignation within me. Resilience, because it allowed me to carry on without bitterness, to find genuine joy in the joy of others. But resignation, too, because it taught me to minimize my own needs, to believe that my happiness was secondary or, perhaps, even unimportant.

I'm not sure I would change that moment in the church pew. I'm not sure I would trade the gratitude I felt for Markie's happiness, even if it meant granting myself the courage to demand more for myself. But I do wish I could have held both back then—gratitude for him and a belief that I, too, deserved to feel loved like that. Because we all do.

That Time I Hung Out with a Drug Lord

So many of my life's stories begin with my adult self reflecting upon a moment, experiencing the full weight of all of it at once. I suspect this is because I've spent a lifetime of hyper-compartmentalizing memories, storing them in neatly sealed boxes, safely tucked away until I choose to open one. Inside these compartments, the stories exist in a strange duality: they are both there, real and unreal. Individually, they carry almost no emotional weight until I open the lid and peer inside.

And then WHAM! It hits me like a ton of bricks.

All at once, everything I knew or should have known comes rushing back, along with everyone and everything I didn't quite grasp at the time.

This particular story is a perfect example of one of those moments. It was summertime in the year I turned fifteen. My best friend, Sydney, had a boyfriend, Shane, and it didn't take long for our one-on-one friend time to turn into a lot of me playing third wheel. So, I was excited when Shane himself made a friend. That meant I wouldn't have to hang out all alone. Though I don't remember being bothered by the solitude, I had started to notice that I was being used to convince both Sydney and Shane's parents that the two of them *could not possibly* be engaging in promiscuous teenage shenanigans...

Sydney had told me that Shane had made a new friend named Tony, and they had been hanging out for a while. It had bothered her because Tony was taking up "her" time. When she convinced Shane that we could all hang out together, she was beyond thrilled, and maybe her excitement clouded the judgment of her father, who was an ex-pastor. As he sat at the same table with us that morning, she let us know that Shane and Tony were both coming over.

The only things we knew about Tony were that he was from a different country and spoke little English, and was around thirty years old. Sydney, Shane, and I were all around the same age: fifteen.

No alarm bells? Oooookay—here we go!

I don't remember the details of how Shane and Tony had met. But it had something to do with his parents, who felt bad for Tony, who was in a different country and had no one to interact with. Or at least that is what Sydney told us that morning, and it only occurs to me in this moment of reflecting and writing about it that that could have been an absolute lie.

In any case, Shane and Tony did come over that day. We hung out, and apart from not really knowing how to interact with someone who barely spoke any English, it was uneventful. Sydney and Shane went to a different room, did their thing, and Tony and I probably played video games.

Gradually, Tony became a regular part of our routine. Over time, Tony's English got better, and though I had the distinct impression that most of the time he had no idea what we were saying, every once in a while, he definitely did. The inconsistency of this was noticeable to me, but when I pointed out the anomaly to the adults, they dismissed it as a normal part of acclimation to a different culture. And I was just an uncultured kid.

Tony had his own car, and he drove us everywhere. So, that probably made the parents happy not to have to haul us around everywhere anymore, and more likely to overlook trivial things that I surfaced, like the inconsistency in his command of the English language or the profession he claimed to have had back home. He'd told me he was a teacher. He'd told Sydney he worked on a farm. He'd told Shane and his parents something entirely different.

At some point over the course of that summer, Sydney and Shane broke up. They'd had a habit of getting into knock-down, drag-out fights over the phone and then breaking up. This time, it seemed like it was for good. Which was fine by me. I was getting tired of feeling like I was being used.

We were at Sydney's house, and her dad wasn't home. It was early evening, but it wasn't dark out yet. There was the familiar stillness in the air, the quiet settling down time of early evening. Birds were still singing a little here and there, but even they were mostly settled into their homes for the night.

We heard a noise outside that sounded like a car door slamming. It was too early for Sydney's dad to be home, so she peeked out a window facing the driveway to see who it was. "Oh my God! It's Shane!"

"What? Why is he here?" I asked, at first confused, but after putting the events of the day together, "Oh my God, I bet he's here to beg to get you back!"

"No, it's for good this time, I swear!" she fired back. "We are not answering the door!"

I peeked outside the sheer drapes from a safe distance so as not to be seen from the outside and saw the familiar goldish brownish hatchback that belonged to Tony, who was getting out of the car as we heard the doorbell ring.

"Why is *Tony* getting out of the car?" I said, loud enough for Sydney to hear but not the boys outside.

"I don't know, but we are going to act like we are not here!" she directed firmly. We carried on like that for a few moments, going from window to window to see what was happening outside, expecting them to leave.

But then we heard BANG! BANG! BANG!—an aggressive banging on the door. As if we hadn't heard the doorbell. Sydney's Dad's house had this elaborate doorbell system like a church organ. I think the neighbors could hear that doorbell ringing. There was no way anyone inside would ever miss it.

"SYDNEY! COME OUT HERE! I NEED TO TALK TO YOU!" Shane yelled, continuing to bang on the door. "PLEASE!"

I took a quick peek out of one of the windows, "Oh my God! Tony is going to the front door! What is going on?! Are all of the doors locked?" I asked quickly and quietly, trying not to panic.

"I don't know!" Sydney replied, her voice shaking.

"What happened, Sydney? *What is going on*?" I asked, desperate for answers for this strange behavior from Shane and now Tony. He was *pursuing* her, and he didn't want to take no for an answer.

"I don't know! I think we should hide!" she said. And she sounded scared.

I didn't wait around to clarify what I heard: I took off to her dad's office and squished myself between a large chest of drawers and the corner it stood in front of. I have no idea where Sydney went, but I could hear similar sounds of clothes smooshing against walls nearby that told me that she was hiding somewhere like that, also.

I don't know how long I was in that corner before I heard a door close. My heart dropped and started pounding out of my chest. I could hear it vibrating up and out of my ears. I tried to focus on controlling my breathing. Why the fuck was I breathing so loudly? The more I tried to lower the volume of my breathing, the louder it became.

I heard footsteps coming down the hall.

I could feel someone else in the room; their movements seemed to break the ear-piercing sound of silence and my own godforsaken loud breathing, breaking it like a fragile bubble and somehow making a safe space for my self to exist again, even though I feared being heard and revealed to be in the room with every ounce and molecule of my existence.

The presence left, and I was again left with the stillness of nothing in the room, pulling back like heavy drapes and what felt like blinking and obnoxious neon green lights at the sound of my breathing that also screamed, "SHE'S OVER HERE!"

I waited there as still as I could, listening to muffled speaking that I recognized as Shane and Tony. Then I heard a door close. Then car doors closing, a car starting, and tire sounds on the pavement up the driveway and into the distance.

A thought had entered my mind that it could have been a trap. One of them could still be in the house, and in that moment, I doubted all that I had just heard, along with the narrative I formed that aligned with it, and I just stayed put. Listening.

After some time, I could hear the smooshing sounds of fabric and flesh against the wall, and my heart sank as I realized it was Sydney, coming out of hiding. She whispered, "Christina!"

I remained hiding. Still. Silent.

"Christina!" she whispered a little more loudly. *One of them could still be in the house,* and I had no way to communicate that to her without giving myself away. She was on her own.

I heard her go through the house, and I waited for what seemed like forever before I felt reasonably safe. If one of them was still in the house, they'd have nabbed her by now. I smooshed myself out of hiding and headed out of the office towards the hallway.

I don't know if she ever told her dad what had happened. I certainly didn't tell my parents. We never spoke of it again.

• • •

Later that summer, Sydney and I were sitting at the table again with her dad, and he was reading the newspaper.

"Oh my God!" he exclaimed.

This happened from time to time with adults in response to some bit of news, and the reasons supporting their exasperation varied from trivial and boring to intriguing. I took the bait. "What?" I asked, with authentic curiosity.

He read the article aloud. I heard the words he said, but they remained on the surface of my brain, almost in an act of defiance, refusing to sink in, to be understood. I leaned in to look at the paper so that I could read the words myself. That didn't help. That's exactly how I had heard them.

The story described a drug lord from El Salvador who had been caught and arrested by local police. This person had held his pregnant girlfriend at knifepoint, and then the rest of the details are hazy. I still don't know how much of the story was true, but the photo was unmistakably Tony.

• • •

The weight of a story, compartmentalized and packed away over time, always seems deceptively manageable—until you open the lid. Like a precious, fragile memento handed down from your grandmother, its significance hidden beneath layers of normalcy, or perhaps more accurately, like a time bomb nestled quietly in the corner, invisible until it detonates, shattering illusions and rewriting histories.

Reflecting upon this surreal chapter of my adolescence, I'm struck less by any perception of danger I narrowly escaped and more by how easily our realities can be shaped by assumptions, convenience, and the subtle dismissals of intuition. The adults around us dismissed our instincts as childish exaggeration, unaware that in doing so, they were unintentionally teaching us to silence our inner alarms.

Tony had been woven into our lives without suspicion, seamlessly becoming a part of our everyday landscape until the day we learned his true story. In hindsight, it's clear that all those inconsistencies—his shifting narratives, his selective comprehension of English—were warning signs we collectively chose to overlook. But that realization only hits now, long after the danger has passed, in this quiet reflection, as the compartments of memory begin to unravel.

Opening the lid on this story means confronting how much we trust others at face value, how we're taught to disregard our instincts, and how easily innocence and naivete can blur the lines between safety and danger. It's heavy, this understanding that life often unfolds unnoticed, quietly assembling truths we only fully grasp when we're ready, or forced, to see them. And it reminds me why I've always stored these stories away carefully, knowing the weight would be waiting patiently, ready to be felt fully only when I was finally prepared to hold it.

15: Moving On: Starting Over, Staying Behind

I
T WAS SPRINGTIME IN 1996 when Dad announced that he had landed a new job in Lansing, Michigan. Initially, I was dismayed and not impressed. I felt as though I had just gotten used to living in Ohio, having established friendships, a spot on the volleyball team, and a life that was going mostly well for me. However, the thought had entered my mind that moving away might solve my problem about having to go to Jackie's on Sundays. The thought of closing that miserable chapter was extremely liberating.

In any case, the weight of my thoughts didn't matter, at least not in our family matters. Dad had accepted the new job, and we'd be moving to Lansing later in the summer. Like when we moved to Ohio, Dad moved first, and would come home occasionally on weekends. Frank stayed behind in Ohio.

The TV station he worked at in Lansing had put him up at the Holiday Inn, so when we came to visit him early in the summer, that's where we stayed, too.

I remember our arrival and first drive through Lansing. It was incredibly dry and hot that day. I've lived in Michigan with its often erratic seasons ever since, so that dry heat could have happened anywhere between March and November.

I remember feeling a bit aghast at what I saw. There seemed to be trash everywhere. Weeds everywhere. Blight, everywhere. It didn't feel like a nice or quiet town like the ones we'd lived in before. It didn't have a big city feel to offer as an excuse like neighboring Rockford to Loves Park, Illinois even Canton to Massillon, Ohio. It just felt like a small junk city. Junky, for no apparent reason.

And I said as much.

Mom offered that it was just one side of town, but as we continued to drive, it didn't really change. I noticed the anticipation and excitement coming from her seemed to drain like someone pulled the plug on it, and any energy she had for either was rapidly circling the said drain.

When we pulled into the hotel, the immediate surrounding area seemed decent enough. Stepping inside felt like stepping into an oasis of another world. It sharply contrasted the perimeter around the Holiday Inn on the South side of Lansing, Michigan. It was neat. Tidy. Clean. Nice.

I'm not sure it did much in the way of convincing Mom, though. I overheard it as one of the first observations she'd shared with Dad when he came down to greet us in the lobby.

"Are there... *other*... sides of town we should explore, honey?" she had asked. "What do you mean?" Dad asked, genuinely not understanding the question and seemingly oblivious to the blight outside. This felt like a red flag. But we knew there was a swimming pool in the hotel with our name on it, and we were promised that we could check it out soon after checking into the hotel, so my mind moved on to other things.

We looked at a few houses with a realtor on that trip to Lansing, and all of them were in areas that I couldn't imagine us ever living in. Back home in Ohio, I was surprised when Mom said that they had put an offer in on a house. I attempted to remember the least offensive house that we'd walked through so I could hope that was the one that they chose, but they were all pretty terrible. Those were the days before the internet, and we couldn't just pull up pictures of the one they'd chosen.

So, I'd just have to be surprised. On the phone with Dad before the move, he announced that we'd be selling most of our things during this move. "We're starting over fresh! And that means fresh everything! Keep only the things you really care about and sell everything else."

Wait, are we rich now? I remember thinking to myself. Sell everything? Buy new things? Who was this person? How would we afford any of that? Still, the idea rang nicely in my ears, and I pinned my energy to that all the way to the summer when it was time to move.

My parents had hired this moving company to pack up our things for us. I didn't have to lift a finger. I couldn't fathom how this was possible. Or what it must have cost. But I didn't question it. I did as instructed and packed up anything really valuable and anything really sentimental, which could only be as large as something that we could haul away inside our family vehicle, in my lap, or at my feet.

I assume that Dad received some sort of up-front bonus for accepting that job, or something. My parents were spending money like I'd never seen them spend money before.

Before we moved to Michigan, Mom's level of thriftiness had a reputation. She was the type who could "squeeze a fart out of a penny." She'd save up shopping for triple coupon day at the local grocery store and irritate everyone in line behind us. We'd stand there for what seemed like forever as she meticulously called out each transaction and challenged anything that seemed wrong, with the line piling up and winding around the store behind us. Back then, cash registers weren't all that sophisticated, and there were often many errors, which did not deter Mom. She'd wait half an hour for a clerk to call a manager over to correct an error of ten cents if it didn't belong.

So, this version of my parents was entirely foreign to me. We had gone up to a local furniture store, and I got to pick out my brand-new bed: a black metal-framed futon. I had never owned a brand-new bed before, and I was excited and then disappointed to learn that I'd have to wait a few weeks for that futon and other furniture to be delivered to the house.

Our first night in our new house was without furniture or any of our belongings, save for what we brought with us. Though we oversaw the moving company pack up our entire house and belongings, they would be a day or two behind us. And it was hot.

For all of that spending we'd done during that first day, it must have burned Mom out. She didn't want to turn the central air on in the house, because running the AC costs money. We didn't have any of our stuff, including any kind of fan that would save us by circulating the 90-degree stale indoor air. It was uncomfortable at first, and then quickly escalated to unbearable.

At some point in the evening, Mom caved and flicked on the AC. "Air conditioning works great!" Dad said, which seemed entirely redundant, so no one replied. My excitement started to grow with the soft whisper of relief whooshing through the vents that evening.

And most of all, I was excited that I would not wake to face another Sunday of going to Jackie's house, and with that thought in my head and upon my heart, I drifted off to sleep.

Life in the Mitten

I can't fully explain the difference in life after moving to Michigan, but I felt it. The air was easier to breathe. The volume of everything—the arguments, the tension, the unpredictability—seemed to turn down several notches. The erratic ups and downs that once kept me on edge had leveled out. With fewer exceptions, I could reasonably predict which version of Mom would be sitting on the couch when I got home from school, and which version of Dad would walk through the door after work. It wasn't perfect, but it was much, much better.

Michigan felt like stability for me. I avoided making friends, wary of the possibility that we'd uproot again. But in a way, that self-imposed isolation made things easier. After bouncing between small-town schools in Ohio, attending an inner-city school in Lansing felt like coasting. I kept my head down, did what I needed to do, and for the first time in a long time, life felt...manageable.

Of course, what I mean is that it was a relatively uneventful life for me. For Bobby, it was a different story. Dad still rode him hard, and Mom still found reasons to kick up storms based on whatever injustice she perceived that he'd committed. The shift that had brought a sense of peace for me didn't seem to apply to him. Eventually and understandably, he decided he'd had enough. He packed his things, and he left, back to Ohio.

By the time he left, I wasn't sure what had changed more— our home, or me. Was it actually easier to breathe? Or was I too busy stepping into my own life to notice if the tension remained?

It was around this time, with the encouragement of my boyfriend at the time—my first real boyfriend, whom I'd been dating for several months—that I finally built up the courage to tell Mom about The Candy Man and Rick. It felt essential to let her know about them and that they'd crossed a line when I was a child.

She was sitting on the couch reading when I approached her, Princess wedged up alongside her. I had told her that I had something important to say. I said it might be difficult to hear, and I asked if she could refrain from interjecting until I was done sharing what I needed to say. She put a finger in her book to mark its place and set it down on the other side of her on the couch. She nodded. I had her attention.

I told her everything, including details I had not shared with anyone outside of my journal.

She sat quietly. Her face expressionless.

When I was finished, I asked if she could keep it between us, because I wasn't sure how Dad would take the news or if I even wanted him to know these things about me.

Her face twisted. "We watched you!" she blurted out.

I blinked, unsure entirely what this meant, but given the context, I assumed she meant that she believed that I was under their constant surveillance and what I had said could not possibly be true. Before I let myself go too far down that emotional rabbit hole, I asked her to clarify, "What do you mean?"

She was visibly shaking, "WE WATCHED YOU! We were ALWAYS WATCHING YOU! You were NEVER ALONE!"

I blinked again, in disbelief. If what she was saying was true, it would have been impossible for my memories to be true. But I checked them. And checked them again, and concluded: I am not sophisticated enough to conjure up memories of such things.

I pushed back, "But I was alone. You guys would go to those flea markets, and you were preoccupied with selling stuff and—" she cut me off. "WE WATCHED YOU!" as if the volume of her voice had power over erasing a reality she couldn't, or wouldn't, face.

At that point, she started sobbing, wailing about what a terrible mother she was, what a good person she used to be, that all she ever tried to do was her best. At some point midway through the spectacle, I got up from my chair. "Why didn't you say something sooner?" she asked, with a tone I worked really hard at not ignoring; she was implying that this was somehow my fault.

"I didn't think you'd believe me," I replied as I walked down the hallway to my room and closed the door behind me.

A Change in Plans

Unexpectedly, in the fall of 1997, Dad got fired from his job at the TV station. He had covered for one of his unionized direct reports, and one of the big boss men didn't like that Dad was an advocate of the people and their union, so he set him up to get him fired.

Such bullshit.

The news buzzed in my ears and vibrated through my body. A feeling similar to being in trouble, like sitting in a principal's office. It felt like huge news. And I had so many questions. What are we going to do about money? How will we pay the bills? We should *sue them!*

But to my surprise, my parents were almost stoic about the whole thing. They must have had some kind of savings that would sustain us until Dad found another job, or maybe he'd received some severance package. Either way, he seemed unbothered.

Maybe he was glad it happened. Or he had gone numb, as I had done when fighting my own self by compartmentalizing the bad things that happened to me.

"We're not going to sue them. They violated the contract, but we're *Christians*. We don't sue." Mom explained, which effectively explained exactly nothing to my seventeen-year-old self.

I peppered them again with the same questions, "What are we going to do about money? How will we pay the bills? I'm sure I don't make enough money to cover the bills!" I repeated myself with exasperation.

"You don't need to worry about any of this. You aren't going to have to pay the bills!" Dad interrupted my tizzy. "This isn't for you to worry about!" he punctuated, ending the conversation.

Left to my own thoughts, I felt incredulous. How were we going to survive? Were we going to get thrown out on the street? I was fairly sure I could survive on my own, but there was no way I could support a family.

Dad kept himself busy through the winter with projects around the house. He tiled parts of the kitchen and added decorative trim everywhere in the house that could support it. And even places that shouldn't have supported it. Eventually, he landed another job in Hagerstown, Maryland.

We'd have to move all over again.

My heart sank. I hadn't made much of an effort to make many friends this time around because I knew we'd just move again, but I was a senior in high school and months away from graduation. But Michigan was good for me. I had a solid job. I had plans to go to the local community college. I had life set and planned ahead of me. What was there for me in Maryland?

I didn't have to twist any arms to get them to let me stay. I wouldn't turn eighteen until August of the following year, but I could stay with my boyfriend's parents until I was old enough to get my own lease. I had started my own savings. I would be fine.

They were able to get Markie transferred mid-school-year, and they were gone, leaving behind the Ford Aerostar van for me to sell as it was likely too old to make the long journey.

I reminded myself a lot of Kevin McCallister's character in *Home Alone* in the early days after my family left me in Michigan. Whatever food my family had left in the fridge and pantry was mine to enjoy, and I took advantage of that freedom pretty much immediately. We weren't allowed to eat whatever we wanted whenever we wanted. Being able to eat anything I wanted just because it was there was a small luxury that I indulged in shamelessly.

I packed up my own things and moved them over to my boyfriend's parents' house, who had an upstairs apartment set up ready for me, like a studio apartment. I finished high school. When I got news that the house was sold, I packed up the rest of the house into boxes, and the movers would take it from there.

Packing up Markie's room was pretty easy, though I lingered a bit, playing with some of his toys. Some of his stuff was still boxed up from our move to Michigan, so it wasn't difficult at all.

My parents' room took longer. They would pay attention to how carefully—or not carefully—I packed away their things, and so I took my time with their stuff more than I had with Markie's. I came upon the files that Dad had kept in his room for as long as I could remember. The court papers that documented the adventure that Bobby and I had out on the road in Florida.

Birth certificates. School pictures. Their wedding pictures.

I can't say specifically why I did it, but I kept their wedding photo album. I took the court documents to work and made copies for myself. I also took Frank, Bobby, Markie, and my school photos. I don't recall any specific reason for having done any of that. I just did it.

My parents had planned to stop by on their way to Illinois to visit with family, and they would help pack up anything remaining for the movers. But since my task was to have it mostly done, it was by the time they arrived.

They had only been gone a few weeks, but when they returned, they already felt vaguely foreign to me.

They were only passing through. They stuck around for an hour, maybe two, gathering up any essentials that they didn't want to risk the movers losing, and they continued on their way.

And then it was just me.

The last time I left the house was bittersweet. I was still living in the area, and I knew I could drive by whenever I wanted, so it didn't feel like goodbye. It was more like, "See ya later." To this day, that house still serves as a sort of memorial of my family as I last remember it; the last time that Mom, Dad, Bobby, Markie, and I lived together under one roof.

Another chapter of the Anderson Family saga, coming to a close.

I had listed the family Aerostar in the *Wheeler Dealer*, and after a few weeks, it had sold for about three thousand dollars. A charming young family had agreed to purchase it after a quick test drive. The husband needed to go to a bank to get the cash, and he'd be back the next day to pick it up. He was so grateful and so excited to be able to purchase that van for his family that I felt deeply touched.

I called Dad to ask if we could give it to them. "Are you nuts?" he said. Not condescendingly or harshly, more matter-of-factly. "Have you got three thousand dollars that you can just throw away?"

"No," I relented, with a sigh of understanding.

The next morning, I got up early to take that van to the car wash. I didn't have three thousand dollars to throw away, but I had a few bucks in change that I could use at the manual car wash to give that thing a good shine so that the family had one less thing to manage or deal with.

That was Dad's daily driving car when they lived in Michigan, and he smoked in it. So even though it had been a few weeks since he'd driven it, it still carried that certain odor in the plastic. I'd gone up to the grocery store and purchased all the interior car-cleaning products that I could find, and I did my best to detail it.

When they arrived the next day, the husband was grateful. "You didn't have to do this," he said. A look in his eyes somewhere between gratitude and disbelief. I was happy to do it. It was meaningful to them, however small.

I took the cash up to the bank, deposited it immediately, and then wrote my father a check for three thousand dollars. Then I mailed it to him.

Chapter complete.

16: Moms

I WAS EIGHTEEN. I had a job working for the State of Michigan, and I was enrolled at Lansing Community College (LCC) studying Computer Science. I had absolutely everything and nothing figured out—especially that last part.

A year after moving 522 miles away to Martinsburg, West Vir-by-god-ginia (as Dad called it), it seemed like life for my parents and Markie was forging ahead as well. Markie was doing well in school, Dad had miscellaneous projects around the house, and Mom had found a church and a Bible study group to belong to. They were making a new home for themselves in the Northeast.

I suppose my relationship with my parents unfolded typically. Though looking back on my life stories, I am unsure if I know what 'typical' really means.

It was spring, and I was wrapping up my first year at LCC. Mom would call once a week to check on me and how things were going. Sometimes I'd hear Dad in the background, sometimes Mom would let him know I said "hello" and I could hear him reply in his distinct silly voice in the background, "Hello there, Christopher-Teeny!"

Dad had a knack for coming up with nonsensical nicknames for us kids, which carried through into our adult years.

My relationship with them evolved into something healthier for me, even if it was just the distance.

I stopped biting my nails, a lifelong habit for as long as I could remember. I'd bite them down so far that they bled, and Dad frequently threatened to make me wear gloves or dip my fingers in some kind of spicy pepper oil.

It always struck me as odd that he cared so much about my nails, given that he also chewed his nails down to almost nothing. Though I don't remember seeing them bleed. Maybe that was part of growing up, developing enough self-discipline to indulge in your bad habits without exposing yourself to harm—in this case, infection?

It was a few weeks away from Mother's Day when Dad called. An unusual but not altogether unheard-of change from Mom's familiar voice.

We went through the typical check-ins. Markie is doing great in school, Dad was doing his hobbies, and Mom had been sick and wasn't feeling well. She couldn't remember having been injured, but she had developed this weird bruise on her shoulder, and she just didn't feel good enough to do much of anything.

"She gonna go see a doctor?" I'd asked. "You know your mom. She thinks she'll be better in a day or two."

The following week, as far as I can remember, went on without anything memorable. In addition to being enrolled full-time in college, I was also working at the State and had a long-term boyfriend to manage. I was living and exploring my own ideas about what life could and should be.

After a week or so, the next call came in with Dad on the other end of the line again.

Mom was even more sick, so sick that Dad had built a makeshift port-a-potty out of a Home Depot bucket and a pool noodle. He was busy telling me all about his creative solution to the problem at hand when I interrupted him, "She gonna go see a doctor now? Dad, if she can't manage to get up to even go to a bathroom, something is really wrong!"

"Ahh. You know your mom. She won't go to the doctor. She's gonna tough it out on the couch."

Who was I, an eighteen-year-old girl, to question the wisdom of my parents?

The next call came sooner than a week.

It was Dad again. Mom was really, really sick. She'd gotten so sick that she became unresponsive, so he called for an ambulance, and they took her up to the hospital.

"I would have called sooner, but I didn't want to worry ya."

The local hospital in Martinsburg didn't have the specialists she needed, so they were going to take her via helicopter to Johns Hopkins.

It is difficult for me to separate my current self from my self at that time. I am rereading my own words with what I know of the events, and everything inside me is willing my eighteen-year-old self to go. GO NOW. *Go be with your family.*

But on the call that day, there was not even the slightest whiff of concern in Dad's voice.

"She's going to be in good hands. They're world-class docs over there at Hopkins."

Was I so absorbed in my own life, my own independence? Was I so young and ignorant that I was unable to comprehend the gravity of the situation?

Mom was at Johns Hopkins for a few weeks. I'd get pretty regular update phone calls from Dad. Each time, I either didn't notice an urgency in his voice or it was actually absent.

She was in a medically induced coma. They had diagnosed her with cirrhosis of the liver, which normally strikes heavy alcoholics, but Mom never drank. And I don't mean she wasn't a heavy drinker—I mean she did not drink. I'd seen her take maybe two sips of wine in my entire life, and that was just to try it. So the doctors chalked it up to either an unknown hereditary condition or a stroke of really bad luck.

I guess in my simple mind, I felt like a diagnosis meant there would be a cure, reasoning that if we know what it is, we certainly know how to treat it.

Her system started shutting down.

Dad called one day with his update and to share the news that her mom and sisters had been there to visit.

"To visit? Why? Should I come out there, Dad? What's going on?"

"They came to say their final goodbyes."

"But she's going to get better. Why would they do that?" I was so mad. I distinctly remember feeling bitterly angry at my family for going to say goodbye. It felt like they had given up on her. Saying goodbye has a finality–it means they gave up! And I wasn't giving up! I was never going to give up! And how dare they!

"Dad, should I come out there to be with you, with Markie?" I asked again.

"There's nothing to do here, Tina. She is in the absolute best hospital in the world. She is being taken care of."

I can connect to my best guess at a father attempting not to worry his daughter while not having answers to either inspire or squelch anxiety.

He was my only real line into whatever was happening there, though. And he still, even after sharing that news about my family, towed that line of neutrality. He did not seem concerned to me.

He had nothing to offer when I shared my anger at her family for showing up to say goodbye. He simply said, "I know. But they are just doing whatever they think they need to do. Even if it is just in case."

All kids probably have some sense that their parents are immortal. Nobody ever thinks about anybody ever *dying*. We live and operate as though death isn't even on the table. Or at least I certainly did in those days.

I grappled with these feelings for a few days. I felt a sense of injustice, even if it was misguided. She shouldn't be there, trapped in a coma, having her family come out to say goodbye, and just be left with that.

I decided I would go out there. The only problem was, I'd never been on a plane before.

It was still early in the internet age, so there were no online airline bookings as far as I knew. I picked up the phone and started calling airlines. It was something like $121 to fly from Lansing, Michigan, to Baltimore, Maryland.

In the sky, above the clouds, I marveled at the vastness of the earth. How small the world seemed below, and a vantage I'd not experienced before. And I prayed. I prayed that I could be of help somehow to Dad, to Markie. To myself? Most of all to Mom. That somehow my presence there would be all that was missing to get her to wake up out of that coma and finally on the track to getting better.

Dad looked tired. Weathered. Markie looked the same as the last time I'd seen him.

Dad was giddy with my arrival. He got straight to work telling me all about the rental car he had picked us up in, that the TV station he was working for was generous in offering to pay for it, and also had given him all the time away from work that he needed to be with Mom.

For an eighteen-year-old with limited life experience, none of that was a red flag to me. Today, at forty-four, I am shocked at my ignorance.

In true fashion, when excited, Dad continued to rattle on, jumping from one topic to the next, and I'm not sure that he took time to breathe. Since I flew into Baltimore, we were heading directly over to the hospital. Dad was rattling on about a home project that Mom had asked him to tackle. I was half listening as he began lamenting about spending so much time driving between home, making sure Markie got to school, stopping in to work as much as he could, and still spending as much time as possible at the hospital, that he had been lacking in his chores back at the house.

I don't think he noticed himself when he continued, "If she makes it out of this, I will build her a whole damn *shrine* if she wants it!"

And I sharply interrupted, "*When* she makes it out of this."

His eyes darted across the road as he drove, which I understood to mean he was pivoting of sorts. "Oh. Yeah," he managed to make both sounds and words tumble out of his mouth. "*When.*"

On the way up to the ICU at Johns Hopkins, Dad tried to prepare me for the sight I was about to see. I couldn't connect to most of what he had said because I never had. And so, I was completely unprepared to process when I did.

There was a figure on a hospital bed, behind the glass wall that we were facing.

Dad was explaining the technology around the air mattress bed thingy she was on. That it was built to prevent bed sores was about all I heard before I faded out of conscious thought while he rattled on in my peripheral hearing.

What I could see was what looked like an overly inflated figure on top of a hospital bed. It reminded me of an overfilled waterbed. This figure, allegedly a human, and allegedly my mother, was arranged feet facing me.

I could guess at what looked like feet under the pale-yellow hospital blanket that covered them. I could see just barely beyond that what looked like dark hair, an element that matched the description of Mom the last time I saw her.

"Can we go in to be with her?" I asked, irritated that I even had to. I didn't fly all the way to Baltimore just to gawk at her behind a glass wall. I needed her to know that I was there. I needed her not to be all alone in there, trapped inside her waterbed sandwich and comatose state.

Dad hesitated. "You can."

He hesitated some more.

"If you really want to."

They didn't want us to go in there if we didn't have to, he explained. She had acquired some incredibly contagious something or other, and they needed to reduce exposure to healthy people as much as possible.

I felt exasperated at this point, as if the words he was saying made any sense to me as an actual or even logical barrier to my going into that room.

"I'm going in!" I said, as calmly as I could, trying to be mindful of any undertones in my speech.

"Okay," he said, as he walked over to the nurse's station to get a nurse.

Next to the glass door was a little rolling set of drawers. She pulled out a gown thingy, pants, shoe coverings, hair covering, mask, and shield thingy.

"Man," I thought to myself. "Is all of this really necessary?"

Dad and Markie had elected to stay out of the room. They had been in there frequently. Which deepened my anger. Only towards Dad. Markie was just a kid, only fourteen. But the way I received things, it was too much of a hassle to put all this garb on just to be in a room with somebody who doesn't even know you're there.

"We don't know that she doesn't know that we're here," I said to myself, quietly enraged that I was alone in my challenge of that thinking.

The nurse pulled a box of gloves out of an apparatus on the wall that contained a line of boxes and motioned for me to put them on.

I can't explain why, after all the other coverings, gloves were what made me stop to ask questions.

"Is that really necessary?" I asked, trying to hide the defiance in my voice.

"Oh, yes. Absolutely every part of you must be covered. You don't want to catch that!"

In my mind, maybe my hands were the remaining part of my humanity? The rest of me could be covered without resistance because she was in a coma and could not see me. So, seeing me totally covered would not have been offensive to her. And she'd be able to hear me, even if my voice might sound slightly muffled from the mask.

But gloves meant she wouldn't be able to feel my touch. Which then, and now, feels incredibly isolating. I was determined to remedy this.

I reluctantly put the gloves on my hands. Noting that no one else was donning the full get-up the same as me, meaning I'd be going in alone. "Anything else I need to know before I go in?"

"Just make sure that you keep everything covered. If anything slips, you need to come out immediately."

As I stepped closer to this figure in this bed, my eyes widened at just how much larger the waterbed became. Left by myself, my curiosity was unchallenged to wander.

That can't be comfortable! What is going on there?

I moved along the right side of the bed, approaching the dark hair I could see from outside and...

There she was. There was Mom.

At this point, none of this should have been a surprise, but in that moment it absolutely was. I gasped. Instinctively, I placed my gloved hand on her shoulder to offer reassurance of some kind, just in an "OH MY GOD ARE YOU OK" kind of way.

The ventilator hissed and whirred rhythmically. Some pumps had similar rhythmic soft beeps. I don't know how long I just stood there, frozen, waiting for my brain to make sense of what I was seeing, until I realized that it probably wouldn't, and decided to interact with her.

Not like everything was okay. Just a lot less like everything was not okay.

"Mom? It's me." I said, as softly as I could. "Dad said not to come out here because everything is OK! I just wanted to see you and spend time with you while you're locked up in this crummy hospital. I'll be here for a few days."

"Can I hold her hand?" I asked Dad who was standing in front of the open glass door.

He looked back towards someone standing at the nurse's station, saying something, before turning back around and nodding yes. "You have to keep your gloves on!"

I know I have to keep my gloves on.

I pulled the blanket up, starting at her shoulder, and was surprised and relieved that her arms had not inflated like the rest of her. I continued pulling the blanket up, following the length of her arm, down to her hand.

I noticed red spots all over her hands and under her fingernails. They were ranged in a perfect order like a constellation. I was struck by how perfectly preserved they looked under her nails.

It's fascinating what the brain will focus on to commandeer the mind in order to avoid what it is not ready to see.

I held her hand in my left hand. Which was awkward. Because it wasn't something that we did, even if I was noticing in the moment how natural it felt to me to do it, and so I persisted in doing it anyway.

Instinctively, I raised my other hand from her shoulder up to her head. Which I immediately regretted as I felt and heard the latex glove pull at her hair. It was too late to take away, and too late to avoid. I was already in that far, so I held my hand there again. Because it felt awkward and because it felt right. I was conscious of my own instinct.

I rattled on about school, work, life, and kept talking to her, as though she could hear me, resisting the urge to call that out and let it have air in the room, the words that circled my mind, "I'm not even sure if you can hear me!" I kept to myself. If she could hear me, I didn't want her to feel bad about it.

Recalling this moment with the 25 years of experience added to it, I would assume an eighteen-year-old girl in the same situation to feel out of control, helpless, a variety of things that I distinctly did not feel.

I felt empowered by being there. It was the only thing I could do, and I was doing it. And that was enough.

I don't know how much time passed while I was rattling on when the doctors arrived to make their rounds. Some sort of neutral update was given, followed by another neutral update to which Dad neutrally accepted with his neutral head shake.

She needed a new liver, and she was on the liver donor list, but this infection meant that they would have to take her off temporarily until the infection was gone.

"Can they take mine?" Markie asked directly, quietly, respectfully.

The doctor replied, unflinchingly, which sparked some of my ire, "No. Unfortunately, living donor transplants aren't widely available, and you'd have to be eighteen or older to do it anyway."

"Well, I don't care. Take mine!" he said, raising his voice.

"Marcus, they can't do it," Dad interjected, shaking his head casually. "Your liver would have the same problem as anybody else's. They will give her medications to clear the infection, and she'll be back on the list in a few days. It's not a big deal."

The doctor let Dad's words hang in the air for a beat. His face suggested to me that what Dad said wasn't entirely accurate, but also wasn't debatable, so he didn't. After a few moments, he left us with his perfectly neutral plan of action and immediate next steps, which all felt perfectly logical to me at the time as a perfectly successful treatment of a perfectly understood diagnosis.

Do we just hear the things we want to hear?

I stayed in the area for a few days. I got to see the new house they were living in, including the level of squalor that Dad and Markie were living in during Mom's absence. I attempted to tidy up a bit, fully acknowledging all that they had on their emotional, mental, and physical plates.

Despite all of the neutral news, they were both a wreck.

I flew home. In the air, I made a similar connection to the clouds and vantage point as I had on the way to Baltimore. Noting to myself I'd never be closer to God than there in the sky, and somehow that felt like my sentiments would be more likely to be heard.

I prayed that Mom would get to feeling better and home as soon as possible. Because Dad and Markie were absolutely lost without her. They needed her.

"That bathroom was disgusting!" I chuckled to myself, noticing that I was talking to Mom.

We all need you.

• • •

Back at home in Michigan, life marched on. I was getting caught up on school that I'd missed. I went on an annual camping trip. I'd get phone calls from Dad with updates, and everything was normal. Neutral.

I was out in the backyard swimming in the pool when the phone rang.

"It's your dad!"

I groaned. I didn't want to get out of the pool. Early June in Michigan wasn't all that warm yet for swimming. Getting out of the pool now meant that I'd get cold and then have to get used to the water all over again. Which was also cold. Begrudgingly, I grabbed a towel, wrapping it around myself, and headed towards the house to talk to Dad.

"Hey Dad! What's up?"

"Tina, they're saying she's only got about an hour left."

My brain could not keep up. It was suddenly performing mental gymnastics and not sticking any kind of landing.

"What?" I asked, as if I was misunderstanding the words I had heard entirely.

Dad grew impatient, "The doctors... they've said she is only going to live for another hour or so. I've got to go and call a few other people and be with Marcus."

I didn't know what to say, and I didn't know what to do.

"What does that *mean*?" I asked again, as if somehow the words I was hearing meant something else.

"Tina, she is dying. She will be dead in one hour. I have to go —I will call you back... afterwards."

And he hung up.

That is the moment that I felt like I got hit over the head with a ton of bricks made of pure helplessness. Dad and Markie were 500-some miles away in that hospital. Mom's clock was ticking, and each second that passed, I felt an ache that grew and echoed stronger, and there was nothing. Nothing I could do to stop it.

I placed the phone back in the cradle and started to head back outside. But it is as if the mental load I was carrying physically now weighed too much to carry, and I felt my knees hit the late spring grass, the dirt below it soft and cushioning the weight of my emotional and mental distress.

And I just sat there kneeling. Not crying. Crying would have been like giving permission to the universe to make it True. For as long as I could deny it, it would not be True. And I just sat there, kneeling, kneeling, kneeling.

Someone helped me back into the house, and I followed along sort of robotically to their instructions. Go upstairs. Get dressed. Go lie down.

Before I went upstairs, I left them with the understanding that I would not be answering any phone.

And I didn't.

But the news still traveled through the phone wire first and into the ears of the receiver, whose mouth shared them with my ears, and then it became True.

My mom had died.

The Questions Left Behind

In 2000, I was nearing twenty years old, and old enough to feel the pull of questions I'd been silencing for years. We'd buried Mom a year earlier, and she had been a force. Her shadow loomed large over my world. But she wasn't my only mother. There was another woman—the one who gave birth to me. The one I'd imagined my whole life was somewhere out there, imagining me, too.

Growing up, my curiosity about my biological mother, Lori, wasn't something Mom welcomed. I learned that lesson well back in Ohio when I once dared to ask her about my family history, wanting to understand the pieces of myself I couldn't quite trace. Her reaction was immediate and explosive.

"That woman was a slut! How dare you talk about that woman in *my home*! You ungrateful little bitch! After all I've done for you!"

Her words stung, but it was the rage in her eyes that shut me down completely. I remember my face burning as I tried to swallow the shame, the sense that I'd crossed a forbidden line simply by wanting to know who I was. But I put myself in her position, and I understood it. And she wasn't wrong to feel betrayed by my questions.

So, I buried the questions deep, carrying them around like rocks in my pocket. There was no room to wonder about Lori while my loyalty to Mom was the price of peace.

But now, with Mom gone, those quiet questions floated back to the surface. I could feel them filling the empty spaces, taking root in the places where her voice used to be. For the first time, I felt free to ask. I turned to Dad, hoping he might have the answers I craved.

"She couldn't have been that bad, right?" I asked cautiously during a phone call, pacing my tiny apartment with the cordless phone pressed to my ear. "You had three—actually four—children with her if you count the other one. She couldn't have been that bad?"

The silence on the other end stretched thin. "What?"

I wondered if he hadn't heard me or if he was attempting to avoid the question.

"Uhh, hey, I'm, uh, actually in the middle of something right now. Can we talk about this another time?" His tone was clipped. Unfeeling. And yet also almost panicked.

"Oh. Sure. Sorry. Didn't mean to interrupt your *life*," I replied, my voice laced with bitterness that couldn't mask the sting of rejection. Surprised by my own immaturity, I hung up, feeling the familiar burn of shame. And just like that, the door to my past slammed shut again.

• • •

I was at work at the State of Michigan when a message came:

Frank had been in Florida for a computer show and stopped by the diner where Lori used to work as a dishwasher. As he piled food onto his plate at the buffet, he asked one of the employees if Lori Anderson still worked there.

"She's dead," the woman replied bluntly. "She died about a year ago."

• • •

I remember the way the ground tilted beneath me. I left work that day in a daze, telling my boss, "I just learned my biological mom is dead." The words felt foreign, like I was reciting someone else's tragedy.

The grief was different from what I'd felt when Mom passed. With Lori, I wasn't mourning a life shared, but a life imagined. I grieved the 10-minute phone call we'd had when I was fifteen, the few scraps of detail I'd clung to, the dream of a mother I'd never known.

Growing up, I'd built Lori up as the perfect mother—the one I never had. In my mind, she was loving, nurturing, and understanding. She was the woman who'd teach me how to shave, talk to me about boys, and hold me close when I cried. She was the soft, squishy presence who'd call me her baby and tell me she loved me "to the moon and back." I imagined us reuniting, picking up the pieces as if we'd never been apart. But that fantasy crumbled the moment I spoke to her on the phone at fifteen.

The conversation had been stilted and awkward, with me bubbling over with excitement and her answering flatly, as though she were navigating something as monotonous as ordering a pizza over the phone. She didn't ask about me, my life, or my interests. I learned only a few mundane details about her: she had a boyfriend named Tony, drove a rust-colored Pinto, and smoked. Marlboro Reds.

That was it.

My dream of her flickered after that conversation, but didn't fade entirely. I still wanted her to be the mother I'd imagined, even if I knew differently.

When I learned she had died, the fantasy shattered completely. I couldn't let it rest—I needed answers. I filed a Freedom of Information Act request, convinced that I needed to know how she had died, clinging to some hope of mystery or redemption. Or connection? Something. Anything!

When the envelope arrived, I tore it open, my heart pounding. There, in stark, clinical text, on her death certificate was the truth:

Cause of death: inhaling substances.

I sat there, staring at those words, feeling the dream of Lori disintegrate. She hadn't died of some tragic accident or illness. She had died recklessly, in a way that didn't fit the image I had clung to for so long.

Lori Mae Anderson had died on May 10, 1999, inhaling substances.

She wasn't the mother I'd imagined. She was someone else entirely—someone I would never get to know.

With Lori, I grieved not just her death but the loss of a dream. It was a pain that went beyond grief. A unique devastation. The questions I'd carried all my life now had answers, but they weren't the answers I wanted at all.

And there is no going back.

So, I did the only thing I could do: make peace with the unknown, with the idea that some pieces of me would remain forever out of reach. It's a fragile peace, one that feels like glass stretched too thin. But beneath it, the questions simmer, quiet but insistent, reminding me that they'll always be part of my story, and I'll never have all the answers.

Just the questions.

Just the loss.

17: Between Life and Loss

I T WAS AUGUST 31, 2002, and near the end of the day, when a thought occurred to me to take a pregnancy test. My then-husband and I were not necessarily trying, but we also were not-not trying. My period wasn't technically even late yet, but I had felt just "off" enough that taking a test seemed like the right idea. As I paced the small bathroom, waiting impatiently for the results to come, I started daydreaming about a potential life that would enter the home that I had personally been excitedly planning for as long as I could remember.

I always knew I wanted to be a parent. Having been so restricted growing up, I initially imagined myself as a parent who would let my kids do whatever they wanted—smoke, drink, stay out late—just because they wanted to. A mindset that I understand now came not from a vision for freedom, but as a reaction to having been controlled.

Why did I want kids? Why did I choose to become a parent? I felt a natural tug at my soul to give another human being an opportunity to have a better life than I felt that I had. By the time I was twenty-two, standing there in that bathroom, trying not to stare directly at the stick as if looking at the results might make them any more (or less) true, I found myself landing somewhere in between who I'd imagined I'd be and who I hoped to become.

I always had awareness that my parents were strict, but it wasn't until I had matured some and was on my own that I began to see some of their rules and boundaries in a new light. Some of them made sense. Some had even served me. I noticed that I was far less likely to cross certain lines, not out of principle, but because I didn't want to disappoint my dad. That instinct kept me out of trouble, but it was rooted in fear, and not out of respect or even love.

But I did feel that I loved my parents. And reflecting on my childhood, though I can see the gaps—how rarely we named or even acknowledged our feelings, how little space there was for tenderness—I also see the throughline. Even in the silence and the mess, I never doubted that I belonged to them or that they loved me, too.

The timer went off. It was the moment I'd been waiting for: was I, or was I not, carrying a new life?

The results were faint, but they were there! Two lines! One strong line, the line that lets you know that the test is "good," and one faint line, the line that lets you know the results. Any evidence of a line, so said the instructions, was a positive result.

I was pregnant.

I couldn't contain my joy. I had read somewhere that you shouldn't tell other people that you're pregnant until you're around 12 weeks because you might miscarry, and then you'll have to deal with untelling everyone. As a side note, I think this is complete bullshit because if you miscarry and you haven't told anyone, you have to deal with that all on your own. But I digress, to each their own.

I took it upon myself to share my excitement in my own way that night.

I picked up the phone and called Dad. We exchanged the usual pleasantries. I got an update on Markie, Dad's new wife, her kids, and the security business he was excited to finally be building.

I shared with him that I was excited too, for a close friend who had recently found out that she was pregnant.

I went to bed that night, starting the never-ending checklist of motherhood that included all the things that I thought I knew, and a desire to desperately soak in all that I didn't.

• • •

The next morning, I heard a familiar sound. It was a message on AOL Instant Messenger. It was Dad's new wife: "What am I going to do?"

Alarm bells started ringing through my ears. A bizarrely phrased question completely void of any context... *this must be a mistake.* Maybe she was talking to someone else and had accidentally sent this to me? I sat there, still wiping the sleep out of my eyes, not wanting to ask questions that I didn't want to know the answers to, and having no clue if or how to respond.

Then, the phone rang.

That familiar sinking feeling when you know something is horribly, terribly, irrevocably wrong set in.

The caller ID of the cordless handset indicated it was Dad's phone number.

Dread sunk in and twisted my guts up in one swift motion. "Oh God," my mind scrambled to put the pieces together; his wife's ominous message and now the phone ringing, "something happened to Dad." A million frantic possibilities flashed through my mind, each one worse than the last.

I picked up the phone, hesitating.

"Hello?" I tried to keep my voice steady, suppressing the near crippling fear clawing at my chest.

"Tina?" The voice on the other end sounded just like Dad's.

Oh, God. Thank God, Dad is okay! What happened then? Something with his wife's kids? Markie? What was going on?

"Dad's dead."

The voice on the other end of the phone solved the riddle abruptly and without warning. The words vibrated throughout my body. I felt electric.

"Wh-what?" I asked, incredibly confused, my brain frantically grappling for a sense of direction.

"Dad had some weird chest pain this morning, and by the time he had asked his wife to get his coat and shoes, he had passed out. Pissed himself right there on the floor. The ambulance came and took him away, but there was nothing they could do. Dad's dead." I now recognized the voice on the other end of the phone as Frank's. It remained Frank's, no matter how much I willed it to be Dad's while he continued to tell me what had happened.

Well, that was a pretty shitty way to find out my dad was dead, I thought, replaying Frank's words over the phone that first day of September. In that moment, it felt like being hit over the head with a ton of bricks. My brain could not— would not—make sense of the words.

Learning of Dad's death over a phone call, the same way I had learned of Mom's, flooded every corner of my mind, my heart, and my soul. It filled spaces that I am convinced no external force can shift or take away.

Grief blasted through me in every stage, all at once. The primal part of me screamed for time to stop, just for a little while. And yet, as it always does, it marched on—carrying with it the life growing inside me and the memory of the life I'd just lost.

In an instant, I stopped my grieving. Not from any great intention set by me, it felt more like a primal urge. I knew I had to get myself under control or I'd lose my baby.

It was pure faith that got me through those first few moments, which rolled into minutes, and then days, as my father's funeral approached.

I don't remember if I flew or if I drove. And that detail is distinctly missing from my memory bank and tells me everything I need to know to be reminded that I did not want to make that journey. I did not want to face a place on a map where my father both lived and no longer lived.

Still, somehow, I got there. Just in time for his wife to be belly-aching about some random thing that Bobby had done. Markie and Frank were already there in West Virginia, so it was just Bobby and I who would be traveling from out of town. He from Ohio, me from Michigan.

He had gotten into town late at night, and rather than knock on a door or wake anybody up, he slept in his car in the driveway. Some kind of paranoia hit the woman whom Dad had married, and she convinced herself that Bobby was there to "take everything away." Like, take *what* away, lady? After Mom died, Dad and Markie lived in that house like a couple of bachelors.

They donated most of Mom's things to the church that she attended, and anything remaining that reminded Dad of Mom, he got rid of, too. Or at least that's how it seemed. There was nothing there that Bobby would have been after, save for photos or mementos, I tried to soothe her.

"I only have two or three photos of your father, and those are all that I have! And he said he wanted your dad's guns!" She cried, overdramatically, over the phone. I took a deep breath. "I bet those are really nice photos, and you should definitely hang on to those. I'm sure that the photos Bobby wants are from our childhood. Not the last year and a half. I'll talk to him about anything else."

She didn't seem interested in reality, or that's my best guess, because even though I presented rational thought to her, she continued to wail about her precious photos that Bobby absolutely was not after. I just let her have it and let it go.

The first funeral day was a smaller family "viewing," I guess, as they are called. For any bit of not remembering how I got from Lansing, Michigan, to Martinsburg, West Virginia, I recall my travels to that funeral home even less. My then-husband would have driven us, as I certainly would not have had any ability to get us there. I was a vessel carrying life, but it wasn't mine.

Having been through the whole tradition of funeral chaos just a few short years prior, I knew that I just had to ride through a few days of a whole bunch of hard truths that didn't matter whether I was ready or even wanted to hear them or not. It felt like an assault on my heart and mind that I had no choice but to suffer through and bear without objection or say-so.

I hate everything about funeral homes. The hushed voices, soft spoken and lowered out of respect and reverence. The place that everybody shows up to to say goodbye to someone who is dead and not there anymore, but if you tiptoe around everyone and everything, maybe you can trick yourself into believing that life doesn't exist anymore. It's a tragically forced and somber circus, and I will personally come back and haunt everyone if that's how people decide to behave at my funeral.

Dad was strict and firm, and not always lively. But when he was—those are the sounds and sights and feelings that explode up out of my chest. That is the Dad I choose to remember the most. Happy, whistling, with his side smile grin, winding up to say something clever or silly.

The person in the coffin had a stoic expression. I recognized it instantly as my father's. I mentally compared this dead Dad against dead Mom, and there was a dramatic difference. Mom didn't look at all like Mom. So much so, I wished I had never looked into the casket. But Dad looked like sleeping Dad. I offered that to anyone within earshot, as

I'd heard said at Mom's funeral, "They did a good job with him!"

What the fuck does that even mean.

He wasn't in some car wreck or holed up in an ICU for weeks. He died almost instantly, and so he looks just like he did when he was healthy and alive, only days ago.

In hindsight, I recognize that moment for what it was: it was my rational brain very much trying to take over from feeling anything on that day. At the time, I felt a powerful sense of responsibility, or duty even, to compartmentalize my feelings, which felt like I was in control. But looking back on myself, especially in those early days, I resembled less someone holding some graceful intention of control over themselves and more like an empty-headed zombie. And I guess, in reality, I was a mix of both.

"Oh, they forgot his cigarettes!" cried Dad's widow, breaking the serenity of my mental escape.

"You gotta go get his cigarettes, he'd want those!" In case I misheard her the first time, I got to hear her clarify, to her young son, I think he was around eleven at the time, who unflinchingly ran off (assumingly) for said cigarettes.

I was stunned. And I stood silent, staring at Dad's dead face, willing myself to remember him this way so that my soul would find peace that he was gone. But I couldn't help recalling my own past with my dad, who lay dead in this coffin, without his cigarettes.

• • •

He'd promised me that he had quit. After some particularly awful coughing episode he'd had back in Ohio about ten years prior, I was legitimately worried about his health. And it made me feel sad. And it made me feel mad. Because I knew that smoking was a choice. And I was twelve or thirteen years old. And so, in only the way a twelve- or thirteen-year-old girl could: I laid the guilt on him thick.

"Don't you want to live to see me grow up? To see me get married? Don't you want to know your *grandkids*?"

And I must have worn him down. Or maybe he connected my experience to his own; his father had died when he was only fifteen. I don't know what got through to him, but it seemed that something had. Through tear-filled eyes, he gave me his soft pack of Basic cigarettes, which held just one or two. And he said he was done smoking. He promised that he was.

Later that summer, we were back in Illinois visiting friends and family, and I stumbled upon a pack of Marlboro Reds. "WHAT IS THIS?? YOU SAID YOU QUIT SMOKING!!" I said through tears. To the outside world, I might have appeared to be playing dramatic, but I can connect to every molecule of those tears, and they were real. I felt betrayed. And sad. And mad.

We'd been staying at my Uncle Ron's house there in Belvidere, Illinois, and I ran away. Not literally, I just walked away. But I had no plans of ever going back. I built up a fantastic defense: if he couldn't stop smoking to save his life, I'd save myself the trouble and stop being his daughter because he was just going to die anyway.

• • •

"You're just going to die anyway." My own words echoed inside my head as I looked down at my poor, dead dad.

Right on cue, the pack of cigarettes appeared, and there was his widow stuffing them gently and lovingly into his shirt pocket.

Marlboro Reds.

My next breath left my body in a laugh at the absurdity. I don't think anyone heard it, and I was grateful. I was not trying to be disrespectful to anyone else's experience. And his wife and her son didn't know my story, so it was easy to dismiss their actions as innocent.

"I told him that I'd make sure he got buried with the good stuff!" She exclaimed, again breaking my mental peace with her voice. And the next breath that left my body came with another laugh, but this one I made sure was noticed, even if she and anyone else who was around me were oblivious to the reason behind it.

After some time, she walked away, but I stood there, glued to his side, staring at his face. I noticed the details of his obviously freshly cleaned glasses, which were perched on top of his nose, and I thought that was also silly because dead people have no use for glasses. But somebody had decided that he needed them on his face, so there they sat perched, the glass reflecting light which restricted my full view of his eyelashes. I decided I might be grateful for this. So, I let it be.

After some time, Frank's girlfriend was standing next to me. Everybody had something to say, and it irritated me because I just wanted to stand there in my space and in peace, and everyone else insisted on sharing their inner whatevers, and I just wanted mine with my dad because I didn't get to have that while he was alive. I didn't get to have that at the end, or in the hospital, and this was my time now.

And still, I let it be.

I watched as her hand reached past me towards his. I was horrified in a non-judgmental way; I absolutely understood then that everybody grieves differently. My "Pro" card is probably lost in the mail, but I had attended enough funerals by now—I knew to expect the unexpected. The horror I felt came from a place of putting myself in her shoes, and I could not connect to a version of myself that would even imagine grabbing the hand or any part of a dead person.

But her hand went right there and held Dad's hand, and she said, out loud, "It's cold."

Now, I am not sure what a person would expect the daughter of the dead man whose hand you are now holding to say or react and having no idea what the expectation she had for me was, I just stood there, frozen, hearing my own heart pound and thud through my ears; standing so still that my body moved subtly with each beat of my heart.

"Do you want to hold it?"

OH MY GOD! I screamed from the inside and somehow still managed to keep there.

"No, thank you." I managed to say, in the quiet, hushed, respectful voice that you are Supposed To Use When At A Funeral.

• • •

After the first day in the funeral home, I was made aware that someone had organized a spaghetti dinner benefit in honor of my father to help pay for funeral expenses at a hole-in-the-wall bar just up the road. There was no part of me that wanted to attend this event, but it would be rude not to, so I went.

I don't remember if I paid to attend or if they waived my fee. It doesn't matter. The key detail that remains of that night was that it coincided with karaoke night. At last, fate mixed the solemnity of death with the calamity of karaoke. Classic!

I didn't want to sing, but I did anyway, mostly out of regret for not having sung at Mom's funeral. My Aunt Donna had asked if I would sing 'Wind Beneath My Wings,' but I just couldn't bring myself to do it. There was no way I was going to be able to pull that off without crying. I give myself a lot of grace for what I was going through at the time, but I count myself as a coward for not doing it anyway, tears and all. And that's okay, too.

So, with all the courage I could muster at twenty-two, I sang Alicia Keys' 'If I Ain't Got You,' which had no connection to my father, but was a song I felt I could sing. The acoustics in the bar's dingy bathroom were kind to me as I practiced a few bars to make sure that I felt confident enough to squeak that one out without getting emotional. And I did.

Frank sang a few songs, as I recall. I don't remember if Bobby or Markie were there, and I don't remember anyone else singing, though I know that they did.

What I do remember is the long, sad, strange faces as they interacted with me. They wanted me to cry and be sad. And I was sad, but I did not cry. And the more they shared their personal stories about my dad with me, the easier it was not to cry. I had no idea who they were talking about. Still, I thanked them for sharing their stories, and somehow ended up being the person responsible for console *them* through their crippling grief at the loss of *my dad*.

The next day at the funeral home, people stood at the pulpit and continued to speak of my father with a familiarity I couldn't share. To them, he was a friend, a mentor, a neighbor. To me, I was distinctly feeling as though he was a distant figure who'd lived a life I'd maybe never been part of. It had only been four years since they left Michigan. I marveled at how time had changed both of us, and quietly acknowledged that if roles were reversed, he wouldn't have known me, either.

So I simply sat there, feeling like the misplaced guest at a stranger's funeral, desperately trying to piece together the man they were mourning from stories that felt like someone else's dad.

The only way I knew to cope with this strangeness was to let it be.

I clung to their stories, even as they drifted further from the person I knew, hoping to find some thread that would lead me back to him. I couldn't be sad for myself, but I could be happy for them, and feel sad for them at a safe distance.

The pastor asked if anyone else wanted to say anything, perhaps one of his children? Did any of us want to say a few words? Anything at all?

What could I possibly say that anyone else here would relate to? I thought to myself, and opted to remain in the silence of my own heart and mind, and chair.

The last stop of the funeral express was the cemetery. We all stood, and I stayed behind while my brothers and other men carried the casket out to the hearse. We followed at some distance behind. There was a part of me that wanted to be nowhere near that casket, and an even larger part of me that didn't think I *belonged* near it.

When we pulled into the cemetery, we were probably six or seven cars behind the hearse. I stayed in the car for some time while cars lined in behind us.

And then I started to hear a noise.

It was faint at first. My brain, no doubt elated by the distraction, got to work trying to make sense of what it was. It grew loud enough that it became familiar to me: it was music.

Not just any music. It was full on redneck, screaming eagle, country music now blaring from what sounded like the vehicle right behind me. I sat stunned for a moment, attempting to reconcile what I heard to the moment in time.

To my right, I could see the tent thing over the area where we were all meant to sit. And the military was there, in formation, in their dress uniforms, guns poised, ready for the funeral. The energy and life and flow and cadence, and rhythm of the music blaring was such a dramatic contradiction to this backdrop. Could I really be hearing what I was hearing? And there was no mistake: the volume was intentional!

I turned back slowly as if I both wanted to see and not see what ruckus was happening behind us. I turned slowly, bracing, but nothing could have prepared me for what happened next: a woman was hanging outside of a sunroof. She threw her hands up in the air and screamed, "YEAH! MARCUS WOULD HAVE LOOOOOOOVED THIS! WOOOOOOO!" as if she were at the sold-out show at the county fair, and not a cemetery.

The spectacle continued as the pastor, in his funeral robe, quickly skittered over to her vehicle to tell her that this was a place of reverence and respect, and could she please turn her music off. In a stunning turn of events, she *disagreed with* the pastor, screaming once more, "Marcus would have LOVED THIS!"

By then I had turned around, but I have remnant of recollection that other people urged her to turn her fucking country music off and she either obliged or someone took her keys away.

For Christ's sake.

After that bizarre interruption, the cemetery ceremony went on like any other I'd ever been to. I stood on the outside of the awning, as the outsider I felt that I was, observing a funeral and last rites of a total stranger. Things were wrapping up, and I was in the clear.

Or so I thought.

The gunshots came first—sharp cracks that shattered the silence and tore through the walls I had so carefully built. I jolted, my body reacting before my mind could catch up. Then, as the echoes faded into the hills, the bugle began to play Taps. That mournful melody drifted through the air like a weightless thing, but each note landed heavily, pulling at something buried deep inside.

Since I arrived in Martinsburg, I hadn't allowed myself to *feel*. I'd locked everything away, as if grief could be postponed or avoided altogether. But standing there, surrounded by the finality of that sound, I felt the weight I'd been holding finally break open.

The sadness hit me all at once. I was no longer just a person in attendance, going through motions I didn't know how to perform. I was his daughter. I was saying goodbye. And I wept.

As I watched the earth swallow his casket, I placed my hand over my belly, where life stirred quietly. I couldn't help but wonder what pieces of Dad would live on in this new life and whether I'd ever fully make peace with the ones he left behind.

"Dad really would have loved this," I said to my brothers afterward, before leaving the cemetery.

"Yeah," they each replied. And we all just stood there, as if we were agreeing to what Dad would have loved in our own way, and also together.

I left my grief there in the quiet of the cemetery. It wasn't denial—it was survival. The life growing inside me demanded my focus, and somehow, I knew that carrying both grief and hope would require setting one down. So, I left it with him.

• • •

My pregnancy was uneventful, save for one scare at around 30 weeks.

A doctor on my prenatal care team discovered I hadn't received my Rhogam injection on time. Because I'm A-negative, if the baby had a positive blood type, my body, a vessel meant to nurture, would see the baby's cells as a threat and try to destroy them.

When the doctor told me, my stomach dropped. The thought was unbearable: the very body meant to keep this baby alive could turn against it. I didn't know how to process that kind of fear, so I clung to anger instead. Anger at the doctor, at myself, at the universe for its cruel reminders of how fragile life could be.

I'd just watched a man I loved be swallowed by the earth. I couldn't lose this child, too.

But as quickly as the anger flared, it passed. The pregnancy went on without further issues.

At my final scheduled appointment, the doctor ordered an ultrasound to estimate the baby's size. By their calculations, the baby could be between eight and ten pounds—a thought that both amazed and terrified me.

I am not built to birth a large baby, so the plan was clear: if the baby didn't arrive by May 20, they'd induce labor.

And that's exactly what happened.

On May 21, 2003, my first child was placed into my arms. The moment they settled against my chest, I felt their warmth—solid, wiggly, and real.

Tears spilled from my eyes before I even knew I was crying. My body ached with exhaustion, but none of it mattered. There, in my arms, was everything.

My heart surged with something I hadn't felt before—so pure, so fierce, and so unconscious that it startled me. An unshakable, unconditional love that anchored me to the moment.

I thought of my own parents just then—how their love had been imperfect, and how life could feel so cruel and so beautiful all at once. I held my baby closer, feeling the weight of them against my heart, and a silent promise began to form: *I will love, protect, and fight for this child with everything I have. Whatever pieces of my parents live on in them, I will make sure they are the good ones.*

In the days, weeks, months, and years that followed, my baby would look back at me with those bright grey-blue eyes, holding all the truths of the universe and their own limitless potential. And in that gaze, I saw something I hadn't dared to believe: my own potential—waiting to be reclaimed, emerging alive again in a world where anything was possible.

Panic Attack

Navigating the months after my father's death and my first child's birth wasn't easy. But then again, ease has never been a part of my story. I compartmentalized what needed to be compartmentalized for the sake of moving forward and living life. I did that with little effort, and to any outsider, things might have looked easy.

Behind the scenes, though, I was wading through some uncharted waters: namely, my father's estate.

I don't remember why, and maybe it doesn't matter, but I was the one designated to deal with my father's widow. Maybe I was the one who took the initiative. Maybe it was because I'm the girl. Or maybe I was the only one who could communicate effectively with someone who was behaving so irrationally.

Whatever the reason turned out to be, that is how it was. I'd spend time sorting out the next steps with Dad's widow, and then call my brothers and get or relay information to or from them as needed.

Mentally and emotionally, I had this process so hyper-compartmentalized that it made me numb. I had to maintain focus on what was immediately around me: my infant child, my husband, and another baby on the way! I also worked full time and had to pay bills and care for a household. I was busy—too busy to get bogged down with anything else.

Where I connect with myself in those days, I connect with feelings of hyperfocus and developing maternal instincts.

So, it took me by complete surprise the day I was talking with Frank on the phone about something to do with the sale of the house, or that Dad's dying without a will putting us in a precarious and needlessly complicated situation that I felt was something more severe than I'd ever felt to date or since.

Frank was rightfully perturbed about something Dad's widow was trying to pull. She had sold Dad's house to this couple who were her (and Dad's) friends. She was paying this couple out of funds from Dad's estate to clean the house, replace carpeting, and other fixes throughout the house. She was double-dipping. Or allowing this couple to do so.

It was around the time that we were coming to this realization when Frank shared with me that he suspected that Dad's widow had something to do with his death. I wasn't sure if he was being rational or emotional when he told me, "You know she would feed him whatever pills she had on hand for any old thing."

He continued, "Oh, you got a headache? Take this! Toothache? Take that! Second Tuesday after a half-moon? I've got just what the doctor ordered!" When I asked how he was so sure, he said, "She had some kinda cancer and had all these leftover painkillers, all these bottles everywhere. I know she indulged in the devil's lettuce, which bothered Dad. I never saw him do it, but it speaks to the questionable character of this woman."

I heard the words he said, but they stayed on the top of my head, not settling in. I had called Frank that day to relay something that he either needed to know or do, and I didn't have the capacity to let anything else in or deter or delay me. We wrapped up the call, I hung up, and I stood there in my kitchen when the information he shared started to seep into my skull, into the ridges of my brain where they most certainly seized it up, constricting it so tightly that I could start to feel it in my chest.

I thought I was having a heart attack.

Instinctively, I placed my one hand over my heart while my other hand gracefully braced me against the kitchen cabinets, and guided me down to the floor, where I lay, eyes wide open, staring at the ceiling.

"Is this how he felt?" I thought to myself, unable to speak or do anything else besides savor whatever time I had remaining to think about my life, which was flashing before my eyes. I closed them tightly as tears spilled out of them and down my cheeks.

I don't know how long I lay there like that before the tightness started to subside, and I felt like I could breathe again, and I could think again, and I realized that I was going to be okay. But I also had no idea what had just happened to me.

Since I was pregnant, I went to the doctor the very next day, where I learned that I had had a panic attack. And that I was no longer pregnant. I had a great doctor at the time, and I remember the concern on his face and that he wanted to help me. It was so palpable that it could have been another person in the room. He was suggesting that I seek some help from a therapist and was particularly concerned that I didn't seem to be concerned after learning about the pending miscarriage.

"This sort of stuff happens all the time," I told him, like he hadn't attended six million years of medical school, and he was hearing it for the first time. "The only reason I even knew I was pregnant was because I took an early pregnancy test, and viability isn't really established until you've hit 12 weeks; and I was only around 7 or 8 weeks," I continued, sharing facts and logic, wearing both like a thick armor. "If I hadn't taken that pregnancy test, I wouldn't have even known about it, and I'd assume my next period was like any other period!" I concluded, like snapping the cage of my iron helmet shut, sealing me off from the outside world.

"This is heavy stuff you're going through. There are people who can help," he suggested, so helpfully and gently. I heard the words he said as he spoke them, but they stayed outside of my armor. I thanked him for the Prozac and the doctor's note excusing me from work for a week, and I went on my way.

In retrospect, this chapter of my life feels so distant, I almost don't recognize the person living it. The way I compartmentalized everything—stoically, matter-of-factly, as if life was something that happened to me rather than something that I actively participated in—is so completely unrelatable to the person I've become.

What shocks me most is the lack of compassion and empathy I had for myself. Only I can truly understand the depths of that time, yet even now, I find it shocking.

Putting that armor on, compartmentalizing, I hadn't put any thought into doing that. It wasn't intentional. It wasn't about appearing strong or even being strong, though I understand why I routinely received that feedback. It was survival—plain and simple. I just did it, as if I had no other choice. Because I didn't.

Dad's estate finally closed sometime later that year. Since he died without a will, his widow received half of everything that Dad and Mom spent their lives building, the other half was divided evenly among my three brothers and me.

Dad's widow wanted to sell off items of value and split the proceeds, but none of us really wanted 'dead dad money,' as Frank had coined it, and certainly not more than we didn't want his widow to get half of it. So, I worked with a lawyer to petition the court as the desire of our father's only living heirs to donate all remaining physical property to various charities in the Martinsburg area, and I never heard from that woman my dad married ever again.

Live, Laugh, Love

It was Easter Sunday, 2005. As was tradition, we spent the morning at church and then the afternoon Easter-egg-hunting and feasting. Everyone was wearing their Sunday best. I had sewn matching Easter outfits for my oldest and myself because I stubbornly refused to buy many maternity clothes; I viewed them largely as a waste of money since you only wear them for such a short time.

A few months after Dad's estate was settled, I'd learned that I was pregnant again—and so by Easter, my second child was due any day. As we packed up the car for the ride back home, I couldn't help but daydream about finally meeting them. Since this was our second child, we opted not to learn the gender ahead of their birth. This pregnancy felt different from the first, and something inside me told me that they were a girl.

Everybody had their guesses. All we cared about was that they were healthy, happy, and perfect.

I also cared about not being pregnant anymore. I had gained much more weight with this pregnancy than with the first and spent my waking hours feeling supremely uncomfortable. By the time we got home, my anticipation had turned to impatience. I was so uncomfortable, I couldn't bear the thought of another day at work with well-meaning people asking, "When are you gonna have that baby?" So, at around 3 p.m., I decided to try a folk tale I'd read about:

Castor oil.

Two tablespoons of it later, I hoped for the best. It turned out that "the best" was spending a few hours that evening in the bathroom. I went to bed very disappointed and very much not in labor.

I fell asleep that night, dreading the thought of having to go to work the next morning.

At 6:00 a.m., I wrote in my journal:

"Is this labor? I don't know... I've been having contractions since 1 a.m. that have been three to five minutes apart. The timing doesn't seem to have changed much, but they have gotten stronger. Everyone else is still sleeping... I didn't want to wake them because I wasn't sure if this was labor or not... but after 5 hours, I am really hoping that it is. At least one of us can get some sleep."

By 9:30 a.m., we were at the hospital. The doctor broke my bag of waters at noon, and things really escalated from there. I remember feeling a bit like a wild animal—primal. I paced the room, noticing myself behaving like the wild cats I'd seen in cages at the zoo. A wild look in their eyes, a vacant expression on their face, pacing as if they know they are both in an unnatural environment and trapped there.

Something inside me knew I needed to move, to break free from the confines of that small, sterile hospital room. "I want to take a shower," I announced, the words spilling out before I'd even thought them through. Maybe the water would distract me from the pain that was quickly taking over my body in waves. Maybe it would give me a moment to feel like myself again.

While in the shower, I started to feel the distinct urge to start pushing. A nurse came in and checked me and said I needed to get back to the bed—"NOW!"

I remember that I waltzed out of the shower into the room and towards the bed, with absolutely no bothers given that I was totally naked. It was I who did that—I have this awareness—but it was like watching someone else do it. Everything about that action violated distinctly "me" things: being in pain in the first place is something I would do privately. By this time in the day, there were nurses, a doctor, my husband at the time, his mother, his sister, and probably ten others. I would never have exposed myself to that many people while also being in pain.

And I certainly wouldn't have waltzed out into a room of all those people completely naked, still dripping wet from the shower!

Everything about that experience was primal. I was not in control, didn't try to be, but I was at the same time very aware of how not in control I was.

I also noticed, as I was there on the bed, pushing, that I was screaming extremely loudly and shouting vulgarities into the faces of the doctor, the nurses, and my family. Then, back as me, I quickly apologized for it in between pushes, "I'm so sorry for screaming!" More pushing, more screaming, more swearing. "I'm so sorry I'm swearing!" And they just as quickly and graciously forgave me for it, "You're having a baby—you're allowed to be a little noisy about it!"

And then, at 1:46 p.m.—eight pounds, two ounces of pure perfection, with a head full of beautiful red hair that glowed like a sunset. As they placed my daughter on my chest, her warmth, her weight, her undeniable presence washed over me. She was solid, real, and mine.

In that moment, the world seemed to pause. Everything I had endured, every challenge life had thrown at me, every fear and uncertainty—it all fell away. Holding her in my arms, I didn't just feel like I'd won something; I felt like I had been given the greatest gift life could offer. My world wasn't just whole, it was more than I'd dreamed it ever could be.

Life, as I knew it, would never be the same, and for the first time, it held a promise of something extraordinary. In her eyes, I saw the beginnings of a new chapter—one filled with love, with purpose, and with the kind of hope that only a new life can bring. She wasn't just a part of me; she reflected everything I was and everything I aspired to be. And I just knew that she'd exceed even my wildest dreams.

Forgiveness, Part One

I was sitting alone in a pew at Trinity Church, a massive non-denominational mega-church in Lansing, Michigan, on a Sunday in 2006. Built just a few years earlier in 2000, Trinity's sleek and modern building accommodated thousands of attendees each week. The first time I attended, I recall thinking it felt more like a "cattle farm" than a church due to the sheer size of its congregation. However, by my second or third visit, I had grown to appreciate this very aspect. There was comfort in the anonymity it provided—I wasn't interested in being tracked, noticed, or having my attendance feel even remotely performative, as it often had during my childhood.

In those days, I was a regular attender, dutifully dropping my children off at their classes before heading to the main sanctuary for my own.

To get to that moment there in the pew, with two small children, then three and one, was no easy feat. My kids were consistently easy-going, so any resistance wasn't coming from them, but rather my own restless need to make sure that everybody had precisely what they needed in order to properly leave the house for a few hours.

With an infant and a toddler, you need the diaper bag, the extra change of clothes, the extra-extra change of clothes, a snack, a bottle, something to keep the toddler occupied with, and a backup in case that lost its novelty, favorite blanky, favorite stuffed toys. Did I grab the extra pacifier and the extra-extra pacifier? Did everybody eat? Is everybody clean and happy?

And then I catch a quick glimpse of myself in a nearby mirror to realize I hadn't even begun to get myself ready yet, and *of course,* we needed to leave the house in less than five minutes.

This silly ritual only seems silly in hindsight. Because I assure you, back then it meant everything in the world to me to be "on time," even though "on time" was something entirely self-imposed. Nobody, not one single soul, would have noticed if I had just stayed home in my pajamas. But there I was, in a swirl of diapers and overloaded with extra things I rarely needed, hell-bent on making it to church "on time."

I checked my small children into their classrooms, and as I walked away down the hallway, I exhaled, feeling the weight of the world lift off my shoulders. Finally, I made my way to the pew where you met me when this chapter began.

In those days, I genuinely looked forward to church. We had a really engaging pastor who could deliver a message without seeming too "preachy." Each Sunday felt like receiving heartfelt advice from a trusted friend. The enormity of the church meant I could attend or not attend without guilt or shame. I was there because I genuinely wanted to be.

That particular Sunday service began like all the others, with the pastor warmly greeting his congregation and offering a quick prayer for those who may have attended in need. I let my eyes wander atop the heads of my fellow congregation, trying to imagine who there needed some healing. Who there was hurting? Who just needed a friend? I willed my heart to extend the grace that I felt and carried with me on every day of the week, and I prayed that God would allow those people to feel it, too.

The music portion of the service began, and it was always my favorite part of the entire production, and why it was so important to me to be on time. I sang the lyrics of the songs from the depths of my soul. Love, healing, patience, kindness. I was there for it all!

After the music portion, the pastor announced that there was a special guest who was going to share their testimony. I always found personal testimonies to be compelling, and this felt like a gift I hadn't expected to receive. I was grateful before they even began to speak that they would allow themselves to be so vulnerable and courageously share their story.

I don't remember the specifics of his story, only the echoes of pain and heartbreak. A trusted family friend had abused him. The details were his, but the tears he shed felt universal —the same tears I had shed, the same ones others in the congregation now shed silently around me.

Then, his tone shifted. He stood taller, his shoulders squared, his head high. He was no longer the crumpled boy sharing his wounds. He was a man, unwavering, resolute.

"I forgive him," he said.

My breath caught.

"You did what?" I thought, my mind racing. My mouth hung open as I stared at him, willing him to explain, and at the same time, not sure that I wanted to hear it. Surely, I had missed something.

"I forgave him," he repeated, his voice steady, the conviction unmistakable.

It was as if my soul left my body for a moment. I sat there, stunned, unable to process what I was hearing. Forgiveness? For *that*?

The pastor joined him onstage, and together they prayed for forgiveness to find its way into the hearts of the congregation. My soul returned to my body just in time to feel the rigid tension melt away. My eyes softened. My breath steadied. This felt right—for them, for these people, for the world outside these walls.

But not for me.

I looked across the bowed heads of the congregation, praying for their healing and peace. "Forgiveness for you," I whispered in my heart. "Forgiveness for you."

But then, from somewhere deep inside:

"Never forgiveness for that."

My prayer stumbled, caught between my heart and my mind. The words rose again, louder this time:

"Never forgiveness for that."

That Sunday, I left church feeling as though I had witnessed something extraordinary and impossible. The young man's story stayed with me, not for its details but for its conclusion. Forgiveness. It had entered my world as a possibility, a concept I could not yet grasp but could not dismiss.

The seed had been planted. But for me, it would still take years to sprout.

This Is Different

It started with neck pain.

A dull, persistent ache that settled into the right side of my neck and refused to leave. It wasn't the kind of pain I could pinpoint to a pulled muscle or a bad night's sleep, but when I walked into an Urgent Care in late fall of 2006, that's exactly what the doctor suggested.

"Probably just slept wrong," he said cheerfully, handing me a sample packet of muscle relaxers before sending me home.

A week later, the pain hadn't just persisted—it had amplified. A sharp, radiating sensation now plagued both sides of my neck and crept into my head, pulsing like an alarm my body was sounding that no one else could hear. Then, a new symptom hit: a headache so sudden and searing it felt like lightning striking the crown of my skull.

I went to the Fast Track that was attached to the hospital where I worked before starting work that morning. This time, the doctor confidently diagnosed a musculoskeletal imbalance, gave me a cortisone shot, and sent me on my way, suggesting that I follow up with my primary doctor if things didn't settle down and consider physical therapy.

This felt so different from any pain I'd had before. But the two doctors I had seen both responded to my symptoms with such certainty that I felt embarrassed to push back. I walked away holding the contradiction of what I'd been told and what I felt, and went to work as usual.

I'd only been at work an hour or two. The pain became unbearable, eclipsing every other sensation. I could barely think, let alone advocate for myself. Desperate, I walked down to the Emergency Room.

I waited three hours before a doctor saw me. X-rays and CT scans showed nothing conclusive, and they were preparing to send me home again. I felt the sting of embarrassment grow with each tick of the clock that I was there. I was sorry for wasting everyone's time, including my own.

Then, Dr. Burton, the neurologist, walked in.

"Tell me what's going on," he said.

Something about his presence cut through the haze of everything that was going on within me. He wasn't rushing. He wasn't dismissive. He was listening.

"I've had muscle pain before. I've had headaches. This is *different*," I told him.

That sentence—one I barely remember saying—changed everything.

Dr. Burton ordered further imaging. A few hours later, a nurse came in to tell me that I was being admitted, and the Internal Medicine team would come around to speak to me once I was settled into my new room. She also let me know that she was going to administer pain medication to make me comfortable. Finally, she asked if there was someone she could call to be with me.

I took deep breaths over the course of the next hour. I texted my then-husband everything that I knew, which, of course, was close to nothing.

They wheeled me to a shared room and pulled the curtain closed as they parked my bed. "Good luck!" the transport technician genuinely offered as he stepped out.

I'm not sure how much time passed between my active suppression of thought and deep breathing and when the flood of white coats entered the room. Dr. Burton's face emerged from the sea of white coats.

The MRI and CTA confirmed what no one had expected: both of my vertebral arteries—the ones that carry blood to the brain and spinal cord—had torn along their inner walls.

Those words used together meant close to nothing to me, but the roomful of doctors staring intently at me like an unsolved mystery made it clear—this was serious.

"The good news," Dr. Burton said, with a calm that felt at odds with the gravity of the moment, "is that we've identified the cause of your neck pain. The bad news is that no one in this hospital—and most hospitals around the world—has seen this before."

He explained: It's rare enough for one artery to tear, let alone both. This kind of injury was typically seen in severe trauma cases—car accidents, violent falls, the kind where the head is forcefully separated from the body.

But I hadn't been in a car accident. I hadn't fallen. I was a long-distance runner, not a stunt double. And yet, here I was with a diagnosis:

Spontaneous Bilateral Vertebral Artery Dissection.

By the time they found it, one artery was completely closed off, and the other was more than halfway blocked. That should have been catastrophic. But my body, against all odds, had rerouted blood through tiny collateral vessels, a backup system that had kept me from having a stroke. And kept me alive.

Dr. Burton was fascinated. "We don't know if you were born with those vessels or if your body created them in response," he said, a note of awe in his voice.

I wasn't focused on the mystery. I was focused on the fact that I was still here.

Over those two weeks, I had encountered well-meaning doctors who dismissed my pain. Their assumptions about my condition—and my inability, at first, to articulate just how different this felt—could have cost me everything.

"This is different," I had said.

And that difference saved my life.

I was hospitalized for a few weeks and on strict bed rest for months while the dissections healed. The only evidence remaining of the event is the network of extra vessels my body built to save me.

Looking back, I see how close I came to slipping through the cracks. It's not lost on me that I was lucky. I had access to healthcare, to advanced imaging, to a doctor who paused long enough to listen. Not everyone gets that.

This experience also taught me something about myself. I didn't walk into those appointments armed with a perfect script or unshakable confidence. I walked in as a person in pain, fumbling through a system that isn't always built to see us as individuals.

And yet, in the end, I did enough. I persisted. I trusted my instincts. I gave my body the chance to fight for me.

I carry this story as a reminder: the human body is remarkable. The human mind is powerful. And together, they are capable of more than we often give them credit for.

18: Finding Myself

BY 2008, I HAD no idea that I was writing a letter to my future self. I was navigating the complexities of family life, raising my children, and grappling with the fear of isolation—something I wouldn't fully face until later in life. But even then, a part of me sensed that solitude held something profound, even if it terrified me.

This journal entry, written in April 2008, feels eerie now, like a whisper from the past foreshadowing what was to come:

> *I am afraid of being alone. Not in a home-alone sense, but in a sense of being all alone with no family or friends. Being alone mentally would also fall under this umbrella of fear for me: I don't want to develop Alzheimer's and not remember anyone or anything in my life. I've heard people joke that people like that don't even realize what they're missing. That terrifies me!*

> *It sounds cheesy and cliché, but I love everything I've experienced in life—even the bad stuff—and I love and appreciate everyone in my life, especially my family. To be without any of it/them would render me a useless shell of a being, and the very thought of it frightens the hell out of me.*

> *Consequently, I put a very high value on what I think others (specifically my family) think of me. My feelings get hurt quickly, and I tend to react strongly when it comes to what someone says to me or about me, or even my perception of what they said. I'll probably need some heavy-duty psychological intervention the first time*

either of my kids tells me they hate me or threatens to move out, or even if I just sense that they are thinking it (I know this is going to happen! I was a teenager once!).

How could I love or embrace this fear... just thinking about it makes me hyperventilate a little bit, but I suppose if I were all alone, I would have time to figure out just who I really am. The people in my life influence me so much, I'd be forced to be just plain old me. Maybe I would achieve self-actualization! It just wouldn't be worth it at all to me.

When I read those words now, I see someone who was clinging to the safety of connection while sensing that her fear of being alone was tied to something deeper. Back then, I couldn't imagine embracing solitude—it felt like losing everyone that I loved. Or worse: losing everyone who loved me. But now, I realize that it was during my loneliest moments that I began to find myself.

Solitude didn't strip me of my identity; it revealed it.

Without the noise of other people's real or perceived expectations or judgments, I was forced to listen to my own voice, to confront the parts of myself I hid or ignored. It wasn't easy, and it wasn't immediate, but it was transformative. That fear of being alone, which once felt like the ultimate loss, became the doorway to something I'd never expected: the discovery of who I *really* am.

The Voice Inside

In the spring of 2011, a reckoning arrived that I didn't know I was ready for. Life had taken me through one twist after another, each one peeling back layers of myself I hadn't fully faced. I was going through a divorce, a separation not only from my husband but also from the life and family that I had desperately wanted. In the midst of the legal process, I found myself seeking clarity and started working with a therapist.

In therapy, I began to speak about the memories, the truths I had buried for so long. Each session was like prying open a door I had nailed shut, each memory a ghost slipping back in, reminding me that healing isn't linear and that it isn't gentle.

I began unearthing things I had never spoken aloud—some I hadn't even admitted to myself. We worked through moments from my childhood that I'd kept hidden behind walls, holding them up to the light, feeling the weight of them fully. The therapeutic process felt like standing in the middle of a storm, letting it strip away everything I thought I understood about myself until I was left with nothing but raw truth.

My therapist suggested I write a letter to my inner child. At first, the idea felt strange, even daunting. But as I began writing, the words poured out of me. It was as if I had finally unlocked a door I didn't even know existed, let alone had been locked. That letter, written on April 5, 2011, became one of the first steps toward reclaiming my sense of self and showing love to the parts of me I had hidden away for so long:

> Little Tiny Tina,
>
> I am so sorry you are so filled with pain. I know you feel alone, hurt, abandoned, abused. I am so sorry that I have kept you locked away for so long. I thought that keeping you locked away from the world would keep you safe, and I had no idea that it would only leave you feeling isolated and afraid.
>
> I want you to know something: you are worthy of love. You *deserve* to feel loved. And I know that you don't even really understand what that means right now, but I want to show you. When you're ready, I want you to feel free. And I want you to feel how loved you really are.
>
> Sweetie, you did nothing wrong. You did nothing to deserve the way you have been mistreated. It's sad, but there are terrible, evil people in this world. I don't think you really know that. I know that your trust has been

betrayed at a time when you have needed people the most. That the two people whom you should have been able to trust left you feeling abandoned and unloved. But I'm here today to tell you that YOU ARE LOVED. I love you so much. And today I am opening the door. You don't have to stay locked away anymore. When you are ready to come out, I am here to listen, and I will protect you. Do you understand that? No one will ever hurt you again because **I will protect you**.

Right now, I know I don't know the extent of your pain, what you've endured. But I want to understand. When you're ready, please tell me. I will listen and we will heal together. You are free, honey. You are locked away no more. Just take my hand and you will be happy again. You will be a child again. You won't cry yourself to sleep anymore. You will feel secure. *When you're ready*. I know you're scared, but you don't have to be anymore. No one will hurt you like that ever again.

After writing the letter, something shifted within me. For the first time, I felt like I was truly listening to that little girl's voice—and hearing her for what she was saying. Days later, I found myself writing a poem. It wasn't planned or forced; it simply poured out of me, a conversation between the woman I was and the child I had been.

> **once upon a time**
> and somewhere out there
> is a little girl whose little head
> hangs low in deep despair
>
> she'd read somewhere in fairy tales
> that one day he would come
> and she's clinging to the notion that
> he'd bring her safely Home
>
> so she sits at a lovely table
> she waits with innocent eyes
> with a beautiful smile and a happy heart,
> she's so alive inside
>
> the first time she was seven
> he was al the "candy man"
> he left confusing stains on her

that pierced right through her skin

oh, she didn't understand,
but somehow felt betrayed
she kept the secret to herself
where no one else could see
he told her it was all her fault
and that no one would believe
her parents moved her far away
still broken and hurt but then,
she was so relieved she'd never see
the "candy man" again

so she sits at an ugly table
she waits with timid eyes
with a crooked smile and a wounded heart
she knows she's dying inside

then when she was eleven
this awful cycle repeated
a family friend had just moved into town
a move that would leave the girl's soul depleted
his name was Rick this twisted man
he told her she was his girlfriend
he'd make her watch pornography
so he could stain her again and again

every Sunday her family would go
and the girl would beg to stay home
but she couldn't say why
and her mother would make her
and she was tortured each time they were alone
she couldn't tell a single soul
this girl so small and thin
he told her no one would understand
and that it was she who "came on to him"

so she sits at a lonely table
she waits with tear-filled eyes
with a painted smile and an empty heart
she knows she's dead inside

and that little girl's still waiting
now sobbing, "Please Love Me"
and the only one to help her;
to really save that girl, is Me

• • •

I had carried that pain like an unspoken truth, tucked away where it wouldn't interfere with the life I was building. Facing it, naming it, and acknowledging that little girl's voice was painful—and it was liberating. I realized that healing doesn't erase the scars; it lets you take ownership of them as a testament to your strength. She had survived, and now, *so had I.*

Reading those words, I felt as though I were seeing myself, my younger self, for the first time. I could finally see the wounds she carried, the years she spent waiting, hoping that someone would come along and rescue her. And as much as it hurt, I realized that the only person who could save her was me. I was the only one who could finally give her the love and validation she had longed for all those years.

In that moment, I saw my pain through her eyes—the betrayal, the loneliness, the desperation for love. But I also saw her resilience, her strength, her ability to endure when it felt like the world was collapsing around her. And I made a silent promise: I would no longer abandon her. I would carry her with me, love her as fiercely as I could, and give her the safe home she had always dreamed of.

This chapter of my life marked the beginning of a long and imperfect journey. I was learning to hold space for both the girl I had been and the woman I was becoming, to let them coexist in a way that honored their stories without being consumed by them. The little girl who once waited at a lonely table now has a seat at mine, where she is safe, loved, and finally home.

Forgiveness, Part Two

Something shifts when you begin to examine yourself with real intentionality. You start to notice things—patterns, truths, blind spots—that had been invisible until the moment they come sharply into focus. Sometimes, it's gradual, like the sun rising over a horizon you didn't know was there. Other times, it's like a flower in full bloom, suddenly demanding your attention from a seed you planted long ago.

In 2009, I was going through a divorce, and for the first time in my adult life, I felt like I was standing completely still. My world was collapsing, and there was nowhere to go, nothing to distract me from the discomfort of it all. I felt like a miserable failure: a terrible wife, an inadequate mother, and even a disappointing daughter-in-law. The voices of doubt and judgment felt deafening.

But then a question, small and unassuming, began to form at the back of my mind: *Does feeling like a failure make me one?*

Certainly, I owned my share of responsibility in the breakdown of my marriage. I had clung too tightly to overly romanticized ideals of what it meant to be married and to have a family. I had made mistakes, overlooked signs, and failed to meet expectations—both my own and others'. But did those failures define me, Tina, the person? Or were they simply moments in my life, chapters in a story that was still unfolding?

The revelation wasn't immediate, but it planted a seed. If I had gotten myself into this place, couldn't I also find a way out?

Therapy became an immensely valuable tool during this time. It was a space where I could hold up a mirror and see myself fully, flaws and all, without judgment. It was also where I began to understand the weight I'd been carrying—not just from my marriage, but from my entire life. I had been shackled to pain and resentment for so long that I didn't know what it felt like to walk freely.

For years, I believed I had forgiven people from my past. I had told myself and others that I had. But what I realized in those therapy sessions was that my forgiveness was incomplete. I had "forgiven" people for *their* sake, as if granting them absolution freed me from any further responsibility.

It was like saying, *"You are free. You may go! However, I will remain here, shackled in the chains of this thick and heavy pain, which will cut into me until I die or for all of eternity, whichever comes later."*

What I hadn't realized, until therapy forced me to confront it, was that the heaviest of those chains were the ones I'd placed on myself.

Growing up, I quietly accepted a simple equation: chaos in the home meant that I—or one of my brothers—must have done something wrong. If there was yelling, it was because of something we did or said. If there was tension, it was because of us. This belief didn't stop with trivial things like spitballs on the bathroom ceiling. It seeped into the darkest corners of my life.

Somewhere along the way, I internalized the idea that if something terrible happened to me, I must have caused it. I must have asked for it—somehow, in some way, simply by existing.

That belief made it easy to forgive others. How could I hold a grudge against them when I believed, deep down, that their actions were my fault?

But myself?

I couldn't forgive myself. I didn't realize I was holding a grudge against myself, and even if I had noticed, back then I wasn't yet old enough to understand that I was too young to take any responsibility for my actions. Or more specifically, my *inactions*. As I grew older, I developed a cycle of self-admonishment: I never stopped it.

One day, while driving home from church, I came across a person standing on the side of the road with a cardboard sign. I had a $20 bill in my coat pocket and felt an undeniable urge to give it to them. Without much thought, I rolled down my window, handed them the money, and continued on my way.

I didn't say anything about it to my children, who were six and four at the time, but a few days later, my oldest brought it up. They had overheard someone say that people who beg for money are crooks who use it to buy drugs or alcohol.

My heart broke a little at hearing such cynicism in their innocent voice, but I also understood the sentiment. It was something I had thought myself at times.

"You may be right," I said, shrugging. "They might use that money to do bad things. But they might also use it to buy food or a warm place to sleep. Giving is about the heart of the giver, not the receiver."

That night, as part of my bedtime ritual, I wrote down the exchange in my journal. When I reread my words, they stared back at me like a revelation:

> *For*giving is about the heart of the *for*giver, not the receiver.

That moment opened a door I didn't know was there. If forgiveness wasn't about the other person—if it truly was about the heart of the giver—then maybe I could stop carrying the weight of others' actions. Maybe I could even forgive the person who had been hardest on me all along: myself.

It wasn't immediate. It took time and effort and countless small moments of grace. But the first crack in the armor was realizing that I didn't need to forgive myself for something I hadn't done. I was too young, too innocent, too powerless to have prevented the things that happened to me.

Forgiveness didn't mean condoning what had happened or pretending it didn't matter. It meant freeing myself from the impossible standard I had set for myself as a child—a standard no child should ever be held to.

Forgiveness doesn't mean condoning bad behavior or becoming a doormat. It doesn't require reconciliation or even an apology. It's not about the person who hurt you—it's about you.

Forgiveness is the act of freeing yourself from the chains of resentment and pain. It's choosing to set down the weight that has been digging into your shoulders, not because the person who hurt you deserves it, but because *you do*.

That moment with my child marked a turning point. I began to see forgiveness not as a weakness, but as an act of profound strength and self-love. It became one of my favorite personal philosophies:

All giving, especially forgiving, is about the heart of the giver, not the receiver.

You Can Do It All, But Should You?

It was a steaming hot August Saturday in Michigan. One of those days when the humidity is so thick that you can drink the air.

I had planned to take my elderly dog and two cats to the vet and had enlisted the help of my two children to assist, then seven and five years old.

My pup had a long history of getting nervous all over the floor at the vet, so we gave her extra time in the dog run before going inside to get everyone signed in and wait for our turn.

We were sitting there, patiently waiting, and things were going smoothly when one of the cats started howling nonstop in her carrier. Eventually, this cacophony starts to blend in with the dull roar of the busy vet's office.

I started to get smug. I was actually going to pull this off!

And then I smelled a change in the air.

My oldest had stood up to comfort the cat and was standing in front of the chair to the right of me.

"Don't move!" I cautioned, knowing something had occurred which would end in an even worse situation were it to be stepped in.

My oldest took a giant step backward...

...right into the source of the smell.

My youngest points to the source and starts laughing at her sibling's plight.

The dog is trying to get away in shame, the sound of the cat howling seems to get louder, and my oldest is now howling and harmonizing with the cat in complete disgust at his predicament.

"Okay... okay. That was unexpected. But you've got this," I told myself in a rapid-fire pep talk.

I snapped into action:

"Take off your shoe. Go outside. Try to clean it off. I'll be out in a sec," I instructed calmly, evenly. Composed.

"Do. Not. Move!" I evenly directed my youngest. Her eyes locked with mine. We had an understanding.

I went to the desk to grab supplies to clean up my dog's mess. When I looked outside, my heart sank.

Guess who decided to scrape nervous dog poo off of their brand-new shoes on the sidewalk *directly outside the front door of the vet's office*?

Yeah. *This* lucky parent's kid.

I handed the leash to my youngest and repeated: "Wait right here. I will be right back. Do not move." She nodded in agreement.

I could barely open the door. My seven-year-old stood so close to the door that I could only open it a few inches.

"Get your ass in the grass," I lowly growled behind my clenched teeth, my patience evaporating, channeling my inner Dad.

Did I mention that the entire front exterior of this vet's office is glass? It's all windows! Every human, dog, cat, bird, and reptile in the waiting room had a front row seat to our show.

Back inside, the staff were cleaning up my dog's mess.

I apologized profusely. They tell me it's no problem, it happens all the time, it's no big deal. I continue to apologize anyway and thank them for their help.

I grab cleaning supplies and head back outside. By some miracle, we had an extra pair of shoes in the car.

We head back inside, and our names are called. Everybody is healthy. Back at home, we (by which I mean, *I*) clean up the shoe. Good as new.

• • •

Thankfully, we can laugh about my imperfect management of this situation now.

This continues to be one of those stories that reminds me: no matter how carefully we plan, no matter how many times we play the colloquial Murphy's law in a loop in our heads, we cannot predict all the things that can go wrong. And even if we can, it still goes wrong... just in ways we never imagined.

If we can arm ourselves with that understanding and approach each interaction, each meeting, each vet visit, each day with grace, we will be best equipped to roll with the chaos that comes.

And if we don't, and we find that we have perhaps bitten off more than we can chew, we can still offer ourselves grace. And have the courage to try planning differently next time.

19: The Weight of Time

THE REMAINDER OF THIS memoir shifts into a more intimate space. The following chapters are drawn directly from my personal journals, written in real time as I lived through the experiences you've been reading about. You'll notice specific dates appear, and this is intentional. These entries weren't written with an audience in mind; they are raw, unfiltered, and were my way of making sense of the world around me, and as I processed it, in words that I was only beginning to learn how to stitch together.

I've chosen to include them largely as they were, because they reflect the truth of my inner world more honestly than anything I can write in hindsight. These pages are less polished, more fragmented, and deeply personal. But they are also where some of the clearest truths live.

The Seduction of Stillness

Depression has always been, to me, intricately linked with time.

It's not simply a matter of feeling sadness or despair in the present—it's the pull of the past, the relentless allure of stepping out of the current and sinking into the familiar murk of what has already been. In this way, depression feels less like an emotion and more like a choice—or at least, the conscious *awareness* of a choice.

I have moments where I'm acutely aware that I could sink into a depression if I allowed myself. It's as if a door opens before me, leading to that timeless, suspended state where the rules of the present no longer apply. The present, with all its linear demands and obligations, loses its grip. In the realm of depression, time stops. Or perhaps, it loops. I know I could step through, close the door behind me, and roll around in the past as if it were mud—and not just any mud, but a luxurious, intoxicating kind. The kind that works its way up under your fingernails but doesn't repulse you. Instead, you stare at it, marveling at its texture, its shimmer, the way it seems to transform into something beautiful, like fine jewelry or diamonds. In that space, even the grime feels like treasure, as it replaces your otherwise sense of void with something, anything. There's an instinct that even the messiest emotions are better than the hollow of nothingness.

But this isn't sadness. It's depression. And there's a distinct difference. Sadness, even when deep and overwhelming, is alive. It carries motion, often tied to a specific event or loss, and it has the potential to ebb and flow. Sadness may sting, but it can also heal; it demands to be felt but leaves space for other emotions to coexist. Depression, however, is something else entirely. It is not alive. In the state behind the open door, there is a sense of satisfaction and familiarity, but once you are there, you feel nothing. That's the lie it tells to get you inside—the promise that nothingness will be easier to face than pain. But nothingness is worse than anything in the world, and you don't realize how awful it is until you're stuck in it.

When I am in there, I am a shell of a person. The things I know that I love to do—the things that make me feel alive—I stop doing. It feels as though I'm watching myself from a distance, blank-faced and joyless. I can observe my own emptiness, but only from the outside. From within, there is no noticing, no self-awareness. Just the hollow routine of existing without truly being.

There is an almost seductive quality to it, this pull of the past. It's easy to imagine staying there, savoring it, relishing the sensations. I could feel the weight of old grief like a familiar blanket, or the sharp sting of regret like an old wound reopening. The emotions might hurt, but they'd also cradle me, providing a sense of strange comfort. The past is unchangeable, static. There is nothing to fix or solve—only to feel, and in feeling, to revel. Depression thrives on this stillness, pulling you deeper into its void where even pain begins to lose its edge, replaced by a numbness that swallows everything whole.

But here's the thing: the longer I stay there, the harder it becomes to return to the present. I've learned this about myself. Time—real time—keeps moving forward, with or without me. The world doesn't stop. And the more I linger in that suspended state, the more it solidifies. The harder it is to pull myself back into the here and now, the harder it is to breathe the air of the present.

This is where the choice comes in. When the door opens, I see it for what it is.

I feel its pull, but I also recognize the risk. The present is messy and uncertain, yes, but it's also alive. It's the only place where I have agency, where I can create, where I can truly live. The past, as enticing as it may feel, is a closed loop. It invites me to sink, to be swallowed by its familiarity, but it can't offer me anything new. The dirt under my fingernails may sparkle like diamonds in that state, but diamonds can't grow. They are formed under pressure, true, but they are static. The soil of the present, on the other hand, is alive. It is messy and unpredictable, but it is fertile.

When I've chosen not to step through the door—when I've stayed in the present—it hasn't always been easy. There's a reason the pull of depression feels so strong: it's a place where it feels like the effort of living can pause. But I've learned that effort itself is life. The push and pull, the motion, the struggle—this is what it means to be conscious, to be alive.

I wonder sometimes if this is why consciousness itself feels so tied to time. To be conscious is to be aware of time's passage, to feel its movement and its weight. Depression tempts me to step outside of it, to exist in a space where time stands still. But I know now that standing still is not the same as living. To live is to move with time, even when it's hard. Even when it's messy.

And so, when the door opens, I acknowledge it. I let myself see it and feel its pull. But I don't step through. Instead, I remind myself that the present, for all its imperfections, is where life happens. It's where I can plant seeds, where I can grow. And that, I think, is worth staying for.

Living Between the Lines

Summer 2012. It began with a weird sensation in my left arm. I wasn't concerned at first—graceful has never been an adjective applied to me without sarcasm, so bumping into something and simply forgetting about it didn't seem far-fetched.

But over a few days, that weird sensation spread. It crept down my arm, into my hand, and then it started to burn. That's when I called my doctor.

After a careful exam, she declared I was perfectly healthy. "Probably just irritated some nerves," she said, with the calm certainty I wanted to believe. She suggested the symptoms would go away on their own.

Instead, the burning intensified. Both hands felt as though I were holding actual fire, the heat searing from the inside out. Benadryl did nothing. The fire evolved into something worse—a sensation like shards of glass tearing through my veins, from my forearms to my fingertips, and then down to my toes, feet, and legs.

My doctor prescribed Neurontin and Norco and started referring me to specialists. Over the next four years, I became a case study.

Neurologists, rheumatologists, immunologists, vascular specialists—none of them could find an answer. I was poked, prodded, biopsied, shocked, scanned, and studied. My pain was relentless, but according to the nation's top medical minds, I was perfectly healthy.

Even the Mayo Clinic reviewed my case and concluded there was nothing they could offer. One rheumatologist, with an unearned cheerfulness, proclaimed, "You're not dying!"

I remember replying, "I'm not living, either."

I resigned myself to a life of pain. The medications helped me function during the day, but nights were unbearable. My family would pack my hands, arms, legs, and feet in ice just so I could sleep.

My timing could not have been worse. The years I spent battling chronic pain coincided with the height of the opioid crisis. Every step in my treatment became a negotiation between my suffering and a system grappling with addiction.

At first, getting Norco was simple: my doctor would e-prescribe, and I'd pick it up at the pharmacy. But soon, e-prescriptions were banned.

The process became a bureaucratic maze:

1. Request a refill from my doctor.
2. Wait for approval, sometimes requiring an appointment.
3. Physically collect the paper prescription from the office.
4. Deliver it to the pharmacy.
5. Wait for it to be filled—or come back later.

Planning ahead wasn't just practical—it was necessary. But as restrictions tightened, I found myself justifying every refill. By 2015, I was reconciling my prescriptions in spreadsheets, proactively defending my need for medication.

I understood the rationale. By 2016, opioid overdoses had claimed more than 42,000 lives, with an estimated 40% involving prescription opioids. The crisis was real, and action was needed.

But in the shadow of that crisis, people like me, who relied on these medications to manage chronic pain, were caught in an impossible place. The system, designed to protect, didn't seem to see us at all.

The stigma worked both ways: physicians prescribing opioids were labeled lazy, and patients taking them were labeled addicts. I felt the sting of that stigma firsthand. In one ER visit, writhing in pain, I was sharply accused of being a junkie. The physician later apologized, explaining the immense pressure he and his colleagues faced. But the pain of this accusation did not subside.

I clung to Norco not because I wanted it, but because I needed it. It dulled the edges of my pain just enough for me to function—to be a mother, a worker, a person.

The exact moment my pain stopped is as mysterious as the moment it began. Around five years ago, I realized one day that I didn't need the ice packs at night. The burning, the glass-shard sensation—it was just... gone.

I don't know why I was fortunate enough to escape addiction despite years of high-dose prescriptions. I only know that, in those years, Norco enabled me to live when I couldn't imagine surviving without it.

Looking back, what stands out most isn't just the pain—it's the loneliness of it. Chronic pain isolates you. It silences you. And even when you speak, the words are often met with disbelief or dismissal.

For four years, I fought not just for answers but for acknowledgment. I learned to be my own advocate, my own voice, my own constant in a world that felt indifferent to my suffering.

The truth is, I don't fault the doctors who treated me or the system they worked within. Everyone was doing their best with what they had. But as a patient, those years taught me that no one else could understand my experience as deeply as I did. No one else could fight for me the way I could.

There's a kind of clarity that comes from that realization—a clarity I carry with me now, in hopefully forever pain-free years. It's the knowledge that, no matter what, my voice matters. My story matters. And I will never be silent again.

My Little Snow Angel

December 18, 2017

When I was pregnant with my first child [in 2002], I ran really hot. This turned out to be a good thing because that pregnancy ran through the winter. After a heavy snowfall one day, I went for a walk out back of their grandparents' property, sat down on a small hill, and just lay back in the snow.

As the snow fell on and all around me, it created a silence that made me pause and pay attention to the deep and profound feelings inside me. I lay there holding my unborn child in my arms, dreaming of who they might become. I remember just knowing they'd be someone incredible and feeling, for the first time, this deep and unconditional love for the life that grew inside of me.

Fifteen years later, as I watch the snow falling gracefully outside, I find myself reflecting on those same feelings. They are just as strong now as they were that day. And over the years, I've had the honor of watching Fitz grow into someone even more incredible than I could have imagined: brilliant, hilarious, feisty, caring, and loving. Fitz will always be my little snow angel.

Zena's Story, A Parallel of Love and Loss

February 9, 2016

When I was a teenager and even into my early twenties, I was mad at my biological mother for giving me up and not being a part of my life. Really mad. How could anybody give anybody up? I had court documents that stated things like, "Children left alone unattended for hours," and "Children found wandering a busy highway," and "Ms. Anderson now understands the seriousness of her situation and agrees to grant full custody to the children's father." But then I never saw or heard from her again. Mad doesn't even begin to describe the emotion that cut me whenever I'd felt abandoned growing up.

When I became a mother myself, I looked into the eyes of my tiny newborn baby and was both baffled and overwhelmed by the amount of love that poured out of me for this human being whom I had only known for mere moments. In the single instant that I laid eyes on my child, I would have fiercely and ardently given anything to love and protect him. And with time, it all started to make sense to me; my biological mother was only able to give me away because she loved me. She loved us enough to recognize that she wasn't the right person to care for us. So, she gave us away.

Today, Zena's owner made a similar, incredibly courageous decision to give her away. As he wiped away tears, I just knew and could feel that though his decision was hard, he did it out of love. He simply could not devote the time needed to care for an animal at this stage in his life. He recognized that, and though it obviously pained him to do so, he gave her to us.

I often wonder now, as an adult, how awful it must have been for a mother to sign those papers giving away all her rights to her children. I tried to be mindful of those emotions this evening as I sat across from a brokenhearted young man who kept reassuring himself that he was doing the right thing. How many times between August 12, 1982, until she passed away May 10, 1999, did she tell herself she was doing the right thing?

While tracking down the owner this past week, I was really looking for closure. With several unreturned phone calls and dead ends, we were pretty sure that the owner was either too busy or didn't want her, but I couldn't in good conscience keep a dog whose family might be looking for her and missing her, even if we had no evidence of that. Finding him today and talking to him this evening finally brought the closure I was looking for. She is ours to love, free and clear.

I never could have guessed, though, after drawing parallels from my own life, the depth of the closure that I would actually find.

I am noticing now that I had titled this "Zena's Story," but in a way, it is also "Tina's Story." I, along with my family, get to love this beautiful, sweet little girl who also just so happens to share the same birthday as me. And she will find that just like in my story, "the right thing" will actually turn out to be the "best thing." And the "best thing" will be a happily ever after she never could have dreamed of.

20: Conversations With Ghosts

July 29, 2019

In the seventeen years since Dad passed, every dream I've had of him has been the same.

He's always in the hospital, unable to talk to me. While I feel relief that he's still alive in those dreams, there's always an undercurrent of sadness because I know he's dying. I suppose this is my subconscious's way of processing the frustration I feel about not being able to say goodbye. His death was so sudden, and I was 550 miles away.

Last night, though, everything changed.

In my dream, Dad wasn't dying. He wasn't in a hospital. He was just... alive. And not only was he alive, but it felt normal that he was.

We talked. We talked a lot. He smiled that sideways smile I haven't seen in nearly two decades, and he chuckled when something I said had him tickled. Hearing that laugh, seeing that smile—it felt like being handed an unexpected box of treasure.

All day, I found myself replaying the details of the dream, over and over, through the starry eyes of someone in love. And you know what? I think it's okay to be in love with a moment, even if it's just a dream.

That dream connected me to twenty-one years of moments I shared with Dad during his life. It reminded me that even though I didn't get to say goodbye, those memories are still mine, and they will stay with me for the rest of my life.

The Sink

January 13, 2022

It only took three seconds.

I was out running errands, my mind juggling a never-ending to-do list, mapping out stops like a game of efficiency. The loop was constant: *Go to the gym, then update my address at GNC, and don't forget to finally take those boxes to the recycling center this time.* My body was on autopilot, my brain preoccupied with the logistics of the next few hours ahead of me.

At some point, I found myself in a public restroom, washing my hands. I approached the sink, placed my hand under the soap dispenser, and watched it obediently whirr out a puff of foam into my palm. Step one: complete. I lathered my hands together and moved on to step two, instinctively holding them under the faucet, waiting for the water to start flowing.

Nothing.

I stood there, still thinking about errands, vaguely annoyed that the faucet wasn't cooperating. *Ugh, great,* I thought. *Now I'm going to have to wave my hand around like I'm conjuring a spell. Maybe jump up and down or whisper the secret password these stupid sensors seem to require.* My brain, still caught up in its endless loop, hadn't yet registered the obvious: this wasn't an automatic faucet. It was manual.

Oh.

I blinked, chuckled at myself, and reached out with my wrist to flip the handle. As water finally gushed into the sink, the humor of the moment started to settle in. There I was, standing expectantly in front of something, waiting for it to do something it wasn't even designed to do.

And that's when it hit me: how many times in life have I done exactly this?

How many times have I stood in front of a person, a situation—even myself—waiting for something to happen, something that was never going to happen, simply because that's not how things were built to work? At home. At work. In relationships. In every one of those moments, frustration bubbled up because I was expecting someone, or something, to operate in a way they simply weren't wired to operate. And yet, I kept standing there, waving my metaphorical hand in front of the faucet, stubbornly refusing to look at what was really in front of me.

The more I thought about it, the clearer it became. The manual faucet wasn't the problem. The problem was my assumption that it should act like an automatic one. And isn't that true of so many things in life?

I've been frustrated with people for not responding the way I thought they should, with situations for not unfolding the way I'd expected, and even with myself for not being the person I thought I should be. But how often do I stop and consider whether my expectations are rooted in reality, or if I'm standing in front of the wrong kind of faucet altogether?

That little moment in the bathroom stuck with me. The simplicity of it, the absurdity, the clarity it brought. It's not about lowering expectations or giving up on what you want; it's about taking the time to actually see what's in front of you, to understand it for what it is, and to figure out how to work with it instead of against it.

All because of three seconds on a Saturday morning.

The Woman of A Certain Age

March 27, 2022

For as long as I can remember, I have appreciated the unfiltered wisdom of the proverbial Woman of a Certain Age.

I have observed and admired this Woman of a Certain Age for calling things like she saw them. Her very existence is both weightless and refreshing.

I look forward to the moment in life when it's my turn to drop the filters, where the wisdom of years and lived experiences that support the sentiments of the Woman of a Certain Age leave them simply unchallenged. For she is: A Woman of a Certain Age. There is no denying her Truths.

In the meantime, and for an undetermined number of decades, I resolve to:

be polite
be gentle
be loving
be caring
be patient
be kind
be accepting
don't be crazy
be rational
be realistic
treat others the way you want to be treated
be useful
be honest
be helpful
tell the truth
be a good listener
be a good friend
be considerate
be good
don't be cocky

don't make excuses
say nice things
say what you mean; mean what you say
be intelligent
(but not too intelligent)
behave yourself
be a lady
be respectful
don't show off
don't make people feel bad
be generous
be sweet
smile
be gracious
have manners
be a good example
be a good host
go the extra mile
be tolerant
be understanding
recognize things are greater than you
be a good human

All of the above are exhausting (though still not exhaustive) and 100% summarized by the Woman of a Certain Age:

don't be an asshole

In this statement, there is a freedom, an unshackling that I feel deep down in my bones but cannot seem to describe adequately in other words, especially if I want a place in polite society.

Is this what a midlife crisis feels like?

Loyalty to Ghosts

May 20, 2022

The day before my eldest turns nineteen, and the past suddenly feels both nearer and farther away than it ever has.

Mom died the year I turned nineteen. Since then, I've lived in constant conversation with her ghost, with both my parents' ghosts, really. I'd go to them for advice, not because I had it in words, but because I had their memories. And for almost two decades, those memories served as a blueprint for raising my two children, comparing, contrasting, and using what I knew to guide them. Anything I couldn't clearly recall, I'd recorded in journals, as if preserving every detail might allow me to unlock some wisdom to share with them.

Now, my child is about to reach the age I was when my mother died. And as I look forward to this milestone, I feel a new awareness creeping in: the ghosts have guided me for as long as they can. It's time to let them go.

I hadn't realized I'd been carrying a nineteen-year loyalty to them until now. For all the good, bad, and even ugly moments they represented, I leaned into their influence like an old, familiar cloak. Their decisions, my experiences—they were woven into the fabric of my parenting choices, sometimes grounding, sometimes confining.

The next day, I would cross into new territory. For the first time, my parenting decisions would stand alone, guided solely by me, without the shadow of my own parents' choices hanging over them. There's a bittersweet freedom in that thought.

Part of me felt a slight panic at the prospect of stepping into this new space without the blueprint I'd relied on, but I also felt a spark of excitement. It'll be interesting, I thought, to finally meet myself fully, to see who I am, as a parent and as a person, without the ghosts whispering in my ear.

Over the past few months, I'd been re-examining other areas of my life through this same lens. People, processes, assumptions—all the ideas and ties that were once solid but no longer serve me—had started to loosen. Letting go of them felt a little like stepping into fresh air after a long time indoors, a mixture of the unknown and the deeply liberating.

As for the word "orphan"—I'm at peace with it. In one sense, it accurately describes my position in the family tree, the generation that came before, now gone. But I've never actually been alone. Far from it. I have been fortunate enough to be surrounded by friends who became family and by the father of my children, a wonderful dad who has been everything they could have wished for. I am deeply grateful for each person who helped raise me and raise my children.

Family tree projects in school turned into a kind of spectacle for my kids—branches growing in unexpected directions, faces they hadn't met, and stories that were complex and unconventional. But it's their tree, and they've embraced its beauty, scars, and all. It's all that they know.

This year, I'll turn a new page. And so will they.

21: Releasing the Shadows

November 13, 2022

It hit me that I'd been pledging loyalty to ghosts in a way that was not just nostalgic, but deeply unhealthy.

Or it felt that way because I finally saw it for what it is—an old interrogation lamp hanging over me, exposing things I've kept hidden, even from myself. At the time, that loyalty might've been my survival mechanism. Keeping my parents on a pedestal was my way of honoring their legacy, their superhero status, and maintaining a kind of order in my memories.

My childhood and my life were built on the secrets that I kept out of loyalty to them—to the story I told myself about them. I'd keep the darker truths buried, protecting their memory as they couldn't explain themselves or defend their reasoning. It seemed unfair to drag out their mistakes, even wrong on some level. So, I crafted excuses, coated the memories in sugar, and maintained an image of them that was as comforting as it was false.

Because I wanted to see them that way. Because I felt I had to see them that way—to stay sane, to believe in some version of "normal." Normal was my holy grail. I wanted to be like everyone else, just vanilla, invisible, and uncomplicated. People wouldn't understand the truth. They'd recoil at the details, as they often have when I'd let the thornier pieces slip. The words and silences, the things done and left undone—it's all too much for the outside world. So, I covered it, layered it with perfumed stories and memories softened by time.

Did I hold on for twenty years, refusing to let myself feel anger, to protect this illusion? It's almost laughable now because I am so, so angry.

I replay memories with excruciating clarity. I remember every detail: the texture of my clothes, the way rooms smelled, how each moment felt. I used to play these scenes back as if they were surrounded by a halo of sunshine, coating even the hardest memories in warmth. But now, at forty-two, I don't see any sunshine in those stories. Only shadows.

They're gone, beyond judgment, beyond defense, beyond apology. There will be no reckoning, no asking for forgiveness, and yet, somehow, I am expected to forgive them. To release them. Because it's the "Right Thing To Do." The *healthy* thing to do.

The truth is, by making so much space for these excuses, I've left no room to acknowledge my own feelings, my own reality. As if my life, my pain, my healing didn't matter.

When I say, "Lori was just not fit to be a mother. She really had no business having kids," I'm not just giving her an excuse; I'm minimizing the effect her neglect had on me, the damage of insecure attachment that taught me to rely on no one. Relationships are built on a need for connection, and I've never needed anyone, not really, not in the way people usually do.

When I say, "Dad didn't know how to be a father. He grew up in an era of hands-off parenting, children seen and not heard." I gloss over the years of one-sided affection, of feeling like love was conditional, something withheld whenever I became inconvenient. I've grown up with an anxiety about taking up space, about being a burden. That has rippled through every relationship I've had since.

When I say, "Mom probably had some undiagnosed mental health condition," I minimize the chaos, the unpredictability, the walking on eggshells. The part of me that's always waiting for the other shoe to drop, testing people to see if they'll crack, if they'll reveal their "other side" like she so often did.

By doing this, by making these excuses, I've taken on responsibility for their actions and reactions. When things went wrong, I told myself it was my fault. "I pushed too far." I blamed myself for both their flaws and their failings, erasing their choices in favor of explanations that absolved them at only my expense.

And yet, in the midst of all the damage, some good came from the broken pieces:

I learned to see the best in people, even when they can't see it in themselves. I can shine a light on their potential, push them to be better, to reach for more.

I'm sensitive to moods and can sense shifts in others' emotions before they can. I've become skilled at asking the right questions, mostly, but not always, at the right time, guiding people back to calm. And I'll put in this effort with people I truly care about.

I'm a good listener, the kind who can sit with someone as they dig deep into themselves. I value transparency and prefer honesty over bullshit. I'll soften the truth for those who are earnestly working toward something, but if you're not? I'll mirror your energy right back at you.

Most of all, I've learned that forgiveness is essential to happiness. I'm committed to working through this mess, to finding a place of forgiveness that's rooted in reality, not fantasy. Because I realize now how far from reality I was.

Forgiving them won't mean excusing them. It won't mean erasing what happened. It will mean reclaiming my own story from the ghosts. Forgiveness will be my own liberation. Not a pardon. A release.

Learning to Consider Myself

November 15, 2022

It's a strange feeling, like stepping into a mirror and truly seeing myself for the first time. I'm struck by how little I've considered my own existence. How little I've allowed myself to feel. It's heartbreaking and humbling all at once, realizing that I never thought I should feel anything—anger, happiness, sadness—none of it seemed to apply to me.

I never thought I had needs. I never thought I was someone worth protecting.

Want to know what infuriates me the most? Inconsiderate people. The ones who bluster around, entirely oblivious to the way they impact others. I thought my visceral reaction to inconsiderate people was about them. But standing here now, seeing myself clearly, I realize it's all three fingers pointing right back at me.

Every time I've scowled, "You inconsiderate person!" I was unconsciously railing against my own neglect of myself. Here I am, forty-two years old, only now seeing that the one person I've truly been annoyed with for being inconsiderate... is me.

I've spent my life building my energy, my sense of self, around the needs, wants, and feelings of others. I know other people better than I know myself. Even strangers are easier for me to read. I can pick up on their behaviors, tonality, expressions, and run them through my mental model, churning out advice like an emotional help-desk. For those who are receptive, I help them become stronger, clearer versions of themselves. And for a while, they keep coming back, as if I have some secret elixir to offer, while I feel my own energy draining away, drop by drop.

Those who don't respond well call me condescending. I'm starting to understand why. I think it's because I see them so well, maybe *too* well, and that can be uncomfortable if they don't feel seen or understood in that way by anyone else, including themselves. It's like holding up a mirror they didn't ask for. And maybe, without realizing it, I've been a little too comfortable looking into their mirrors because I'm so unfamiliar with looking into my own.

But here's the thing: Nobody has it all figured out. The ones who know they don't are the ones who might actually be closer to understanding themselves. The truth is, I will never claim to have myself entirely figured out either. I can't. Every day, I'm meeting new people who reveal new dimensions, new behaviors. Every day, I'm seeing something I didn't know, which means I will never know everything. Not about the world, not about people, not about myself.

And maybe that's okay.

I'm realizing now that my boundless curiosity, my need to understand everyone around me, stems from an insecure attachment. It's rooted in the hope that someone, somewhere, will come along, read me the way I read others, see my needs, and fulfill them. But that's not how this works, is it? I'm the one who has to meet my own needs, to see myself, consider myself, as I've done for everyone else.

In doing so, I'm discovering something new. This ability I've cultivated—the capacity to read people, to understand them, to help them see themselves more clearly—it's a skill. A gift, even. It's just been misdirected for too long. I've been using it to unlock everyone around me, while keeping the door to myself bolted shut.

Now, it's time to use this gift for myself, to turn this key inward. It's time to stop looking to others for my reflection and to see myself clearly, unfiltered, for who I am. To consider myself, my needs, my wants, my feelings. To recognize that my life, my existence, matters just as much as anyone else's.

And that feels like one of the most important things I'll ever figure out.

22: Generational Breakthroughs

June 10, 2023

Achievement.

This word has been echoing in my mind for days leading up to my youngest's high school graduation.

Growing up, achievement wasn't exactly a family priority. If a bar had been set, I certainly couldn't see it. For reasons I'm still unpacking, it seemed like my family just didn't put much stock in the concept.

When I got a "D" in school, Mom would say it meant I "didn't give a Damn," and honestly, she wasn't wrong. I Didn't. And since she Didn't seem to either, I Didn't push myself to change it.

I did just enough to stay on the volleyball team and avoid being held back. I spent my time where I wanted: with friends, tinkering on my computer, reading things that interested me, and writing. Things that mattered to me, even if they didn't add up to what others might call "achievement."

By the time my own high school graduation had rolled around, my parents were already living 532 miles away. I had to ask—and eventually convince—them to make the long drive back to Michigan for the ceremony. Money was tight, and let's face it, graduation wasn't exactly at the top of anyone's list. But they came.

Sitting in the Breslin Center at Michigan State University, watching my youngest accept her diploma, I couldn't help but think back to that day so many years ago. The last time I was in that space for a graduation ceremony, *I* was the one in the cap and gown, sitting among my peers, staring out at a future I hadn't fully imagined.

And Mom and Dad were sitting in the audience, probably thinking some of the same things I was thinking now.

If only seventeen-year-old me could have met the version of me sitting in that audience last night.

I thought about my own kids, Liv and Fitz, who have now *both* not only graduated but done so with *high academic honors.*

I still can't wrap my head around that. It feels like a kind of success that wasn't even meant for me, something so far outside the realm of possibility when I was their age. And yet, they did it.

They *achieved.*

If only my parents and seventeen-year-old self could meet these two extraordinary people today.

As I watched Liv cross the stage to accept her diploma, something primal and unstoppable burst out of me—a loud, enthusiastic "YEAAAAAH, LIV!" that I barely recognized as my own voice. My heart is still overflowing this morning as I sit here sipping my coffee (and soothing my vocal cords), reflecting on both of my kids and everything the future holds for them.

They're breaking the generational patterns I grew up with, shattering the limitations that once felt so inevitable. They're chasing dreams and achieving things I never imagined possible—and I'm noticing that these things are possible not just for them, but also for *me.*

23: Pathways to the Self

January 12, 2023

I've been on a journey toward self-awareness for about a year. It has not been fun, and it has not been easy. You have to face the things within you that make you tick, and frequently it's not pleasant. But it's part of the process. Yay.

Years ago, I dabbled in "inner child work," but recently I discovered another method of visualization that felt fresh, intriguing, and a little daunting. The idea is simple in theory: whenever you have a visceral reaction to something, like being annoyed when someone refuses to address hard things (one of my triggers), you meet your inner child in an imagined safe place to understand where that reaction first started.

Though there's no exact science, research suggests that our emotional and personality foundations are more or less established by age eight. Kids with painful pasts often carry those scars into adulthood. It's as if childhood hardships mold us into adults with a whole set of unconscious habits and triggers, deeply rooted in memories we may not even fully remember.

With this information, I realized it made sense to dig around in my own childhood to understand these triggers, to acknowledge old wounds, and to decide whether to heal and move on, or to let the wound remain if it still serves a purpose.

I knew I'd have to confront feelings buried for decades. It would be like sitting down with myself from a lifetime ago and finally allowing her to speak up, to be heard. With that in mind, I decided to try a guided visualization to meet my inner child. The process required a sort of meditation, but here's the problem: meditation often puts me right to sleep.

So, I approached it with caution, remaining conscious of each step. I wouldn't call it meditation; it felt more like stepping into a carefully built memory, *somewhere between real and imaginary*. A half-dream, half-memory space.

The visualization began with my present self walking down a path. The guide encouraged me to notice my surroundings, to immerse myself in the sensory experience of being outside. I could imagine every detail effortlessly.

It was a sunny summer day. I envisioned a paved path winding through the woods, the kind where the warm sun filters through the leaves and casts dappled shadows on the ground. A gentle breeze brushed my face, carrying the smells of earth and pine. Nearby, I could hear a small lake, the sounds of bugs and frogs and birds creating a soundtrack of simple, natural life.

After a while, I spotted an opening off the path, something hidden—an entryway, like in *The Secret Garden*. A door covered in vines led to a tunnel. The visualization prompts encouraged me to step inside.

The tunnel was familiar in a way that grounded me. It was like an under-road walkway I'd been in before—arched concrete, slightly damp, with graffiti here and there. The temperature dropped about twenty degrees, and there was the occasional drip of water echoing off the walls. The guide suggested I might want to adjust my surroundings, but I stuck with this image. It felt secure. I continued walking until I reached another opening.

The next part of the visualization involved creating a place where I would meet my inner child. The guide encouraged us to imagine a house—a space with walls, doors, rooms. A safe place.

But I couldn't build a house. I tried to envision it, but nothing felt right. Any room I thought of brought an odd anxiety, and my mind rejected it. Instead, I found myself in an endless white space, boundless and bright. No walls, no doors, no furniture. Just pure, open white, stretching in every direction.

It didn't feel empty, though. It felt safe. Vulnerable, sure, but safe. I wouldn't be hidden here. There could be no secrets.

The first time I attempted this visualization, I didn't meet my inner child. I couldn't quite reach her. She lingered somewhere out of view, unwilling to step forward. I left the exercise feeling like I'd brushed against something important but wasn't quite ready for it. The second time, she was there, but still hesitant.

The third time, she finally came out.

She was so small. So sweet. A little spark of joy and curiosity, eyes wide with wonder. She had this boundless energy, an excitement about life and all its possibilities. I sat there, just looking at her, overwhelmed with relief, joy, and something I hadn't felt before—a deep, profound connection to myself.

Sitting on my couch, back in reality, I cried. Not out of sadness, but out of relief.

Excitement.

It's strange to meet yourself like that, to connect with a part of yourself that feels lost and forgotten. It was as if I were meeting a long-lost friend who'd been waiting for years to finally be seen.

I wonder if my safe place will evolve over time or if it'll always stay that blank, open white space. Maybe someday I'll build a floor, or walls, or add a door or a bed. Right now, the idea of it makes me anxious, but maybe that'll change as

I continue this journey, finding a sense of safety within myself. One step at a time.

For now, I'm honoring my inner child's need for openness and light. And I can't wait to see where this journey takes us —her and me, together.

24: The Fall and Rise

IT WAS LATE SEPTEMBER, around 4:30 a.m. I had already been awake for probably thirty minutes before deciding to get out of bed well ahead of my alarm. I headed down the stairs to start my morning rituals: start coffee, let dogs out, get dog and cat food ready, feed animals, drink coffee, sit on the couch and reflect, read, maybe write.

When I opened the sliding glass door to let the dogs out that morning, the early fall wind lightly danced across my face and called to me, inviting me to take in the last bits of fresh early morning air before colder mornings set in. I stepped outside, closed the door behind me, and sat down on the top stairs of my deck. I took a deep breath and exhaled, willing away all my worries.

At the time, I was a technology executive for a nonprofit healthcare IT company, and while the work was enjoyable, it was incredibly stressful. In those days, I'd often use my early morning reflection time to help me cope with the day-to-day of my work life. My kids were grown adults, so besides my animals, work was my chief responsibility. At the same time, I was doing a lot of work on myself, so I was working hard at maintaining a life-work balance. This was a battle I was starting to lose.

I sat there for only a few moments, long enough to let the dogs sniff around and do their business before they wandered back up the stairs and were ready to go back in for their breakfast.

Back inside, I counted one, then two dog shadows follow me in, and closed the sliding door. Then I fumbled with the lock. I was incredibly confused about why I could not figure out how to lock the door. I had awareness that I had locked that door probably a hundred thousand times, and I was confused about why I could not work the simple mechanism at that moment.

The next thing I knew, I heard an incredibly loud crashing sound. My heart dropped to my stomach. The only other person in the house was my daughter, and she was upstairs, assumed to be sleeping—had something happened to her? My brain worked at reconciling the sound with what could have happened, and I thought to go upstairs to find out what had happened.

I realized that I was lying on the floor. A buzzing sensation coursed through my body as my brain tried to make sense of how and why I was on the floor, and then the connection had been made: the crashing noise was me! Immediately, I felt relieved that Liv was okay, and I slowly got myself up from the floor and got the dogs and cats fed. I picked up my coffee from the Keurig and headed to my office to get my workday started.

I sat there for probably an hour before a thought entered my head that I should think about getting checked out. I couldn't really afford to miss work, I had way too much work to do. Going to the ER seemed out of the question, as it would most certainly mean that I'd be there all day. After my spontaneous vertebral artery dissections, every visit to the ER with symptoms of anything serious garnered attention from clinicians that I learned to expect would result in extra time.

I was probably fine. It was probably just stress, I told myself as I continued to work. I had gotten up early that day because I needed to get a lot of work done. But I hadn't felt stressed that day. In fact, I felt quite the opposite—the fresh air had made me feel focused and relaxed. I couldn't identify any feelings of anxiety or stress. I felt in control. Waking up early was supportive of those feelings of control. You can get so much work done while everyone else in the world is asleep.

It was around seven in the morning when I could hear Liv getting up for her day. I had talked myself into taking an Uber to the hospital to get checked out. I had passed out, but I didn't know why or if it would happen again, so driving myself seemed like an unwise choice. Liv was in cosmetology school, and while she had 'vacation days,' taking them meant adding time until she graduated. And I was fine—going to the hospital was just a way to confirm that everything was perfectly fine.

Having my own parents die of avoidable causes added a layer of checks and balances to my decision-making process when it came to my own health. I was, am, and will forever be determined not to die for some stupid, avoidable cause, and especially not one supported by something stupid like pride or ego. Or that I was too preoccupied with work, that I elevated that above continuing to be alive and for my kids to have a living mother.

It is worth noting that I am not afraid of death or dying. Probably having experienced death so closely to me and my own near misses has supported my acceptance of death and dying as a consequence of life. I don't want to die. I assume that I will live to an obnoxious age, one hundred and nine is the number I like to say. I just refuse to be a participant in my own death, if that makes sense. I'm not by any stretch of the imagination a perfect mother, but I am a mother. And my kids deserve to have me in their lives for as long as the universe allows it.

But they will not live out their days with this feeling that I have: of being robbed of the opportunity to watch my parents grow old. Of being robbed of the opportunity to continue to learn and grow through my family stories, and learn who my parents were. Or for them to learn who I am.

Who I continue to become. Of being robbed of the opportunity to face them, with any pain they have caused me, and ask, "Why?" and get an answer. And vice versa! Or confess to me the stories of their youth of which I may not know. Or things they noticed that I did or said that supported them. Or deflated them. Or whatever!

So, I calmly let Liv know the plan in the hallway outside her bedroom. She was concerned. "I can take you to the hospital, Mom—it's not a big deal."

My natural state is deflection. So I did.

"Thank you for offering, but all of this is really okay. I am sure that it is just stress-related, and I'm just going to get checked out to confirm that. No big deal. I will call you if anything important comes up, but really—I feel fine. This is just a silly thing, like all the other silly things."

I don't know that she was convinced, but she would have known that I wasn't going to back down and that I would keep my word to call her if anything important came up. Nobody wants to go sit in a hospital ER all day just to learn that everything is okay.

At the hospital, in ER triage, my blood pressure was quite high. I've always been textbook, so this was mildly concerning to me, and while I was making a mental note of that, the triage nurse chimed in, "Being in the ER can be stressful and cause blood pressure to go up; we'll check again in a bit." But I had been in the hospital probably over a hundred times. I worked there for sixteen years! Hospitals did not cause my blood pressure to spike.

Still, I actively choose not to worry about things unless there is something to worry about, and so it was easy to leave that bit of information as a mental note. A sort of clue that may or may not have something to do with the mystery that the medical team was tasked with solving.

Because of my symptoms, they got me in a room pretty quickly. Well, they got me in a *chair* pretty quickly. I was disappointed to learn that to save money, this hospital was getting patients seated in hospital chairs in this large room with pathetic, flimsy privacy screens between them. There is absolutely no privacy, and people are walking back and forth through the area nonstop. The experience was incredibly dehumanizing.

I pulled the warmed hospital blanket up over my head as I reclined my chair and attempted to get settled in. Different people came in to take blood, to take me to imaging, and back. Mostly, I sat there, trying not to exist.

In the chair next to me, I could hear an older woman who had asked to use the bathroom. She said she couldn't walk. The nurse she had was not as kind or as patient as mine. She tried to convince the woman that she could, in fact, get up to walk and that the bathroom was "right over there."

The woman's voice rose to an exasperated level. She was, from what I could tell, trying to contain her sense of urgency, and so I also sensed that her biological urges were circumventing her own patience. "I can't walk! I can't walk!" she replied over and over again. It sounded like the nurse was going to get her a wheelchair, and the woman objected, "There's not going to be time! Get me a pan!"

I am sitting two or three feet away from this commotion, both of us women 'protected' by the equivalent of a barrier the size of about half of a twin-sized bed sheet. I pulled my legs into my chest, raising my arms up over my ears under my blanket, in a physical manner of trying to give this woman some goddamned privacy.

The commotion escalated. The voices raised. I thankfully couldn't see or smell what happened next. I was able to put together that she didn't make it entirely to the portable commode. I heard her sobbing after the nurses and aides left her. I wanted to say something so that she would feel less alone. But I wasn't sure that was what she wanted, or if that would make her feel more humiliated to know someone was there. So, I did the only thing that I could do and went inside my own head.

I was scared. I didn't have any reason to be scared except that I had absolutely no clear reason to have passed out that morning. But I don't know, I tried to rationalize with myself, maybe the buildup of stress works like a pressure cooker. And even if I didn't feel stressed at that moment, was the thing already ready to burst?

My blood pressure kept going up. This has never happened to me before. A nurse added something to my IV to help lower it.

Intrusive thoughts streamed into my consciousness that I couldn't fight back. If I was going to die, at least I had done everything I could to stay alive. But my son Fitz didn't know that I was there! I texted, "Hi! I love you! I'm thinking about you! How was the festival?" I felt relieved by his quick response, and our ensuing text conversation felt like an umbilical cord tethering me to life, and I felt peace thinking, 'whatever happens, everything is going to be okay.'

I received a notification on my phone: lab and imaging results are in.

Being a technology executive in the healthcare industry, this was an intriguing side quest that I allowed my brain to go on while I waited. I had not even spoken to a doctor yet, but here were the results of labs and imaging studies, waiting in my hands behind a patient portal application!

Dare I look?

I worked in healthcare for the entirety of my career, twenty-three years. I'd worked alongside enough clinicians to know that the patients who are most informed about their conditions and treatments are better off. But there is a point when curiosity and the internet muddied the value and crossed lines into destructive, rather than constructive.

I waited a few minutes. Someone somewhere would have received a similar alert on some device. A nurse, a doctor.

Someone. That someone would receive that notification and come over to me to discuss the results. I waited.

And then I talked myself into looking. Because what could the harm be in looking?

I had this inner tension that I can't really describe. I was excited to get to see results before even talking to a doctor, at the same time as being aghast about it. I love technology, and I love the fact that this is an option... but should this be an option? I proceeded. Rationalizing that I'd rather face words on a screen than an unknown person's face.

Labs: normal, normal, normal, normal.

I texted Liv, "Everything is coming back normal!"

Feelings of relief started to roll in, like a gentle tide. I felt myself relax and sink a little into my recliner.

CT scan, Impression: No acute intracranial process. Whew! ...I think? I'm not entirely sure what this means, but it seems like good news. I see there's more, and I scroll. History, additional history, comparison, technique, yada, yada. Words I don't understand but read as 'normal.'

Findings: No evidence of acute intracranial hemorrhage, mass effect of midline shift.

I don't know half of those words. But that sounds like good news. I keep reading.

There is prominence of the sulci and ventricular system due to cortical and central atrophy.

Uh, this seems like a grey area. I don't know what these words mean, but I sense a shift in the tonality or expression of the words.

Subtle hypodensities involving periventricular and deep white matter, compatible with chronic small vessel ischemic change.

And I still don't know what the words mean, but the sense I had in the last sentence shift has grown greater with this one. Well, shit. This does not seem good, I think to myself.

Do I wait for a doctor to explain this to me? Or do I consult with Google?

I don't know right away. I read and reread the words in an attempt to will myself to know what they mean. I was unsuccessful.

I remember there are more results. Maybe there is something there.

CT Angiogram Head and Neck with Contrast, Impression: Focal 7.9 mm aneurysmal dilation along the distal LEFT ICA, otherwise normal CT angiogram of the neck.

FUCK.

I couldn't stop the tears from forming in my eyes. I willed my eyes to contain them—this room was so busy, and people were walking through nonstop. I did not want anyone to see me cry. I also hate crying, and what was I even crying about? I barely knew what the words meant. But the words I did know about this aneurysm in the neck dragged me back to 2006. I'd been here before. I'd had and conquered these fears before.

And now they had resurfaced like zombies, erupting from the ground to reclaim space in my life, once again. And all of this was happening while I sat in this stupid chair in this cheap-ass hospital, surrounded by blissfully unaware, stupid fucking happy people waltzing through with their stupid fucking happy lives and these stupid fucking privacy screens are an absolute goddamned joke...

A woman in a lab coat appeared. I watched her eyes glance at my hands, which were still holding my phone, my browser set to Google. "Hi, I'm Doctor So-and-so. I see you have the news. We're going to discharge you to follow up with your primary care physician and a cardiology consult. Probably a

Holter study..." Her voice, her face, the room faded to black. I faded to black.

"Sound good?" The light and her voice erupted back into my awareness all at once. My eyes squinted, and if ears have a similar bracing of harsh contrast, they did that too. "Yeah," I replied, wanting to just get out of there as quickly as I possibly could.

Willing myself not to just get up and leave on my own. Googling what it means to leave a hospital before being formally discharged.

Wondering if it would be all that terrible to disconnect myself from an IV. My subconscious soothed me with a reminder that I would not emotionally or mentally bear that additional drama very well. And I sat there for what seemed like an eternity as a good little patient until I was formally discharged.

The days and weeks that followed were something of a blur. Follow-ups with my doctor, with specialists, all blending together.

An aneurysm is something you can potentially live with forever with no issues, but I'll need to get scanned every year to monitor it. Due to my age and personal emphasis on being healthy, the brain thing was most likely a degenerative condition that would mean eventually I'd forget everything. Which would be one of my greatest fears. Not so much for myself, even if that sounds terrifying. But for people whom I love, and who love me. To have to look at me and forget me while I still live, and forget them.

Inspired by the risk of forgetting my own life story and having it disappear entirely, I picked up my dedication to retelling to my kids and anyone who would listen, and writing it all down. It couldn't have been for nothing. It mattered. We mattered! I mattered!

At a rescan in November, a miracle happened: brain imaging was normal.

Whatever shrinking was happening had not only stopped but also unshrank! I was and continue to be incredibly relieved. And I feel gifted by the universe for another chance at life and living with my full mental faculties. It will not have been for nothing.

The aneurysm is growing and will continue to be monitored annually until it is surgically removed, or for the remainder of my life.

I don't know what that aneurysm has planned, but I'm living to 109, baby!

Not My Job

October 14, 2023

My therapist looked me straight in the eyes the other day and said, "It isn't your job to figure out what's going on with other people."

In that moment, the words hit me like a thousand bricks—all at once, crushing me yet somehow lifting a weight I hadn't realized I'd been carrying.

It was such a simple phrase, but the range of emotions it triggered was anything but simple. The insight was liberating, but it also left me exposed, as if some core part of me had just been cracked open. I knew, almost instantly, why this struck so deeply. I've spent most of my life in the habit of figuring out other people, to an almost obsessive degree. I'd leaned into this skill, this "superpower," because it made me feel safe. If I could anticipate others, I could dodge their hurts, avoid their disappointments, and keep myself perfectly armored. It was a strategy that allowed me to get exactly what I needed from people, or to know when to cut my losses and walk away.

It was a survival mechanism. And it had worked. I'd survived.

But now, I realized, I didn't need it anymore. I wasn't that vulnerable child or teenager, navigating turbulent emotional waters. I didn't need to play mental gymnastics to feel safe and secure. I was safe, with or without it. I was fully capable of looking after myself, of setting boundaries and voicing my needs without endless analysis.

This "superpower" had once been a shield, but now it was a prison, isolating me from real, mutual connection. My compulsion to understand everyone else had blocked me from truly being understood, because I had been doing all the emotional heavy lifting for everyone around me. By filling in their blanks, I had left no space for people to show up authentically. If I was always figuring out how to connect with them, I never allowed them to connect with me. I'd made myself both their therapist and their puppet master, pulling the strings to create a sense of safety and control that, in the end, kept me isolated and unfulfilled.

It dawned on me how much this pattern had shaped my relationships. Since the day my parents moved away, I'd sharpened this skill, driven by the need to navigate each new relationship as safely as possible. And while it did give me a filter for who could be in my life, it also created an exhausting dynamic. I became everyone's counselor, and those who didn't appreciate that role either drifted away or clashed with me.

For a long time, this "weeding out" seemed like a gift. I prefer the company of people who are open to growth, who embrace the journey and the messiness of life. People stuck in their ways, resistant to change, drained me. They felt like vampires, sapping my energy. I learned to spot them quickly —another side of this so-called "superpower"—and avoid their stagnant energy.

But this new revelation opened my eyes: even with the people who *were* growth-minded, I had missed the mark. It wasn't my job to figure them out either. It was my job to show up authentically and allow them the space to show up for me, just as they were. Anything less was a performance, an endless exercise in control.

I felt the truth of it deep in my bones. The fear-driven need to "figure people out" had served its purpose, but it was no longer serving me. I didn't need to navigate life as a series of mental puzzles, piecing together other people's inner worlds to feel secure. I could feel secure within myself, independent of others' reactions or behaviors.

There's a powerful freedom in stepping back and trusting others to do their own emotional work. I want to build relationships where I can depend on people to show up for me, where I can simply *be*, without maneuvering to protect myself or them. The connection I'm craving isn't a one-sided mental exercise, it's mutual and vulnerable, and real. It's built on trust, not control.

It isn't my job to figure people out. It's my job to simply be present, to bring my whole self into relationships, and to allow others to do the same. For once, that feels like more than enough.

The Sound of Security

October 14, 2023

I absolutely adored my dad.

To me, he was a superhero—a figure of boundless strength, someone who could do no wrong. In my eyes, he was a protector, a man whose love was unbreakable, whose power could move mountains and cradle my heart at the same time. I believed that his strength was my safety net, that his happiness could anchor our entire family.

It wasn't until years later, through conversations with others, through therapy, that I even considered that what we endured was *abuse*. As a child, I assumed every family was like ours. I saw Dad as a superhero despite everything. I didn't have a frame of reference to see it any other way.

I think many kids grow up with this kind of hero worship for their dads. And if your dad dies when you're twenty-two, and you're pregnant with your first child, that hero image gets locked in even tighter. There's no one left to defend or explain their choices, no more conversations to fill in the blanks. So, I filled them in myself—with sunshine, glitter, and excuses. I made his memory perfect because I needed it to be.

When he was happy, my whole world felt safe. He'd whistle, completely absorbed in his own little world, seemingly oblivious to everyone else. It was easy to overlook how solitary that happiness seemed to be. He'd be whistling away, making one of his bizarre soup concoctions or fiddling with some gadget by his well-worn recliner, and for those moments, I felt like everything was right in the world.

Even on the coldest winter car rides, he'd whistle Christmas songs, each of us wrapped in our bulky coats, breathing warmth into the old Buick faster than the heater could. No one would talk; he was lost in his own world, even in a packed car. But so long as he was happy, I could bask in that sound like it was sunshine on my face, thawing me out from the inside. That whistle was my signal that everything was okay, that I could relax and stop bracing for whatever might come next.

And in those moments, I'd keep my distance but stay close enough to soak it in. I wanted to drink up his happiness like a warm breath of spring air after a too-long winter. If I stayed out of his way, it might last longer. But I still wanted to be near, to feel the world safe and secure under the spell of his personal contentment.

Growing up, my sense of security hinged on his moods. If he was at ease, I felt like I could breathe. But even in his happiest moments, I learned that the best thing I could be was invisible. Or if not invisible, then useful.

Sometimes, when he wanted to relax, he'd drop a hairbrush in front of me, run his hand through his hair, and lie down in front of me without a word. Brushing his hair became an unspoken expectation, something all of us kids did at some point, but when it was just Markie and me, it felt like my "job." I'd sit there, brushing, waiting for the signs that I'd done well. If he drifted off to sleep, it was good. If he sighed or made a sound that felt weirdly intimate, it was great. But if he reached up and ran his hand through his hair, that meant I wasn't done. Sometimes he'd add, "Five more minutes," and I'd have no choice but to keep going.

The whole ritual left me feeling like my worth depended on what I could do for him, even when it made me uncomfortable. It was never about what I wanted or how I felt; it was about making myself useful and pushing past my discomfort. I learned that love and security meant sacrificing my own needs, that the measure of my value was my ability to make others comfortable, and to expect nothing in return.

No one directly told me to think this way, but it was there in every growled, "Tina! When are you going to learn to keep your mouth shut?" Over time, I learned that speaking my mind, sharing my feelings, anything that might disrupt his personal sense of peace and calm, was a risk I couldn't take. Whatever I thought or felt didn't matter; my job was to maintain his happiness.

I'll never know who he really was or what made him the way he was. But despite all I didn't know, and even the things I did, I still love him with all my heart. Even now, years after his death, I find myself thinking about moments that would've made him proud. And in those moments, I can only feel proud on his behalf.

And I'd give just about anything to hear that whistle again.

The Mark of Rage

October 16, 2023

The lasting mark of physical violence, I knew him as Dad. It's been a reality I've avoided staring at too closely for far too long. There's a part of me that's been looking past these memories, holding them at arm's length, because there's no answer to why they happened—just the impact they left behind. And now, I need to be real and honest about them with myself.

Dad wasn't an angry man, not in the way that he stormed through life seething. He had a range of emotions, most of them what I would have considered "normal." He could be hardworking, dedicated, blissfully happy, even vulnerable at times. It's just that his anger was different—when it flared up, it was wild and unbridled. And it could happen without warning. There was no visible fuse; he didn't simmer in a way we could read. He'd just explode.

I know that in his happier moments—when he was whistling, cooking, or lost in his own little world, nothing much could shake him. Those moments were a haven, the times I felt he was untouchable in his joy, and they became my emotional refuge, too. But even then, there was a cautionary edge to it. I learned to be mindful, to be small, and to avoid setting off whatever might be lying dormant beneath the surface.

There were (exceedingly rare) times I saw him cry. I remember one time after a particularly explosive fight with Mom, another when I told him I was scared he'd die young from smoking. I can still picture him gathering us in the basement, on his knees, with his hands holding Mom's, promising us he'd quit, saying he didn't want to leave us like his dad left him. It was a rare, tender moment where his love for us shone through, unfiltered by anger or frustration.

I never laid a hand on my own kids. The fear that I'd somehow inherited his rage, that it might spill over and hurt them, kept me vigilant. I knew that if I ever crossed that line, I couldn't come back the same way he couldn't. I don't judge others for using discipline that's measured and controlled, but for myself, because it was my personal experience from the receiving end—I assumed I would never be able to compartmentalize that way. I'd rather not even risk it.

Even now, I can feel the way my body used to brace itself, that familiar tingling, knowing exactly what was coming and knowing there was no escape. I remember the physical sting, the outline of the belt, the thick edges, the holes, the cracks, the welts and bruises it left behind. I knew that whatever I'd done, the punishment would go far beyond the crime, that the anger in those moments had little to do with me and everything to do with something I couldn't name.

The only thing worse than my own punishments? Watching or listening to my brothers' ordeals, deeply feeling compassion and empathy for what they were going through, and feeling powerless to stop it. I think Dad did go easier on me because I was the girl. At least I was only hit with a hand or a belt. My brothers weren't as lucky—ping pong paddles, dowel rods, whatever was in reaching distance seemed to be fair game.

He kept a display case of dowel rods outside his workshop. Frank had to pass by it every day on his way to his room. Whether it was intentional or not, the whole thing was deeply unsettling, a quiet reminder of the threat always looming.

Sometimes, Mom would try to intervene.

I remember her calling out, "That's enough! He has a test tomorrow." She was talking about Bobby. And somehow, the fact that he had a test was the piece of information that mattered. I remember feeling so relieved for Bobby that it stopped, even if it took something as arbitrary as a test. But when he walked away, his face wasn't relieved. He looked broken. That's a look I can't shake.

There were times I even volunteered to take the punishment, just to end the waiting, to keep my brothers from going through it. I'd confess to things I didn't do, spin stories on the fly to justify why I'd done them, anything to get it over with. I was just a kid, desperate to return to a normal that wasn't normal at all. I don't know what my parents thought of me, this little "troublemaker" always at the center of some mess, but really, I was just trying to protect myself and my brothers however I could.

No one else was going to.

What I needed was for them to see themselves clearly in those moments, to recognize that they were out of control, and to protect us from that unbridled rage. I needed them to understand their own triggers, to make sure their love for us outweighed whatever demons they were battling. I needed them to choose us, to prioritize our safety over whatever fueled their anger.

But that didn't happen, and I'm left with the marks it left on me. The way my body learned to brace, the way my heart learned to be small, and the way my mind learned to excuse what shouldn't be excused. And now, all these years later, I'm left here to try and make sense of it on my own. Just as before.

25: Back to My Roots

December 1, 2023

I changed my last name back to Anderson. I haven't been Tina Anderson for over twenty years (since October 2001, to be exact!), and the moment felt nothing short of exhilarating. Sitting with the SSA agent, giddy with anticipation, I could barely contain my excitement. As I drove home, I reflected on what those twenty-two years without my family name had meant and how they had shaped me.

My first thoughts were filled with gratitude. The family names I had borrowed during those years weren't just placeholders; they represented two wonderful, loving families who had welcomed me with open arms. They showed me what warmth and laughter could look like within a family. Of course, no family is perfect, but these families had an abundance of *consistent* love, and for that, I'll always be grateful. Those names became part of my journey, part of the seasons I spent learning, growing, and healing.

As I drove, I passed the church where I was married for the first time. Memories of my twenty-one-year-old self came flooding back—the excitement in the days leading up to the wedding, the nerves about pulling off such a big event, and the overwhelming joy of starting something new. Dad had walked me down the aisle alongside my Aunt Donna. I laid a single rose on the piano in memory of Mom, and the handful of family members who attended from my side, who filled just two or three pews in a sea of somewhere around three hundred guests.

I was so eager to embrace my new last name that day. It felt like stepping into something bigger than myself, a family that loved and adored me as much as I loved and adored them. My life felt full of promise. I didn't imagine then that it would ever end.

But it did. Divorce came. And with it, bittersweet emotions.

I remember sitting in the courtroom, tears streaming down my face—not because I doubted my decision, but because I mourned the hope and joy I had felt on my wedding day. The judge paused the hearing to ask if I was okay. I laughed through my tears, nodding, "I'm fine. I want this." And I did.

We were making each other miserable, and there was no path forward together, and we both knew it. Still, thinking about the contrast between the excitement of that first day and the finality of that moment in court was stark. I hadn't yet noticed that two clashing emotions could coexist.

I kept that last name for practical reasons; it matched my children's. But it also reflected the stigma I felt about divorce. A different last name would be an admission, a signal to the world that I had "failed" at marriage. I felt stained by divorce.

Years later, when I got married again, I took my second husband's name, eager to start anew. But on our wedding day, as I wrote my first husband's last name on the marriage certificate, I felt a familiar sting of shame. It was a reminder of what I was leaving behind, a question of where I truly belonged. I brushed it off as wedding day jitters and dove headfirst into the idea of being loved and cherished unconditionally. But I hadn't quite considered myself in the equation.

That marriage, too, ended in divorce. By then, I had become an expert in hiding myself. My intensity, my vibrancy, my authenticity—all in the name of "making it work." I believed

I should be or do anything to make someone else happy, even if it meant dimming my own light.

Looking back at photos from those years, I see a version of myself that barely resembles me. The light in my eyes had faded; my smile grew tired. I was alive, but I wasn't *living*. I was contorting myself into shapes that fit someone else's expectations.

When I finally walked into the courtroom for my second divorce, I didn't feel the bittersweet mix of emotions I had felt the first time. I felt relief. I spent years hiding who I was, and I was ready to stop.

Changing my name back to Anderson felt like reclaiming a part of myself I had long buried. It's not just a name; it's a connection to my roots, to the family that shaped me, and to the parts of me that I now embrace fully. Going back to Anderson means acknowledging my intensity, my vibrancy, and my capacity for feeling deeply. It means rejecting the idea that I must hide or shrink to fit into someone else's mold.

I think about the Andersons who came before me—people who likely dimmed their own lights to survive in a world that wasn't ready to embrace their full selves. I see how that pattern may have carried through generations, aging us prematurely and breaking us quietly. Squeezing the life force out of us too early. But I also see the strength in choosing differently.

Reclaiming my name is my declaration: I will no longer dim my light.

I will honor the parts of me that feel deeply, that express boldly, and that take up space unapologetically. This is how I break the cycle: by being wholly, authentically me. By building a life where my light shines brightly, surrounded by those who dare to let theirs do the same.

I'm not just going back to my roots—I'm planting new ones, grounded in self-acceptance, self-love, and the unwavering belief that I am enough, just as I am.

26:The Weight of Memory

GROWING UP, I WOULD lie in bed at night, imagining myself at any point in the future. What kind of person would I be? Would I have a family? A home? A career? As hard as I tried, I could never quite "connect" to my future self, but that didn't stop me from trying.

Now, with little effort, I can connect to the past versions of me—the girl who lay awake, imagining the future. I can vividly recall the sounds of birds chirping in springtime, their wings fluttering as they bathed, the rhythmic tapping of curtains against an open window: *tap... tap... tap*. The clanging of pots and the bubbling of water from the kitchen, the hum of life happening in the house, and the world around me.

The sound of crickets in the summertime takes me back to the stillness of those evenings. My wet hair would drip against the back of my nightgown after a shower, the faint chill of it clinging to my shoulders as I sat in the quiet three-season room with my family, the air warm and heavy after a full day outdoors. I remember the smell of the summer, what I wore, where I was, who I was with, and how I felt. The sights, sounds, and sensations are all there, suspended in time, as if I never left them.

I can feel the sun's warmth on my face as it poured through a window, illuminating tiny specks of dust, suspended midair, dancing in the golden light like fragments of forgotten memories. Those specks were magic to me. They twinkled like pixie dust, conjuring fragments of thought and feeling. Even now, they pull me back into those moments.

I wonder if that little girl knew how often I'd return to her world, retracing her steps to find my footing. She didn't have all the answers, but she has something I still hold on to—an unwavering sense of wonder, a belief that life is stitched together by moments like these. And maybe that's why I remember her so clearly: she reminds me to look for magic, even in the dust.

The Surprising Depth of Me

It began with a simple exploration of what I thought were familiar pathways in my mind. Yet, something shifted. As I peeled back layers of old survival mechanisms, as I examined the stories I'd told myself to keep moving forward, I found myself standing in a space I didn't know existed.

And then I cried.

But it wasn't the usual kind of crying. These weren't tears prompted by someone else's words or actions. They weren't fueled by grief, anger, or even joy. Instead, it was as if my soul said, "Hey, look what else I can do!" These were tears of *amazement*.

For most of my life, I've clung to the sentiment that things were never as bad as they could have been. That mindset became a survival mechanism, a way to minimize my own experiences. My life was hard, but everyone's is. And it could have been so much *worse*. I'd given myself and others an unspoken pass—a way to dodge accountability—for what wasn't done or what wasn't said. It was a quiet mantra that had kept me afloat: "It wasn't that bad."

But as I reflected on those words, I started to notice their weight. They'd carried me this far, yes, but they'd also tethered me to something. Something unfinished. Something unresolved.

I've often thought about the adults in my life who should have known better. They made mistakes, missed chances, and failed to see things they should have seen. And yet, I've accepted their humanity because, after all, aren't we all flawed? Isn't it unreasonable to expect perfection? It's a thought that has given me peace—or at least, the illusion of it. But it's also been my excuse to avoid facing the ghosts of what *wasn't*.

What I've realized, though, is that acceptance isn't the same as forgiveness. Acceptance is a form of letting go, but forgiveness requires something deeper. It requires confronting the raw truth of those unfulfilled expectations, of the hurt that lingers in their wake. And forgiveness? It isn't about granting a gold star for what was done right. It's about acknowledging the pain of what was done wrong, and deciding that I don't need anyone else to fix it.

That's when it happened—that moment of visceral, soul-deep relief. I noticed myself in a way I hadn't before. The tears came not from sadness but from the sheer release of holding myself in full view. It felt...good. Not because anyone else had made me feel good, but because I had given myself that gift.

And I've wondered: Is this what people feel all the time? Have I been missing out? Was I daydreaming in class that day they taught us how to do this? I don't know. But what I do know is that it's new for me. It's as if my soul decided to surprise me with its capacity, showing me something I didn't know I had. And I stood there, amazed, thinking, "So this is what else I can feel."

The realization wasn't just emotional; it was physical, too. It felt like the weight of my stories shifted. Not just the weight of what happened, but the weight of how I've carried those stories. How I've framed them, folded them up, and tucked them away in compartments. Opening those compartments always felt dangerous, like a Pandora's box I might never close.

But this time, it felt different.

The weight of the story was still there, but it wasn't crushing. It was grounding.

I'm not saying I've figured it all out. There's still so much I don't understand—about myself, about forgiveness, about the ghosts I still carry. But for the first time, I've experienced what it feels like to see myself with clarity and kindness. Not in comparison to others, not for the sake of others, not in the shadow of "it could have been worse," but simply as *me*.

And that is a revelation I will never forget.

Learning to Choose Myself

I used to think leaving meant failing. That belief sat at the center of me for so long, like an immovable stone, cold and heavy in its certainty. Relationships, I thought, were about endurance, weathering storms, fixing cracks, and building bridges over impossible chasms. So, when I found myself standing at the edge of yet another ending, I didn't see courage. I didn't see self-respect.

I saw failure.

And it took years to unlearn that.

Years to realize that leaving wasn't about giving up but about stepping into something far harder: the unknown. Each relationship I left taught me something new. Each one showed me, in its absence, what I needed and deserved but hadn't yet articulated.

For example: honesty—not just the absence of lies but the kind of honesty that feels like light pouring into a darkened room. I didn't know how to ask for it at first, because I didn't know I was missing it.

I just knew the creeping doubt that settled in my chest every time actions didn't match words, every time an answer felt just a little too polished, a little too rehearsed. It wasn't until years later, when I found myself in the quiet of my own company, that I realized what I had been asking for all along: "Show me who you are and let me decide if I want to stay."

Then there was accountability.

That lesson came the hardest because accountability requires two things: vulnerability and effort. It's the willingness to say, "I messed up," and the follow-through to do better next time. I fought for it—not with those words, exactly, but in the subtle ways you fight for something you need without knowing you need it. "Please just tell me when you'll be home," I said once. He looked at me like I'd asked him to read my mind. Maybe I had. Maybe that's what happens when you grow used to silence where accountability should be.

Each relationship added something new to the list: respect, consistency, and presence. Subconsciously, I was building a framework for what I needed, brick by brick, heartbreak by heartbreak. I wish I could say the lessons came easily, but they didn't. They came in the form of nights spent waiting for a call that never came, arguments that felt like circling the same unanswerable question, and the quiet, persistent ache of being in a room with someone who wasn't really there.

I learned to fight for these things. And when I realized they were never there to fight for, I learned to accept this as reality, and to leave.

Walking away wasn't easy. It never is. There's a special kind of heartbreak in leaving someone who, for all their flaws, you still love. But each time, I left knowing I was honoring something in myself that I hadn't known existed before. I was learning to choose me.

I used to wonder if I was asking too much. Was it unreasonable to want honesty? To expect someone to be accountable for their words and actions? To hope for respect, consistency, and presence? I told myself to be patient, to wait for them to meet me halfway. But patience, I've learned, has its limits. There's a fine line between waiting for someone to grow and waiting for them to be someone they're not. The latter isn't love; it's a slow erosion of self.

I don't see those relationships as failures anymore. They were classrooms, each one teaching me a little more about who I was and what I needed. They showed me the bare minimum I'd been willing to accept and the courage it took to demand more. And in the end, they gave me the greatest gift of all: the ability to choose myself, over and over again.

It's not just about knowing what I deserve; it's about being unwilling to settle for less. That's what love is, I think. Not just the love we give to others but the love we give ourselves —the kind that says, "This is my floor, my foundation, my standard. Anything less is not my home."

27: To My Children

September 7, 2010 – today

To my beautiful children, whom I will always love with all that I am:

I have so many hopes and dreams for you. Whatever path you choose, wherever your life leads you, I will be there to support you. Every step of the way, every decision you make... you are two of the very few people on this Earth who could never disappoint me so much that my love for you would ever waver. I am so proud of who you are today and feel so wholly blessed to have each of you in my life.

Don't be afraid to dream. If anyone mocks you or deflates your dreams, run. These kinds of people are toxic to your being.

Be spontaneous. Play in the rain. Laugh until you cry. Love even when it hurts. Never take anyone or anything for granted.

Always be completely genuine so that when someone tells you that you are beautiful, you know they are talking about everything that you are, not just your outward appearance.

Be passionate about life. If a moment moves you so much that it takes your breath away, take the time to write it down and lose yourself in it for a while. A dream. A sunset. A kiss. Your newborn baby's first breath, first cry, first smile. When life is moving so fast you don't know which side is up, you can look back on these memories and reminisce about how you were once so swept away. These musings can help carry you through difficult times. They will remind you that you are alive.

Real friends will never hurt you on purpose. That's not to say the truth won't hurt sometimes, especially when it's what's best for you. Someone who will take the risk of telling you the truth over saying whatever will make you feel good is a true friend. You can have more than one. Make sure you reciprocate it. I hope you will do this for each other.

When you fail, take the time to recognize why you did before jumping back up again. Know that it's okay to make mistakes. Learn from them. There are some things you just can't learn in life until you've failed at them—sometimes more than once.

Always know that your Daddy and I love you very much. And you never have to wonder if we know how much you love us. No matter what you ever do or say, we know. You'll hear us say from time to time, "You'll understand when you're older." Talk to us about it when you do get older.

Don't be in such a hurry to grow up (you'll understand this when you're older!) As a child, be a child. As a teenager, be a teenager. As a young adult, be a young adult. As an adult, have and hold the courage to be yourself.

Make sure you make time for your family and friends. There is nothing sadder than family reunions that only take place at funerals.

Be true to yourself. Life won't always be rainbows and butterflies. But if you can wake up in the morning with a smile on your face and the strength to do it all over again, then you've really accomplished something. I'll always be there for you. Never forget that.

Love,
Mommy

Epilogue: The Lasting Imprint

When I began this memoir, I was carrying a story so heavy it felt like it might consume me.

I wanted to preserve the memories of my childhood, of the people who shaped me, and of the person I became despite (and because) of them. I wanted to make sense of it all: the chaos, the love, the pain, the perseverance. But as I sit here reflecting on the journey this book has taken me, I realize that what began as an attempt to untangle my past has transformed into something far more profound.

This memoir isn't just a record of where I've been. It's a testament to who I am now and who I'm still becoming.

For so long, I felt tethered to the ghosts of my past—not just the memories of my parents, but also the invisible forces of shame, fear, and resentment that shaped my choices and beliefs. They loomed over me, casting long shadows over my relationships, my parenting, and my sense of self. At times, I've carried those shadows like burdens, and at other times, I've hidden within them, too scared to step into the light.

But through writing, I found something I didn't know I was searching for.

Through writing, I found freedom.

Not the kind of freedom that erases the past but the kind that allows me to hold it with compassion and curiosity instead of judgment. The kind that transforms scars into reminders of strength and resilience.

Each chapter of this memoir carries a piece of that transformation. In revisiting life's darkest corners, I found humor in the absurdity. In reliving moments of solitude and fear, I discovered courage. In confronting anger and betrayal, I unearthed forgiveness—not just for others but for myself. And in chronicling the generational patterns I once feared I'd never escape, I found the joy of watching my children break through them, shattering ceilings I didn't even know were there.

What ties all these threads together is a simple, profound truth: healing is not a destination.

It's a continuous journey—a series of small, imperfect steps forward, often taken during setbacks and struggles. It's about choosing, every day, to let go of the chains that no longer serve us. It's about carrying the lessons of the past without letting them define the future.

I've learned that forgiveness doesn't mean forgetting. It doesn't mean erasing the pain or absolving those who caused it. Forgiveness is about freeing ourselves from the weight of resentment. It's about choosing to set down the anger and shame we've carried for so long, not because they don't matter, but because *we* do.

To my children, Fitz and Liv: You are my greatest teachers and my greatest joy. Watching you grow into the incredible people you are has been the privilege of my life.

You've shown me what it means to break cycles, to dream boldly, and to live authentically. My hope is that this book offers you a window into my heart, a deeper understanding of where we come from, and how far you have already exceeded your own origin stories. It may take some time before you agree, but I am grateful that you got to see my flaws, because they showed you that perfection isn't realistic, and it isn't the goal. Being real, being resilient, being you—that's what matters. Never doubt that you are loved beyond measure.

To the readers who have journeyed through these pages with me: Thank you for bearing witness to my story. I hope that it resonates with you—that it reminds you of your own resilience, your own capacity for growth and forgiveness. Life is messy and unpredictable, but it is also breathtakingly beautiful. Even in the darkest moments, there is light to be found.

This little light of mine, I'm gonna let it shine.

With love and gratitude,

Tina

Acknowledgments

This memoir would not have been possible without the collective support of so many remarkable people. I am deeply grateful to all who have shaped my journey, whether by mentoring my craft, offering critical feedback, or surrounding me with unconditional love and care.

First, I want to thank those who helped bring this story to life in its written form:

Abe El-Raheb – Your keen editorial eye and thoughtful, nuanced feedback brought a new dimension to my story. You helped me uncover gaps I couldn't see on my own— especially in the way I've structured the narrative in silos, mirroring how I've stored up my memories. While those compartments once brought comfort, I never anticipated how opening them up for readers would also open them in full view to *myself*. Thank you for helping me recognize that.

I also can't overstate how much it meant that you responded not just to the writing, but to the human behind it. That subtle distinction built a kind of trust that made all the difference.

Collaborating with you has been a gift, and I look forward to continuing to create together.

Caroline Barnhill, Nicole Sanders, David Ruane, Trish Ruths, Anna Demmer, and Ben Curl – Thank you for showing up so generously with your time, attention, and honesty. Each of you brought a unique lens to this story, and I'm deeply grateful for the clarity and compassion you offered along the way. Your feedback didn't just help me refine the manuscript—it helped me see the story more clearly through someone else's eyes. As you were the first humans I trusted to read this, your thoughtful reflections gave me the courage to keep going. That was a vulnerable and vital part of the process, and I'm so thankful to have had you in the room with me, even from afar.

Gustavo Caraballo – This book would not exist without you. For years, this story sat unfinished, uncertain, too heavy to carry alone. I did the writing, yes, but you are the reason I made it to the finish line. When I dove back into these pages—again and again—you held me up, sometimes quite literally. When the emotional toll felt like too much, you were my backbone when I lost sight of my own.

And then, of course, there's the cover. Your creative brilliance brought this story to life in a way that words alone couldn't—capturing its heart, its weight, and its hope. No one's picking up this book without that cover. And no one's reading it without the support and strength you gave to me behind the scenes. Inside and out, beginning to end, *you* are in every part of this.

Thank you for loving me. For creating and protecting a space where I could fully and finally be myself. And for welcoming me so completely into your family—Ryleigh, Laylonie, your parents Gustavo and Debra, your sisters Ana and Lis, your brothers-in-law Mike and Christopher, your nieces Elise and Autumn, and your nephew Ian.

I am endlessly grateful.

I found you.

• • •

This is also a heartfelt tribute to the people who were with me through it all and believed in me through life's most challenging and beautiful moments:

Frank, Robert, and Marcus – Whoooooeee! What can I say? *We made it.* Who knew the bare minimum could feel like such a wild ride? I'm so grateful I never had to walk this road alone. Growing up with you taught me the beauty of shared experience—even when it meant laughing at the absurdity just to survive it. Thank you for allowing me to share bits of your stories as they've intertwined with mine.

Bruce and Betty – Thank you for taking me in as family, long before and long after my parents moved away. Your steady presence has kept me afloat in moments of despair and reminded me, again and again, of what truly matters: the kind of family that shows up.

Rose and Wil – I am forever grateful for your open hearts and for treating me as one of your own. Rose, you sat with me in hospitals for countless hours and advocated on my behalf, asking the hard questions so that I received the best and right care. The unwavering love and support from both of you mean more than I could ever say out loud.

Aunts Donna, Joanne, and Mary Lou – Thank you for always loving and accepting me exactly as I am, and continuing to do so to this day. You showed me early on that family isn't limited to blood, and that kind hearts and open arms matter more than anything. Also, sorry for all the swears scattered throughout these pages. (You raised me better.) And shout out to my cousins Jeff and Val—you're part of this, too!

Fitz and Liv –Watching you grow into yourselves—boldly, beautifully, and unapologetically—has been one of the greatest privileges of my life. Your patience, humor, and grace have reminded me, again and again, of the importance of growth, even when that journey meant navigating life's more absurd corners. The way you live so fully as *you* has felt like permission to finally do the same. Thank you for walking this road with me, for learning alongside me, and for graciously allowing me to keep learning from you. I love you more than words can hold!

Dave, Amina, Andy, Pauline, Melissa, Ryan, Kari, Cathy (Cat Pee!), Stacy, Steve, Joe & Jess, Marty, and Kristy – You might not have known you were being observed (well... at least one of you did!), but you and your families modeled a new way for me to understand what family could be. Some of you even asked, "What's up with your family?" as we navigated these realizations together. I'm sorry—not sorry—that it took me so long to see it for myself. I'm deeply grateful for your kindness and gentleness while I caught up, in my own time.

Mom, Dad, Lori – I recognize that every part of who I am —the tough lessons, and even the things I'd rather forget— owes something to you. This memoir holds most of what I ever wished I could say to you if you were still alive. Without the foundation you provided, imperfect as it was, I wouldn't be the person I am today.

I miss you. I think of you often. And I carry forward the lessons—both the hard ones and the silent ones—that have shaped my path. It was in the gaps, in the spaces between what was said and what was left unsaid, that I noticed the part of you that gave me the chance to get to be me.

To everyone who has touched my life, your influence has been vital in helping me become someone I get to love to be. Each of you has contributed uniquely to the light that continues to guide my path. This memoir is as much yours as it is mine—a testament to the enduring truth that it *truly does take a village,* including the wise therapists and guidance counselors who helped me make sense of the mess and meaning along the way. Thank you!